The Blue Guides

Albania

Austria Austria
Vienna

Belgium and Luxembourg
Bulgaria
China
Cyprus
Czech and Slovak
  Republics
Denmark
Egypt

France France
Paris and Versailles
Burgundy
Loire Valley
Midi-Pyrénées
Normandy
South West France
Corsica

Germany Berlin and eastern
  Germany

Greece Greece
Athens and environs
Crete
Rhodes and the
  Dodecanese

Hungary Hungary
Budapest

Southern India
Ireland

Italy Northern Italy
Southern Italy
Florence
Rome
Venice
Tuscany
Umbria
Sicily

Ne⋯⋯⋯⋯⋯s
Amsterdam

Poland
Portugal

Spain Spain
Barcelona
Madrid

Sweden
Switzerland
Thailand
Tunisia

Turkey Turkey
Istanbul

UK England
Scotland
Wales
Channel Islands
London
Oxford and Cambridge
Country Houses of
  England

USA New York
Museums and Galleries of
  New York
Boston and Cambridge

Residence of the Greek Ambassador, Sofia

Bulgaria

by James Pettifer

BLUE GUIDE

A&C Black • London
WW Norton • New York

First edition, March 1998

Published by A & C Black (Publishers) Limited
35 Bedford Row, London WC1R 4JH

A CIP catalogue record of this book is available from the British Library.

ISBN 0–7136–4101–0

Published in the United States of America by
WW Norton and Company Inc.
500 Fifth Avenue, New York, NY 10110

Published simultaneously in Canada by
Penguin Books Canada Limited
10 Alcorn Avenue, Toronto
Ontario M4V 3BE

ISBN 0–393–37196–X USA

Cover photograph: Bachkovo Monastery. Photo Melanie Friend/ Hutchison Library. **Title page illustration**: St George and the Dragon, Rila Monastery.

James Pettifer is a writer specialising in the southern Balkans, He has reported on events for *The Times* and many other publications in Britian and abroad. He is a member of the Royal Institute of International Affairs and was a Senior Associate member of St Anthony's College, Oxford from 1993–96. He is a Research Fellow of the European Research Institute, University of Bath, and Visiting Professor at the Institute of Balkan Studies, Thessaloniki. His most recent books are *The Turkish Labyrinth,* and *Albania—From Anarchy to a Balkan Identity* (with Miranda Vickers). He is also author of *Blue Guide Albania.*

Printed Butler and Tanner Ltd, Frome and London

Contents

Introduction 9
Acknowledgements 10
Explanations 11

Macedonia~nomenclature and
   language 12
Glossary 13

Practical information

When to go 14
Passports and formalities 14
Bulgarian embassies and missions
   15
The Statistical Card 16
Visas for the business visitor 16
National tourist information 16

Tour operators 16
Skiing 17
Walking and climbing holidays 18
Special interest holidays 18
Camping 18
Health spas 18

Getting to Bulgaria

By air 18
By rail 20
By bus and coach 21
By car 21
By sea 22

Hitch-hiking 23
Currency regulations and custom
   formalities 23
Money 23
Students 24

Arriving in Bulgaria

Tourist information 25
Accommodation 25
Restaurants 25
Food and drink 26

Notes for the business visitor 27
Organised crime 27
Useful addresses 28

Getting around Bulgaria

By rail 29
By bus and coach 30
By tram 30
By car 31
Car hire 32

By air 32
By bicycle 33
By motorcycle 33
Taxis 33

General information

Foreign embassies and missions in
   Bulgaria 34
Emergency telephone numbers 34

Health and health insurance 34
Crime and personal security 35
Self defence and weapons 36

Women travelling in Bulgaria 36
Disabled travellers 36
Public holidays and festivals 37
Opening hours 37
Visiting archaeological sites and
  museums 38
Telephone and postal services 38
Telephone codes from Bulgaria to
  foreign countries 39
Newspapers, magazines and the
  media 39
Antiques and memorabilia 40

Academic institutions 40
Religion 40
Public toilets 41
Narcotics 41
Electricity 41
Drinking water 41
Time 41
Naturism 41
Sport 41
Hunting and fishing 42
Social customs and etiquette 42
Night life and relationships 44

Language

Alphabet 45
Greetings 46
Useful expressions 46
Name... 46

On the street 47
A little grammar 48
Food and drink 48
In the restaurant 49

History of Bulgaria

Eurasian pastoral nomads and the origins of Bulgaria by
  Professor Sir Dimitri Obolensky FBA 53
Bulgaria and the end of Ottoman rule by Professor Richard Crampton 59
Bulgaria and the end of communism by James Pettifer 67
Greek influences in Bulgarian life and history by James Pettifer 68
The Turkish minority in Bulgaria by Dr Hugh Poulton 71
Bulgaria and the Macedonian Question by James Pettifer 74
Bulgarian culture and folklore 74
Bulgarian wildlife and ecology 78

Select bibliography 79

The Guide

Sofia 83

Central Sofia and ancient Serdica 86
The city centre east of the Sheraton Hotel 96
The University and the Orlov Bridge area 104
Outer Sofia 108
  The Central Railway Station area 108
  The Intercontinental Hotel and vicinity 109
  The Hotel Rodina and vicinity 109
  The Ambassador Hotel and vicinity 110
  The Military Museum and the National Palace of Culture 110

Environs of Sofia 111

Mount Vitosha 111
Boyana 113
Dragalevtsi 115
The Royal Palace at Vrania 116

The Dragoman Pass, Vidin and the northwest 118

Sofia to the Dragoman Pass and Serbia 119
Sofia to Vidin via the Iskar Gorge 120
Sofia to Vidin via the Petrohan Pass and Berkovitsa 125

Svishtov and the central Danube 131

Sofia to Pleven 131
Pleven to Svishtov 133

Ruse and the eastern Danube 138

Ruse 138
The eastern Danube valley 142

Varna, the northern Black Sea coast and the Shumen region 144

Varna 144
The Black Sea coast from Varna to the Romanian border 151
The Black Sea coast south of Varna 157
The Shumen region and the First Bulgarian Kingdom 164

Burgas and the southern Black Sea coast 169

Burgas 169
Burgas to Sozopol and the Turkish border 173

Plovdiv and region 179

Plovdiv 179
North and west of Plovdiv 185
East and south of Plovdiv 189

Stara Zagora, Veliko Tarnovo and the central mountains 196

Stara Zagora and environs 196
Veliko Tarnovo and environs 201

Melnik and the southwest 208

Melnik and region 208
The Rila mountains 217

Pernik, Kyustendil and the western borderlands 220

Pernik and environs 221
Kyustendil and environs 221
Excursions into the FYROM 227

Index 229

Maps and plans

Ancient Roman provinces 75
Ancient Thrace and the Black Sea Coast 55
Burgas 171
Plovdiv 183
Ruse 141
Sofia 88–89
Tarnovo 203
Varna 147

Introduction

Bulgaria is an important Balkan country with outstanding mountain and coastal scenery, interesting antiquities, and a long and complex history. Under communism Bulgaria was generally seen in the West as a mass tourism destination, linked to the development of the Black Sea coast resorts, and skiing was promoted in some centres. Although individual travel was allowed in the later communist period, and motoring holidays were possible after the mid 1960s, very few people actually did visit the country independently by road, or the Black Sea coast on cruise ships. The history, culture or monuments of Bulgaria have never been very well known in the United States or Great Britain.

Large numbers of travellers have always passed through Bulgaria on the road and rail routes to Turkey and the East, but most of them made little contact with Bulgaria or Bulgarians. The study of **Bulgarian culture**, **history** and **language** is confined to a very few specialised institutions in academia in Britain and the USA. Even important and dramatic archaeological discoveries, such as the great Thracian tombs at Kazanluk, are not very well known. Business contacts under communism were also fairly limited. There has been some increase since the one party state collapsed in 1989–90.

Political turmoil in the Balkans after the end of communism has not assisted Bulgaria. After 1989–90, a period of economic chaos ensued, with widespread food and power shortages, and visiting the country seemed unwise. The war in neighbouring ex-Yugoslavia followed, which has fundamentally affected perceptions of all the Balkan countries, and will probably do so for the foreseeable future. The conflict and its confused aftermath has isolated Bulgaria psychologically, and to a degree physically, from many European links, as the war interrupted many traditional routes between Bulgaria and Western Europe, so that, for example, the old Orient Express rail route from Belgrade became totally inoperative for a time. United Nations economic sanctions against the old Yugoslavia had a serious effect on the Bulgarian economy and little real compensation was paid by the international community. Bulgaria did not benefit financially from the Dayton settlement. In 1996 a major economic and currency crisis developed that had the advantage of making Bulgaria a very cheap country for Western tourists, but this has affected badly nearly every aspect of national life.

There is a great deal more to Bulgaria than the mass tourist resorts, and in this *Blue Guide*, I have tried to provide a sense of the rich heritage from the **Thracian, Classical, Byzantine, medieval Bulgarian, Ottoman Turkish** and **National Revival** periods, and the remarkable mountain and coastal scenery and countryside. There are historic towns and fine beaches on the Black Sea coast which have not been spoiled by building development, and are well worth visiting. Specialist tourism is developing in some areas, such as bird-watching and hiking.

As a first post-World War II *Blue Guide* to Bulgaria since the excellent French-language *Guide Bleu* of 1933, and Frank Fox's pioneering volume *Bulgaria* published by A&C Black in 1909, I have to some extent focused the book on the Classical and Byzantine heritage, which has been inadequately covered in many communist period Bulgarian books, and on the parts of the country, such as

Sofia and the Black Sea coast where functioning decent hotels and restaurants exist. This is no longer the case in some provincial towns in the interior, the central mountains in particular, although it is hoped to include them more fully in future editions when social and economic conditions may have improved. Some Bulgaria *aficionados* may notice omissions in this context, but the practical background for the ordinary traveller needs to be borne in mind.

I would be most grateful to receive any comments visitors may have on the text, as up-to-date information on many topics has not always been easy to obtain, material on many places and buildings is still dominated by books from the communist period, or even before, and site guides are often scanty and sometimes non-existent. The museum situation is fairly unpredictable and while I have tried to include up-to-date information on opening times, do not be surprised to find local arrangments changing at short notice. Many museums in provincial towns are closed by property restitution disputes.

I would also like to add that I am not a hiker or hillwalker and while I have endeavoured to describe routes correctly, the descriptions are based generally on secondary sources rather than personal research.

It should be borne in mind by all users of the book, and visitors to Bulgaria, that many matters of 20C—and earlier—Bulgarian history are highly controversial and this affects the way monuments and historic buildings are perceived. What are regarded by some academics as errors are often actually quite legitimate differences of opinion over ideology or historical interpretation. This particularly applies to elements of the Ottoman heritage.

All factual mistakes are my own responsibility.

Acknowledgements

Inevitably, when writing a *Blue Guide*, the writer has many debts to numerous friends and colleagues, some specific and local, others more general and indefinable. My deepest gratitude for help with this volume must go to two sometime members of the diplomatic corps in Sofia, Janet Gunn and Anastase Sideris. Both have shared their deep knowledge of Bulgaria with me and have been of great practical assistance and inspiration.

I am also very grateful to the following: Ivan Stancioff, Michael Christides, Jane Govier, Stefan Tavrov, Assen Navachkov, Professor Frank Walbank FBA, Douglas Ellis, Robert Mickey, Lily Netsova, Sue Comely, Vasil Atanassov, Ilko Shivachev, Ivan Donchev, Christopher Cviic, Yonko Yonchev, Gueorgui Dagardadin, Dr Kyril Drezov, Rosemary Thomas, Milena Milotinova, Borislav Velinkov, Andrew Lance, Georgi Danailov, Professor John Koliopoulos, Dimitar Georgiev, Kamen Velichkov, Mark Nelson and Brian Brown of the *Wall Street Journal*, Vassil Jivkov, Dimitar Dereliev, Julian Chomet, Professor Basil Kondis, Tanya Barron, James Munro, Christo Drumev, Michael and Iliana Saraouleva, Peter Robinson, Dr Emilia Drumeva, Miranda Vickers, Jane Gabriel, Eddie Shirkie, Professor Thanos Veremis, Dr Rossita Gradeva, Jane Hibbert, the staff of the *Slavyanska Besseda Hotel*, Richard Thomas, Tom O'Sullivan, Dr Alexandra N. Dipchikova, Haroula Christodoulou, Paul Calverley, David Alford, Stanimir Tzvetkov, Dr Georgi Svechnikov, Dimitris Caramitsos-Tziras, Yalcin Oral, Colonel Mike Dove, Zhivko Nakev, Mike Dineen, Rada Sharlandjieva, Vencislav Again, Dr Bozhidar Samardjiev, Dr Asparouh Velinov, Boyana Hadjimishev, Maya

Marinova, Sylvia Beamish, Professor Averil Cameron FBA, Alexander Dinevski and Dragan Ivanovski.

Very special gratitude is due to Professors Richard Crampton and Sir Dimitri Obolensky for their wise advice and encouragement and to Philip Goodenfor his sketches and photographs. George Menev and Ivanka Nedeva provided endless practical assistance in Sofia. Dr Elizabeth Close of Flinders University in Adelaide and Dr Nevena Georgiev were kind enough to provide expert advice on linguistic matters. *The Times* Foreign Desk, in particular Richard Owen, David Watts, Denis Taylor and Graham Paterson, contributed to the success of the James Bourchier commemoration at Rila in January 1996, as did Mercia MacDermott, Gareth Jones of Reuters, the *Mati Bulgaria* society, and Jane Collins of the *Reuters Foundation* in London. Judy Tither has been an expert and patient editor.

I also owe thanks to Professors Archie Brown and Alex Pravda of the Russian Centre at St Antony's College, Oxford and Professor Basil Kondis of the Institute of Balkan Studies, University of Thessaloniki, for the hospitality in their distinguished academic homes, and the use of their libraries and research facilities.

Explanations

This book is divided into chapters, each covering a major city and/or a geographical region of the country. Excursions, diversions and important background information are presented as indented text.

Distances are given throughout the route or sub-route in kilometres. Although every effort has been made to ensure accuracy, outside the main centres they should only be regarded as approximate.

Heights of mountains are given in metres and are believed to be accurate.

Main roads are shown as on the numerous general road maps of Bulgaria that are internationally available, and distances can be regarded as accurate. Road quality is generally as shown on the maps but expect damaged road surfaces in many places.

Minor roads. There are thousands of kilometres of minor roads in Bulgaria, which are not shown on maps, especially in mountains and forests. Some are very poor and a four-wheel-drive vehicle is needed to navigate them successfully. **Avoid minor roads wherever possible. Carry a compass and a complete spares kit**.

Many very small **villages** and **hamlets** are not shown on most maps, nor is anything to do with the Bulgarian military, even the most innocuous establishments, such as military housing estates. The Bulgarian military have very good, detailed maps of the whole country which can sometimes be found on the black market or on Sofia street bookstalls, and are well worth buying.

Place name spelling. There are often variations in the spelling of many Bulgarian place names when translated into English. For instance, I have found the Black Sea coast resort spelt *Nesebur*, *Nessebur*, *Nesebar* and *Nesbar*, all in official or semi-official publications. I have adopted one form for all places mentioned in this book, but do not be surprised to find others in use. Some town names have been changed since the end of the communist period i.e. **Dobric** was known as *Tolbukhin* from 1950 to 1990. The communist names are still used by some people, mostly older supporters of the old social system, and it is worth finding out what they are from pre-1989 maps.

The Turkish minority often use the old **Ottoman** place names for some towns and cities, ie, **Ruse** is often called *Ruschuk* in conversation. The same process applies with Greek-speakers, especially on the Black Sea coast, where **Sozopol** becomes *Sozopolis*, or *Sozopoli*.

Urban street names. Many street names have been changed since the communist period, but the older names are often in local use, and the whole situation is very confusing to the foreign visitor, and also to Bulgarians travelling in unfamiliar regions of the country. Outside Sofia and big towns, many names are not marked at all.

Statistics. Statistics such as population figures have been taken from the most up-to-date sources available. It has often been difficult to obtain accurate figures, and while every effort has been made to ensure accuracy, those given in this book should be independently verified if required for scholarly or business purposes.

This particularly applies to politically controversial statistics such as the size of ethnic minorities. Economic statistics are generally reasonably reliable, but business visitors should bear in mind the large scale of the unrecorded 'grey' cash economy in Bulgaria when using them.

Macedonia~Nomenclature and Language

With the end of the second **Yugoslavia** between 1990 and 1995, the territory adjoining **Bulgaria** to the west that was occupied by the old Socialist Republic of Macedonia has attempted to gain international recognition as an independent state. Much controversy has been generated about the name of this state, with Greece strongly resisting the attempts of the government in Skopje to be recognised as the 'Republic of Macedonia'. Bulgaria has recognised the 'state', but not the 'nation', as it does not recognise the 'Macedonian national identity' claimed by the Skopje government or the 'Macedonian' language.

In this *Blue Guide* I have from time to time used the name 'Macedonia' to denote the general geographical territory, which covers parts of modern Albania, Bulgaria, Greece, the Skopje-based state and south Serbia. The abbreviation FYROM (Former Yugoslav Republic of Macedonia) is generally used for the state itself. This is the name recognised for international use under the United Nations brokered 'small package' agreement signed with Greece in autumn 1995.

The use of this, or any other term, for the 'Macedonian' territory does not imply any view on the vexed question of the 'Macedonian' identity, but is only a convenient verbal usage for the purposes of the *Guide*. For background, see the section on the **Macedonian Question** (p 74).

In general, Bulgarians see 'Macedonia' as primarily a geographical term, and concepts of a 'Macedonian nation' or 'Macedonian language' as products of the political ambitions of the leaders of Titoist Yugoslavia.

Glossary

BANU Bulgarian Agrarian National Union
BKP Bulgarian Communist Party
Bulevard Boulevard
Ceta armed band
EU European Union
FRY Yugoslavia
FYROM Former Yugoslav Republic of Macedonia
IMRO Internal Macedonian Revolutionary Organisation
Mafiya Mafia

Manastir monastery
Most bridge
Nomenklatura communist elite
Nos cape
Pave boulder
Ploshtad square
Roma gypsies
Sobranje assembly
Sveti/Sveta saint
Ulitsa street
Voivode military leader

Turkish-language terms

ada island
bazar market
bey Ottoman landowner
bounar drinking fountain
chechme fountain
chiflik farm
dagh mountain
deniz sea
derbend defile
dere stream
eski ancient
ghazi military leader
gueul lake
hammam baths
han inn or mansion
hisar fortress
kale fort
kapou door

kopru bridge
konak big house, usually administrative
köy village
liman port
pashalik Ottoman administrative area
sandjak Ottoman administrative division
sou water
souq market
tash stone
tekke Dervish shrine
tepe hill
turbe tomb
vilayet Ottoman administrative division
yeni new

Thracian root words often found in Bulgarian place names

Apa water
Berga mountain
Bria town or settlement
Burd ford
Dava town
Diza fortress
Kella spring

Pan swamp
Para market place
Sara stream
Stur village
Upa river
Zura water source

Practical information

When to go

Bulgaria has a **moderate continental climate**, with warm summers and cold winters, but there are many microclimates and wide regional and local variations in the weather. Many parts of the country have special factors affecting temperature and precipitation which can produce very marked differences in climate within a few kilometres. These include proximity to the River Danube, exposure to freezing cold northeast winds in the winter from the Eurasian steppe, and to the Black Sea. The mountain ranges are always very cold indeed in winter, with deep snow lying for several months of the year, although the Rhodope climate is less severe than that of mountains elsewhere in the country.

The valleys of the southeast and southwest, leading down to Greece, with the Struma, Mesta and Sazlijka rivers, act as channels for warmer air from the Mediterranean region to flow into the heart of the country, and in a mild winter these areas can be very temperate and pleasant. Spring and autumn are often the best times to visit for general tourism and business, and to go to the interior of the country, although it can be very wet on occasion. April, May, June, September and October are recommended, when the climate closely resembles that of France north of the Midi. Winter travellers generally concentrate on the ski resorts, although Sofia and Plovdiv can make enjoyable centres for city breaks then. Summer can be very hot and humid, in Sofia particularly, although temperatures rarely reach Mediterranean levels for long, and the Black Sea coast thrives during these months. The Plain of Thrace becomes very hot and dusty in high summer. Air temperatures on the Black Sea can be high as early as late May, but the sea does not really warm up fully until early July. The main beach holiday season there ends in mid-September, although in a good year it can be very enjoyable several weeks later.

Drought has been a national problem in Bulgaria in recent years, as elsewhere in the Balkans, although the situation has improved somewhat recently.

Passports and formalities

Since spring 1997 all **EU** (plus EEA—Swiss, Norwegian) and **US** citizens **do not** require visas if they visit Bulgaria for a period of 30 days. Package holiday buyers do not generally require separate visas, check that the operator is arranging the necessary documents well before departure. Individual visas for non-EU nationals are obtainable at Sofia airport and at border crossing points, but it is much cheaper and easier to buy a visa from the Bulgarian Embassy in the country of residence of the traveller. Transit visas are also available, for those staying less than 30 hours. These are cheaper. If a visa is purchased at the border, you may have to pay as much as $US30 or $US40 more. Bulgarian border officials may not have 'change' in hard currency; bring plenty of brand new, small denomination, hard currency notes (see p 24).

The visa section and other consular services of the Bulgarian Embassy in London (see below) are open on weekdays from 10.00–13.00. Personal applicants can usually be dealt with on the spot, although you have to pay an additional fee. Allow at least 10 working days for a postal application. Business visitors need to apply for a separate visa, and business postal applicants should allow at least two more weeks for documents to be processed (see below).

Tourist visas are normally issued for a month's duration, and have three months' travel validity. Bring two passport-sized photographs, and the fee in cash, cheques are not accepted. Adults and children over 16 travelling on the same passport should expect to pay visa charges for each person travelling. Children with their own passport pay the full fee, irrespective of age.

Bulgarian embassies and missions
Albania: 12 Ruga Skenderbeg, Tirana 1
Cyprus: 15 St. Paul Street, Nicosia
France: 1 ave Rapp, Paris 75015
Germany: Leipzigerstrasse 20, Berlin 1084
Greece: 33 Stratigou Kallari Street, Paleo Physico, Athens 15452
Iran: Vali Asr, Ave Tavanir Nesami Ganjavi, 82 Tehran
Romania: 5 Strada Rabat, Bucharest
Russia: 66 , Moscow
Switzerland: Bernastrasse 2, 3000 Bern 6
Turkey: 124 Ataturk Bulvari, Ankara.
UK: 186-188, Queens Gate, London. SW7 5HL, ☎ 0171 584 9400/3144/9433, fax 0171 584 4948 , telex 25465
USA: 1621-2 Str NW, Washington DC, ☎ 202 3877969
UN Mission: 11 East 84th Street, New York, NY ☎ 7374790

The Statistical Card
Bureaucracy is a fact of life in Bulgaria, as elsewhere in Eastern Europe, and begins at the borders, in fact the cynical traveller may well feel it finds some of its most perfect expressions there. On arrival in Bulgaria, the visa will be validated at the point of entry, after the traveller has filled in a **Statistical Card** issued by the Bulgarian immigration authorities. If arriving at the airport, warn friends waiting to meet you to allow time for these formalities, which can take as long as 45 minutes if the terminal immigration officials are busy. This important document must be kept with the traveller's passport during a visit, and it is a legal requirement that it is stamped at the hotel where the visitor stays. If you are staying with friends or a family, registration with the police is required, at the nearest police station to their house or flat.

In practice, these regulations are sometimes not very vigorously enforced, especially in a short stay and some hotels forget to stamp the Card. If staying with friends for an odd night or two, it is worth getting them to write their name and address on the yellow card, with dates of residence. This theoretically contravenes the Ministry of the Interior rules, but is common practice.

NB. It is very important indeed not to **lose** the **Statistical Card**, as even if it does not have a full complement of residence stamps, it must be surrendered at the point of exit from Bulgaria and considerable difficulties can be encountered with officialdom if it is lost. A fine of $US50 per day of residence can be levied. Card irregularities can affect future visa applications.

Students and business visitors who intend to reside for any length of time in Bulgaria should seek advice from the British Embassy in Sofia about residence registration. The Embassy is at 65 Vasil Levsky Street (☎ from UK 00 359 2 980

1220, fax 00 359 2 980 1229). The consular section is open in the mornings on weekdays from 09.00 to 12.00.

Visas for the business visitor

Business visitors who intend to make frequent visits to Bulgaria can apply for a multi-entry visa, but this should be done at least six weeks before travel is intended, through the Bulgarian Embassy in the normal country of residence. It is a good idea to seek the support of the local Commercial Attaché in any application. With the application it is necessary to submit a letter from a Bulgarian business organisation, making clear the fact that regular business contacts have been established. It often helps in obtaining a multi-entry visa if a single entry business visa has been obtained and used first, and that that visit to Bulgaria went smoothly. Visas are issued with three and six month validity periods.

National Tourist Information

UK: Sofia House, 19, Conduit Street, London W1R 9TD, ☎ 0171 491 4499.
USA: 41 East 42nd Street, Suite 508, New York, NY 10017, ☎ 212 5735530.
Switzerland: 5 Schaffhauserstrasse, Zurich 8006, ☎ 411 362 8089.

Generally speaking, brochures on the main centres are in good supply, and helpful, but information is often somewhat out of date in some respects, and should be checked independently if planning a holiday tour or business visit. This is particularly important in Sofia and the larger cities where conditions change frequently. Information on private room rentals is often very difficult to obtain outside Bulgaria. In Sofia, the *Sofia Quick Guide* is a very useful English-language monthly publication, containing many addresses, information on cultural and business events, and street maps. Also *Sofia City* and *Sofia Guide*, all of which are easily found at the bigger hotels.

The British-Bulgarian Society, c/o Finsbury Library, 245 St. John's Street, London EC1 4NB publishes a useful small magazine on contemporary Bulgaria, and sometimes organises Bulgarian events in the UK and special interest tours.

Tour operators

The largest specialist tour operators in the United Kingdom is **Balkan Holidays** 19 Conduit Street, London W1 ☎ 0171 493 8612, fax 0171 493 2680, part of the Bulgarian Multigroup conglomerate. Many package operators include Bulgarian destinations in their brochures. See below for information on special interest holidays in Bulgaria.

Skiing. The largest skiing specialists is also **Balkan Holidays** (see above, or for group skiing reservations, minimum 10 people, ☎ 0171 499 1315). The Snowline Bulgaria enquiry number in the UK is ☎ 0839 400409. Other companies with skiing packages include **Enterprise** (☎ 0171 572 7373), **Falcon** (☎ 0171 221 0543), **Global** (☎ 0171 464 7515), **Inghams** (☎ 0171 789 7081), **Phoenix Holidays** (☎ 0171 485 1883), **Schools Abroad** (☎ 0444 441300) and **Skiscope** (☎ 0444 441300). A useful booklet *Ski Guide Bulgaria* is published by Balkan Holidays which gives information on the resorts and basic information on ski runs and facilities.

Visitors planning to ski with small children are recommended to book at

Borovets or Pamporovo, where there are specialist tuition facilities for young beginners. The minimum age for the ski schools is six years. All Bulgarian resorts have slopes suitable for beginners and intermediate skiiers, and English-speaking instructors. All resorts have mountain rescue teams. Most ski hotels are based on half board booking, although Bansko and Borovets both have bed and breakfast accommodation so that you can take advantage of local restaurants.

Generally speaking, Borovets is seen by most visitors as the oldest and most accessible resort, with very active *après-ski*; Bansko is near a remarkable historic area of the country, and the beauties of the Pirin National Park; Vitosha is convenient for Sofia, and Pamporovo often has the most winter sun and the best weather. Cross-country skiing is available in many different places, and is growing in popularity. The greenhouse effect is beginning to affect resorts, especially Pamporovo, and it is worth taking advice about likely snow conditions before booking, especially at either end of the season.

Walking and climbing holidays. Bulgaria is one of the best countries in Eastern Europe for walking and more serious hiking holidays. In the late 19C, Bulgarians began to hike and explore their forests and mountains, and the Bulgarian monarchs, especially Tzar Ferdinand, were keen walkers. The pursuit was also encouraged under communism, and it was a task of the Young Pioneers to clear the mountain trails each year of undergrowth.

Nowadays there is an extensive network of trails and paths covering very large areas of forest and national park in every area of the country, although they are not all in good repair. Ski runs are used by walkers in the summer in some places. Routes in the more popular areas, such as Mount Vitosha outside Sofia, and the Rila mountains, are usually well signed, but anyone planning to venture anywhere off the beaten track needs to purchase good maps and a compass and binoculars beforehand. Good quality ex-Soviet equipment can be bought very cheaply in the Sofia flea market. Isolation alarms or flares should be carried in autumn and winter (see below p 101).

The **Pirin Travel Agency**, 30 Stamboliiski Blvd, Sofia (☎ 870 687) handles bookings for the Bulgarian Association and runs a network of chalets for hikers. Chalets usually offer only shelter, not food or drink or cigarettes. A useful book for the serious walker is *A Walker's Companion* by Julian Perry (pub. Cordee, London), which gives detailed directions for some of the most spectacular long-distance treks in Bulgaria.

NB. Great care should be exercised in the mountains in the spring, autumn and winter months, where fog and thick low cloud can descend without warning, and blinding snowstorms and whiteouts can occur. It is advisable to walk with a companion. Avoid shepherds' dogs.

Special interest holidays

By far the most popular tours in this field are those organised for British bird-watchers. Bulgaria is rich in migration sites and native feathered residents and migrants. Information on companies and learned societies active in this field is best obtained from the magazine of the Royal Society for the Protection of Birds, available from RSPB, Sandy, Bedfordshire.

A Bulgarian company with a good reputation with British birdwatchers is **N. P. Dilchev**, 20A 'Cherny Vrah' Blvd, Floor 5 Apt 5, Sofia 1407, ☎ from UK 00359 2 65 55 25, fax 00359 2 80 37 91. This company can conduct tours in French as well as English. They usually include visits to one or two archaeological sites. A very useful English language book is *Where to Watch Birds in Bulgaria*, by Petar Iankov, published by the Bulgarian Society for the Protection of Birds. It is on sale at the Natural History Museum shop in Sofia.

British Museum Traveller Ltd, 46 Bloomsbury Street, London WC1B 2QQ, ☎ 0171 636 7169 organise specialised archaeological tours with experts which have a very good reputation. Last available prices were for 1996 when an 8-day tour cost about £995. **Swan Hellenic** cruises sometimes visit Varna and other ports and coastal sites on their Black Sea cruises. A number of river cruise companies, mostly based in Germany and Austria, run boats down the Danube.

Camping and caravans. Camping and caravaning is widespread in Bulgaria, and although visitors are only supposed to camp at recognised sites, in practice there is little to stop discreet and sensible camping in the woods and countryside. **Take care to avoid fire risks, particularly in the pine forests**.

There are about 110 recognised campsites, most of them dotted about along the Black Sea coast and in the coastal hinterland. Amenities of sites vary, from the quite good to the basic and unkempt. Standards are highest on the Black Sea coast. Charges are low. Security is often not terribly good; in terms of petty theft problems, valuables should not be taken.

A list of sites is available from Balkan Holidays, but given the condition of some non-coastal sites, it is not necessarily very helpful.

Health spas. Health spas are very numerous in Bulgaria, and although some of them are not in the most up-to-date condition, they are important holiday centres and tourist attractions. Some have a very good reputation indeed for therapeutic care, such as Sandanski for asthma. Details are given in the text where appropriate. In many places treatment or use of the facilities is not allowed without a full medical examination and diagnosis, and if intending to take a cure, it is worth finding out what information is required by the Bulgarian doctors before departure.

There are numerous thermal bath centres dotted around all over the country, and they are well worth patronising. Most have men and women admitted on different days of the week.

Getting to Bulgaria

By air

In view of the distance from the United Kingdom, much the easiest way to get to Bulgaria is by air. Services from the UK are completely dominated by **Balkan Airlines** and **British Airways**. A very few charter operators go to Bulgaria, generally linked to skiing trips, but it is often very difficult to buy tickets without buying a whole holiday. In practice, virtually all air travel from the UK is on the two scheduled operators, and there is no real charter market. London to Sofia takes about three and a half hours. Out of high season it may be worth considering buying a whole package holiday to Bulgaria, even if you are intending to travel independently within the country, as the whole cost of the holiday can be much less than some flights.

British Airways (☎ 0181 897 4000; World Offers 01345 222111) offers a good service from London Gatwick at 10.15, currently four times a week, on Sunday, Monday, Tuesday and Thursday. The aircraft returns to the UK from Sofia in the afternoon. Providing you stay a Saturday night, ticket prices are reasonable, and between October and April there are often very good value cheap offers. Otherwise, prices seem to be designed for the business traveller on expense account, and can be expensive, especially if booked at short notice. Gatwick can be very busy indeed in the summer and at weekends, and plenty of time should be allowed to cope with the M25 and for airport formalities. The BA central offices in Sofia are in 56 Alabin Street, ☎ 981 7000/1 and in the Sheraton Hotel; at Sofia airport ☎ 973 3031. BA have a reliable air cargo service, with good security in Sofia (☎ 01345 222777).

Balkan Airlines has the advantage of flying from Heathrow (enquiry number at Heathrow, ☎ 0181 759 1818), but with an older fleet than British Airways, and with less good food and service. It is odd that a country that produces such good wine as Bulgaria should find it so difficult to serve much of it aloft. Prices for weekday travel are similar to BA, but often with cheaper weekend offers. In both cases, the price for a return ticket with a Saturday stopover in the summer is currently in the region of £310, but this can vary considerably sometimes. There is a small additional airport tax to pay. Balkan Airlines contact numbers in Sofia are telephone booking ☎ 684 148, head office ☎ 79321, fax 652997; cargo 796 104. Chasters ☎ 654947, fax 798057.

Most major European airlines fly to Sofia, such as **Austrian Airlines**, **Lufthansa**, **Swissair**, **Aeroflot** and **Olympic**, from the hub airports in their respective countries. **Swissair** has a very good reputation. Balkan fly to the USA (to New York and Washington). Their address in the USA is Balkan Holidays, 41 East 42nd Street, Suite 508, New York, NY 10017, ☎ 212 5735538. Many Americans coming to Sofia take a BA transatlantic flight to Gatwick, then the BA Gatwick–Sofia flight. **Varig**, the Brazilian national airline, flies to and from Sofia to South America.

For those travelling to Sofia, or the southwest of the country, and with a little more time, it is well worth considering the exceptional value **British Airways** daily flight from London Heathrow to Thessaloniki, in northern Greece. This seems always to be at least £100 cheaper than direct flights from London to Sofia, and on occasion is as much as £150 cheaper. The road journey to Sofia only takes about five hours, and is a beautiful and interesting trip. There are fast regular coach services linking the two cities (see p 109). Good value and reliable BA ticketing for Sofia and Thessaloniki is available from **Griffin Marine Ltd** in London (☎ 0171 814 9977, fax 0171 814 9978: Mr T. Sirianos).

It is possible to reach Sofia via the **JAT** flights from Heathrow to Belgrade, which are also usually much cheaper than London–Sofia direct flights, then travel by train or coach to Sofia. The **British Airways** London–Belgrade flight is very efficent, but rather expensive. There is no Belgrade–Sofia air link at the moment, although that may change in the near future. A visa to enter F R Yugoslavia is required, current price $US15 which must be purchased before departure in the traveller's country of residence. **JAT** tickets are reliably available from Pilgrim Tours, 37 Maddox Street, London W1 (☎ 0171 495 1323). The

Yugoslav Embassy in London is at 10 Lennox Gardens, London SW7 (☎ 0171 370 6105), open 10.00–13.00. A letter of invitation from a FRY resident must accompany the application form. Visitors arriving without a visa will be detained and possibly fined. Carry ID at all times in Yugoslavia.

There are cheap flights from the UK to Istanbul. The Turkish capital has good coach links with Plovdiv and Sofia from the Istanbul international bus terminal. The journey takes about a day to Sofia (see below). Istanbul–Sofia air links exist, with Balkan and Turkish Airlines but seem rather expensive at the moment. A Turkish visa can be bought easily at point of entry, current price £10.

The main non-state carrier within Bulgaria is **Hemus Air**, which operates a small but useful regional network with flights to cities such as Tirana, Leipzig and Bucharest, and some internal flights.

Travel to Bulgaria via **Bucharest** airport is not recommmended, as cheap connecting flights are not usually available and other transport links are poor. Travel to Sofia via **Athens** is well worth considering in the autumn and winter, when BA and Olympic Heathrow–Athens tickets are very cheap indeed, then use the linking Balkan or Olympic flight north to Sofia, which take about 50 minutes and is not expensive. Greek trains are improving and can also be used.

Some Balkan Holidays flights go direct from the UK to Varna and Burgasin the summer season, and Plovdiv is used for skiing trips going to Pamporovo.

By rail

Until 1991 this was a popular route for students and backpackers in the summer, but the war in ex-Yugoslavia threw the international lines from Europe into chaos. The through route of the old Orient Express via Belgrade was closed for some of the time, and the Belgrade–Sofia service (assuming the traveller could reach Belgrade at all) was running irregularly and with serious security problems on the train.

After the signature of the Dayton agreements in autumn 1995, and the lifting of some UN sanctions on Serbia, the situation has improved marginally, with better rolling stock on the Belgrade–Sofia line, and a regular service being established. There are plans under the programme for Yugoslav reconstruction for a renewal of the whole railway system in the Balkans, but what will actually materialise remains to be seen. It is possible to reach Sofia by train from Thessaloniki in Greece, but although scenic, it is a very slow journey indeed, often with long delays at the border at Kulata.

In extremis, as for instance during the Greek lorry blockade of the border in December 1996, it is possible to leave this train at the border and travel by road to either city.

NB. For the time being the international trains running north of Belgrade, in Serbia, Bosnia and Croatia, are better avoided, except by the dedicated rail enthusiast. This is not simply because of politics and war. As elsewhere in Eastern Europe, security from the theft point of view is often not very good, especially on sleeper services. If you do use the trains, carry adequate supplies of food , drink, cigarettes and toilet tissue. It is a good idea to go with, or find, a travelling companion. **Avoid carrying valuables**.

The telephone number for central rail information in Sofia is 31 111.

By bus and coach

There are no London–Sofia through services operating at the moment, but **coach travel** is nevertheless a practical method of reaching Bulgaria for those with some time to spare. All options involve changing buses en route: it is not necessarily much cheaper than flying. Bear in mind food and accommodation costs when calculating the cost of bus travel over several days.

The most practical route from the UK is to take a through coach from London to Greece. *Time Out* and similar London magazines carry advertisements for services. (Try **Magicbus**, 20 Filellinon St, Athens ☎ 3237471-4.). Change buses in Greece, either taking a KTEL bus to Thessaloniki from the central long distance bus station in Athens, or a private coach, and find the Sofia bus from the Hotel Vergina in Via Egnetia Street (port end of the street not far from the railway station) in Thessaloniki. This excellent service on modern coaches makes a good link with the BA London–Thessaloniki flight (see p 19). It is a beautiful and interesting journey north up the Struma river valley. At the moment, buses leave Thessaloniki at about 07.00, and return from Sofia about 14.00 on the same day. **Recommended**.

Direct coach services run to Sofia from several German cities, including Berlin, Munich and Frankfurt. Information is available on these services in Sofia from Simex (☎ 814986) and Ercona (☎ 807384). Neckerman is the main German tour operator in Bulgaria, with about 70 per cent of tourists coming from the eastern areas of the old GDR.

There is a reliable coach service each day to Sofia from Skopje, in former Yugoslav Macedonia, leaving from the car park near the Old Station in Skopje at 08.15 in the morning, and returning to Sofia later in the day. The Hotel Bristol (near the Old Station)is a convenient place to stay overnight in Skopje if you use this service (see p 228). In Sofia this coach runs from the depot in Damian Gruev Street, twice daily (see p 110). The scenery in the border mountains is very impressive.

In the winter it can be very cold en route, especially at the Gjuesevo mountain border crossing;take plenty of warm clothing.

By car

It is possible to drive to Bulgaria through Germany and Central Europe by car, but given the length of the journey and the serious practical problems often involved in driving through Romania—and the very badly congested Danube river crossing at Ruse—it is preferable to take a route through eastern France, Switzerland and Italy, then a ferry , from Ancona, Brindisi or one of the Adriatic ports, to Patras in Greece, then on to Thessaloniki and follow the Vardar valley north into Bulgaria.

NB.Although the war has formally ended, driving in FR Yugoslavia, Croatia and Bosnia can be very dangerous. **AVOID**.

In Bulgaria, full documentation and spares kit should be carried. Snow chains are often needed in winter in mountainous areas, and studded snow tyres are worth considering if travel outside the main centres is planned. Heavy duty tyres should be fitted in any event. A steel plate to protect the sump is worth considering if the car is low-slung. Unleaded petrol is becoming more widely available but supplies cannot be guaranteed. Driving conditions after heavy storms can be atrocious, with roads turning into near-rivers, and potholes becoming hidden. There a few natural gas filling stations in some places.

The address of the Union of Bulgarian Motorists is 3 Positano Place, Sofia, ☎ 883978. There are local offices throughout the country. The National Centre for Road Aid (open 08.00–17.00, Sun 14.00–22.00; ☎ 983 308).

Motorists must, by law, report traffic accidents to the police. The emergency number for the traffic police is ☎ 166.

NB. A car must be registered on the **Statistical Card** at the border (see p 15). This is important and failure to do so may lead to a vehicle being impounded in Bulgaria. A transit tax is levied on vehicles entering the country, currently 2000 leva for a car, 12,000 leva for a bus, and 20,000 leva for a truck. If drivers do not pay this charge on entry, they are fined a total of five times the entry fee on exit. Special tolls are levied for people entering the country from the Danube bridge at Ruse, and for the use of the bridge.

If you are planning to live or work in Bulgaria it is worth considering buying a heavy, strong car such as a Mercedes Benz that will cope with the rigours of Bulgarian roads. Four-wheel-drive vehicles are a great asset in many places. Avoid purchase of potentially stolen second-hand vehicles.

The road assistance telephone number is 1286.

Greek–Bulgarian border posts. In addition to the existing crossing at **Kulata**, an agreement negotiated by both governments in September 1996, and now ratified, envisages three new border crossings, at **Exohi**, linking Drama with Gotse Delchev; **Ehinos** near Zlatograd in the Rhodope Mountains; and at **Nymphea**, linking Haskovo and Komotini.

The new border posts will require various EU financed road and construction works, due to the mountainous terrain, and it is far from clear when they will actually open, although all three are supposed to be functioning by the year 2000. Local enquiries are recommended before trying to use any of these routes. In practice, there are numerous small cross border tracks across the Rhodopes which a pedestrian can use. Although the practice is illegal, many shepherds and rural inhabitants of both countries do use them frequently.

River Danube crossings. The main ferry route across the Danube links Calafat, in Romania, with the northwest Bulgarian town of Vidin (see p 128). The only bridge is at Ruse, across to Dzurdzu (see p 141). A new ferry has opened in 1997, between the Romanian port of Becket, and Orjahovo. Although functional, it has been affected by acrimonious disputes about high truck taxes on the Romanian side, currently about $US258 per vehicle. Both ferry timetables can be irregular, especially in the winter, but normally you do not wait longer than two hours. Pedestrians in a hurry can often find someone with a small boat to take them across for a few dollars. There is also a ferry crossing at Silistra.

By sea

There are a number of British shipping and international transport companies with business with Bulgaria, and goods or personal effects can be container loaded and shipped to Bulgaria. There are no scheduled passenger services from the UK, but in practice it may sometimes be possible to buy a cabin on a cargo ship operating to Bulgaria. Passenger services also operate from Burgas and Varna to Istanbul. Varna to Istanbul takes about 13 hours. If moving goods, it is best to take professional advice from a shipping agent in London. **Balkan and**

Black Sea Shipping, 72, Wilson Street, London EC2, ☎ 0171 247 7594 are experienced general shipping brokers in the region. Many Greek shipping and road transport companies in Thessaloniki have Bulgarian routes for cargo.

Hitch-hiking

Hitch-hiking is possible to, and in, Bulgaria, but a companion is needed, and almost anything can, and does, happen on the Bulgarian roads. Only for the brave and determined who can speak some Bulgarian.

Currency regulations and customs formalities

It is forbidden to import Bulgarian currency into Bulgaria. Also forbidden is the import of narcotics and firearms, although hunting weapons and ammunition are permitted if declared on entry. The export of works of art is not allowed. Visitors may import duty free goods to the value of $US300. Animals, pets and livestock can only be imported or exported with a permit issued by the veterinary authority. If importing a video camera or high technology equipment of any kind, it is wise to declare it on entry to Customs officials, and to have receipts or other proof of ownership. Keep receipts for all items bought in Bulgaria of any value.

Normal duty free allowances apply to visitors leaving Bulgaria. The Bulgarian Customs Office is at 1 Aksakov Street, Sofia 1000, ☎ 800402, fax 800723. The Sofia Airport Customs Office is at ☎ 79321.

There is a duty free shop for travellers arriving at Sofia airport, as well as in the departure lounge. It is worth bearing in mind that, for some inexplicable reason, it is often difficult to find Bulgarian products in these shops, particularly quality *rakia* such as *Grozdova*, which needs be purchased in Sofia shops.

If you like Bulgarian **cigarettes**, buy them in the same way, as, for instance, Bulgarian-manufactured *Camel* sell at less than half the price in Sofia kiosks than in the airport duty free shops. Cigars, pipe and rolling tobacco are often hard to find in Bulgaria, bring supplies from UK if required. In contrast, cigarettes are often very good value indeed at road border crossings, with quality Greek cigarettes such as *Karelia* and *Assos* only about $US5 for 200. Wonderful Turkish cigarettes like *Yeni Harman* are on sale at the Turkish border. Local peasants and craftsmen also congregate around these shops in summer, goods such as lace, honey, embroidery, wine, wood carvings and paintings can be well worth buying.

Outstanding quality modern ikons that do not contravene the export regulations can be bought from D&M Export-Import Inc (Mr Vassil Loutchev), based in Los Angles, California, who will arrange purchase and transit, ☎ 213 661 3934 fax 213 661 3638, and from some market stalls and souvenir shops.

Money

The national currency is the **leva**, which used to be divided into 100 **stontiki**, but the latter have disappeared with inflation. Bank notes are issued in 1, 2, 5, 10, 20, 50, 100, 200, 500, 1000, 2000, 5000, 10,000 and 50,000 leva denominations.

NB. It is best to change money with the banks or exchange bureau. It is technically illegal to use the street moneychangers although the law is not widely enforced. At the time of writing the exchange rate is officially fixed at 1000 leva to 1 Deutschmark. Depending on inflation expectations, it is possible to get a 10 or 20 per cent better rate for hard currency with street moneychangers. Transactions should only be made in daytime, in public places. Money-changers are adept at folding notes double to swindle their customers.

There are significant quantities of forged dollars circulating in Bulgaria, as in other east European countries, and travellers should familiarise themselves with the informal checks that can be made on bills, ie, the rough patch over the top centre watermark on genuine notes. Pre-1991 bills, with the 'thin' top edge should not be taken, as they may be rejected, even if in perfect condition.

Visitors should bring brand new, small denomination notes, preferably either US dollars or German marks, for their own use. Most British banks now operate a quality standard for Russia, with either brand new or virtually brand new notes. It is worth insisting on this standard before leaving home, as endless trouble can be caused in Bulgaria by old or torn currency, or notes with tears or writing on them. **NB**. Do not bring hundred dollar bills, as they are notoriously difficult to change outside central Sofia.

NB. Anyone doing business in Bulgaria should purchase a machine to detect counterfeit notes and dollar bills. Any currency in a business transaction should be checked for authenticity.

Travellers' cheques can be cashed in Sofia and the main tourist centres at branches of the National Bank and some hotels and exchange bureau, but it is unwise to rely on facilities being available. The same applies to Eurocheques, which are often very difficult to use outside a few places in Sofia. Credit cards are becoming more widely used, with a few Bulgarian banks being linked to the main international networks, and others operating their own credit and cheque guarantee cards. Credit card fraud is not uncommon, and is another argument against their use. Some Bulgarian banks are of doubtful solvency, avoid using them, or their credit cards.

In general, hard currency notes—'cool cash' as people say in Belgrade—is the strongly recommmended payment method, and it is nearly always much cheaper to pay in cash for goods or services than to try to use cheques or credit cards. Many hotels will give prices in hard currency but require the currency to be changed into leva before a bill can be paid.

Students

Although in theory an International Student Card entitles the holder to a number of discounts in Bulgaria, such as lower museum entrance charges, and reductions in public transport fares, in practice these are often difficult to obtain, as in Bulgarian eyes, most charges are already very low for visitors with hard currency. It is certainly not worth buying an Interrail card in the UK for rail use in Bulgaria either, given the current low level of train fares (see below, p 20). The **Pirin Agency**, 30 Stamboliiski Blvd, Sofia, ☎ 870687 has information on youth hostels and hiking tours.

Arriving in Bulgaria

There are few tourist information facilities at road crossing points into Bulgaria. Sofia airport has an information office and can assist with booking hotels. Duty free offices at road crossing points can be very good value for certain goods, particularly cigarettes. The main car hire companies have offices at Sofia airport.

Tourist information

CICM, 8 Sveti Sofia Street, 1000 Sofia, ☎ 9812716, fax 9812186, telex 23829.
Balkan Holidays, 5 Blvd Vitosha, Sofia , ☎ 835111, fax 800134.

Accommodation

It is best to book hotel accommodation in advance of arrival. The tourist guides and brochures available in foreign tourist offices usually give telephone and fax numbers. Generally speaking, there is no problem in finding somewhere to stay in Sofia unless there is a major international conference or similar event in the city. If you have friends in Sofia it is a good idea to ask them to call at the hotel to confirm the reservation in person. It is difficult to book provincial accommodation in advance, but outside the high summer season it is usually easy to find somewhere to stay.

In some places private rooms have to be found through personal contacts, and cannot be booked from abroad.

Restaurants

The restaurant situation in Bulgaria is complex and rather unpredictable, although with luck, it can be rewarding. Excellent wine and *rakia* are available everywhere, the trick is to find the food to go with it. The old state restaurants have been privatised, and there are plenty of conventional Western cheap food places such as pizza bars, even in remote towns. In Sofia there are some very good private restaurants, often in the outer suburbs, and many reasonably priced establishments serving standard Bulgarian food dotted about all over the city. Foreign cuisines are increasingly well represented. The same applies to bigger towns and cities all over the country. Pizza establishments are ubiquitous.

The picture is far from clear overall; some medium-sized towns are gastronomic deserts, with virtually nowhere to eat at all, and the traveller should be prepared for difficulties in the winter, where visitors are not expected anywhere except in the ski resorts and Sofia. In small towns and villages do not expect anything whatsoever, and be grateful for whatever is available. Many poorer Bulgarian families cannot ever afford to eat out at all, and in the old industrial centres and some other poorer districts, there is no economic basis for a restaurant culture of any kind. When on the road, it is worth carrying at least a basic picnic kit, as fresh food in Bulgaria is often excellent and avoids the use of some dismal restaurants. A 'Swiss Army' knife is indispensable.

Prices are generally low, except in fashionable Sofia and Black Sea eating places. Culinary standards vary enormously. Pork is much the most popular meat, good quality lamb or beef can be difficult to find. Fish is also difficult except at the coast, and is often expensive. Most Bulgarian vegetables and fruit are very good indeed, in season, but are often not well harvested or marketed, and quantity rather than quality is common. In this context it is worth bearing in mind the shortages that plagued the communist period. Herbs and spices are very good indeed. Yoghourt, herbs and honey are outstanding. Olive oil is difficult to obtain anywhere; it is worth bringing some from the UK if required.

Organic agriculture is widely practised in the countryside, but organic goods in shops are not branded as such yet. The best products are found in street markets rather than in traditional shops. Although meat hygiene standards are reasonable, butchers are often unskilled, and it is not uncommon to have to do D-I-Y butchery before entertaining.

Hotel restaurants are reliable in Sofia, but are often expensive for what is offered. The *Sofia City Guide* has advertisements that are worth following up (see Sofia, p 95) for detailed recommendations.

Street food vendors selling meat products should be avoided on hygiene grounds. BSE is not yet a problem in Bulgaria and beef is generally regarded as safe.

There are virtually no specialist restaurants or other facilities for vegetarians in Bulgaria, but in spring, summer and autumn there is usually plenty of fresh non-meat choices on most menus.

Food and drink
See p 51 for Bulgarian vocabulary.

As is to be expected given the geographical position of Bulgaria, there are many complex influences on the cuisine. In general, the overall background is Turkish, after the hundreds of years of Ottoman occupation, but with a foundation from the Tartar and central Asian world, and many local and regional influences. The cuisine of the Westernised elite is French in inspiration, as in most of southeast Europe. There are the familiar and depressing manifestations of American 'food culture', with burger bars and fast food establishments. Fish is the most important part of the cuisine of the Black Sea.

The customs and traditions of the Orthodox Church are another important influence on some aspects of the cuisine, with a pre-Easter fast becoming more common with the revival of religion in the post-communist period.

Meals generally start with a *meze*, the dominant element of which is a tomato and cucumber salad topped with cheese, the national *shopska* salad. Grilled meat is the standard main course, followed by fruit, cheese and pastries. Coffee is excellent, in the Turkish style. Herbal tea is quite widely drunk.

Wine
Bulgaria has been justly famous for many years for the quality of its wine and **grape-based spirits**. These wines are generally known outside Bulgaria as reliable, good quality reds which can be found in every supermarket in Europe for a reasonable price. There are some exceptional quality wines produced locally that often do not find their way onto the export market, and experimentation is usually rewarding. On the other hand, some of the lowest quality wines are also reserved for the domestic market, and are better avoided, except for cooking.

Wine has been produced in Bulgaria since antiquity, and the ancient Greek god Dionysus, the god of wine and the theatre, had his origin in the Thracian pantheon. The adequate rainfall and hot summers give a climate that strongly resembles many wine growing areas in France, and among reds the Merlot and Cabernet grapes are the most widely grown. Whites are of less consistent high quality, and a little more care needs to be taken when purchasing. Chardonnays are generally very reliable. *Khan Krum* is a well known quality white. **Domaine Boyar**, London E3 3 RU, is a prominent British supplier (☎ 0171 537 3707).

Beer

Bulgaria has a long brewing tradition, centred on interior towns such as Shumen, Pleven and Stara Zagora. The first beer was brewed in the 1850s in Shumen. Under communism much standardised lager was produced, and still is, of very mediocre quality. However, small private breweries are now starting up, and in one or two cases are producing much better quality, partly bottle fermented beers. Heavier dark beers are also produced, which are well worth sampling. Recently privatised *Kamenitza* in Plovdiv (Belgian owned), and *Ledenika* (Vratsa) currently produce the best beer.

   NB. Non-brand spirits should be avoided, unless you know the producer, as adulteration is not unknown. This seems to be a particular problem with vodka.

Spirits

Bulgarians love drinking and apart from **rakia**, produce many excellent **brandies** and good **slivowitz**, the latter mostly in the northwest adjoining Serbia. Vidin is a good place to buy it. Decent **ouzo** (anise), locally called *mastika*, is also made, and **gin** and **vodka**. Gin can be surprisingly good and 'authentic', but Bulgarian 'whisky' is better avoided.

Notes for the business traveller

Under communism, Bulgaria was open to some Western businessmen within the framework of the planned economy, and Bulgarians have long been familiar with the way capitalism is supposed to function. Under the old regime, the best-known British visitor was the late media tycoon Robert Maxwell, who was active in publishing and as a patron of the arts in the country for many years, and formed a close personal relationship with the communist leader Todor Zhivkov.

   Nevertheless the business culture is not fully Westernised and the recent economic difficulties affecting Bulgaria have led to the withdrawal of a number of companies from activity in the country. That said, many British and American companies are active and successful in Bulgaria, as well as numerous businessmen from other European Union countries such as Germany and Greece. Germany was the largest foreign investor by size in the country, over-taken in 1997 by Belgium. The Greek business presence is very pervasive in many spheres, such as the food industry. Russian links have declined with the end of communism but are still a factor in many industries, such as Black Sea tourism, food, timber and defence manufacturing.

   NB. Generally speaking, small and medium-sized companies often achieve most in Bulgaria, there is a considerable cultural gap between the Bulgarian business world and that of many multinationals. Xenophobia can be a serious problem, many, if not most, Bulgarians dislike the ethos of the 'yuppie' world of finance capital and interna-tional consultancy. People employed by businesses of this kind in Bulgaria need to be aware of local psychology, material poverty and cultural traditions. Unfortunately this has not been the case with many foreigners in this field in recent years, which has affected Bulgarian

perceptions of Western business in very negative ways. EU-financed consultants often seem particularly insensitive to the vast sums they are paid in comparison with local experts in the same field.

Business in Bulgaria requires careful preparation, and basic documents, such as legislation on foreign business in the country,should be obtained from the Chambers of Commerce in London. The newsletter *BBCC Chronicle* published monthly by the British Bulgarian Chamber of Commerce is very useful, and the Chamber can provide up-to-date information on joint ventures, which British companies are active in Bugaria, accurate statistics and trade fair information. A local partner is in practice essential for many businesses, although in some spheres association with a Greek partner can be almost equally effective. Contact the Greek Embassy in Sofia for advice (☎ 00 359 2 446 123; fax 446 507). Another useful publication is *Bulgarian Business Adviser*, from Global Communications, 34 Vladayska Street, 1606 Sofia ($18.95).

The British government sponsors the Know How Fund scheme for Bulgaria, as elsewhere in eastern Europe, and this can be a very valuable source of finance for feasibility studies, management training and other business development activities. In Sofia, contact Mr Peter Hardman, ☎ 00 359 2 980 1220. The Know How Fund Office is in part of the British Embassy complex.

Organised crime, insurance fraud and extortion
Organised crime is a fact of life in Bulgaria as elsewhere in Eastern Europe, and serious pitfalls can await the unwary. Advice on the security aspects of business in Bulgaria should be obtained from independent experts.

NB Under no circumstances whatsoever should local security or bodyguard firms be employed without independent personal recommendation from a trusted friend or business associate. Many firms consider it is worthwhile commissioning background investigations of all local businesses where money is involved and the principals are not known to them. The use of one of the Greek or other foreign banks operating in Bulgaria is recommended for financial transactions.

Insurance is a field particularly influenced by organised crime, and great care is needed in the choice of local insurers to avoid extortion rackets. Seek professional security advice in this field.

Control Risks Ltd, 82 Victoria Street, London SW1H 0HW (☎ 0171 222 1552, fax 0171 222 2296) offer expert advice on the security aspects of business in Bulgaria.

Useful addresses
Balkan Holidays, 5 Blvd Vitosha, Sofia, ☎ 835111, fax 800134.
Bulgarian Business Chamber, 14 Alabin Street, Sofia, ☎ 878417, 879611.
Bulgarian Chamber of Commerce and Industry, 1A Suborna Street, Sofia1000, ☎ 872631, fax 873209.
Bulgarian National Bank, 1 Prince Battenberg Square Sofia, ☎ 886447.
Bulgarian National Radio, 4 Blvd Dragan Tsankov, Sofia, ☎ 854620.
Bulgarian National Television, 29 San Stefano Street, Sofia, ☎ 43481, advertising ☎ 801296.

Bulgarian Telegraph Agency (BTA), 49 Blvd Tsarigradsko Shosse, Sofia, ☎ 880286.
Bulgarian Tourist Association, 5 Triaditsa Street, Sofia 5, ☎ 874059, 874593.
Multigroup plc, Baaerstrasse 43, CH 6300-Zug, Switzerland, ☎ 41 41 712 0850, fax 41 41 712 0860.
Sofia Stock Exchange, Blvd Bulgaria, NDK, Hall 13, Sofia, ☎ 802026.
Sofia-Public Notary, 1 Blvd Patriarch Evtimi, Sofia, ☎ 802501.

Getting around Bulgaria

By rail

The railway system in Bulgaria is rather rundown but still functions quite well in most places, and is by far the cheapest way to travel by public transport between the main centres. **Trains** are anything from slightly grubby to filthy but run reasonably efficiently and fast. Lines such as those between Plovdiv and Sofia, and Ruse and Sofia, are obviously particularly useful for the lower budget traveller, but are also definitely worth general consideration as they spare you the real risks and difficulties of Bulgarian road travel, particularly in the winter. First class is cheap by Western standards and is worth paying for if available.

Some cities are much better served by rail than others, often for no apparent reason, and it is well worth studying a *Cook's Rail Guide* before coming to Bulgaria if intending to use the network ouside the main inter-city routes. Burgas, Varna, Vratsa, Plovdiv and Ruse are all served by express services. Fast trains run between Sofia–Vidin and Sofia–Blagoevgrad. Do not count on any food or drink being available. Toilet conditions on some Bulgarian trains often seem to have changed little since the times of the Sultan. Security on the trains is generally no problem, at least in daytime, but it is wise to avoid flaunting items such as expensive cameras and laptop computers.

Sofia central railway station is a grim, forbidding 1970's edifice, with incomprehensible announcements, even for those with good Bulgarian, and a shortage of signs. A proper Information Office for foreign travellers is urgently needed. Security needs care, especially at night when women and unaccompanied males should avoid the place, unless wishing to buy good quality cheap cannabis that is sold then. Lebanese Black is widely available in Bulgaria.

If unfamiliar with the station, it is essential to arrive in plenty of time for a journey. Tickets for international destinations are on sale from a small window at the far left end of the entrance hall, for internal destinations from the windows backing onto the platforms. An escalator leads down to the platforms. Although platform signs are meant to show what trains are running, in practice they do not always do so, and confusion over platforms is a common reason for missing trains. The train indicators in the main entrance hall can also be misleading. A few local trains run from small platforms at the far left end of the main platform complex. There are small shops and kiosks in the arcade below the station platforms, some with useful services such as barbers and chemists shops, others with food.

A general Bulgarian timetable has now been printed, which is very useful, price 200 leva from ticket windows at the station.

By bus and coach

Bus and coach travel is improving in Bulgaria. Vehicles are generally quicker and cleaner than the trains, but more expensive, although cheap by Western standards. The main coach park for long distance buses in Sofia is between the main station and the Novotel, on the north side of the city (☎ 525004), see p 109. Buses for **Thessaloniki** leave from the side of the hotel, **Istanbul** and other routes are covered from the car park about 400m away towards the station. Some international services for destinations such as **Tirana**, **Belgrade** and **Skopje** run from the bus office at 23 Damien Gruev Street (☎ 525 004). This is a small street quite near the Hotel Rodina, see p 110. The **Hornit Travel Agency** shop in the basement of the Sheraton Hotel can assist with bookings for these services. **Plovdiv** and **Burgas** are also good centres to base a bus and coach travel holiday.

A **state bus service** still functions but mainly in **Sofia** and other large centres. Vehicles are slow and antiquated. There are four main bus stations, in the north, south, east and west of the city. Privately-owned coaches dominate all inter-city and international travel. They are usually fairly modern and clean. There are no regular timetables for most services, but coaches wait in the park until they are full. If planning to take a long journey it is strongly recommended to take a taxi to the Novotel and go to the park early in the morning—buses start running as early as 06.00 and many services do not run in the afternoons or evenings. Prices are generally very reasonable and the standard of most coaches is quite good. If you wish to buy a ticket to go to Thessaloniki, you must produce a passport when buying a ticket. **Avoid overloaded vehicles**.

Luggage space is sometimes restricted and security of bags needs watching. Valuables should be kept in a small hand luggage bag on the coach. Coaches do stop from time to time for food and toilets, but it is worth carrying some food and drink in the hand luggage. If you wish to go to **Greece** but miss the main through coach, it is possible to get down there at most times of day by taking a bus to Sandanski, then a taxi to the border at Kulata (see p 213).

By tram

The trams are a cheap and useful way to get around in Sofia and one or two other large cities, providing you know exactly where you are going. They are invaluable on some semi-suburban routes, and run very late at night. Security is generally fairly good, with trams being used by unaccompanied women into the small hours. Tickets, which are very cheap indeed, are bought from kiosks near the tram stops, or from the driver, and validated on the tram. In suburban parts of Sofia, taxis often queue near the tram stops at night. Pedestrians need to take care near tramlines, especially in winter.

By car

Motoring in Bulgaria is easy, from the point of view of formalities, but the number of cars on the road should not deceive the visitor into thinking that Bulgaria is an easy place in which to drive. A motoring holiday is quite feasible, but should not be undertaken lightly or without adequate planning or awareness of the difficulties that may be encountered. Third party insurance and a green card are legal requirements, but comprehensive insurance is essential.

The condition of the roads varies enormously, from modern highways that are in good repair, to mediocre asphalt roads that are often badly potholed, to dirt tracks that make heavy demands on even the strongest vehicles and on drivers who are used to Balkan conditions. All variants can be encountered on a trip of a few miles duration. Bulgarian drivers are not always skilled. Travel in the winter can be very difficult indeed in even the most developed regions and the cities, and much of the rest of the country can be brought to a standstill by one of the heavy snowstorms that occur in most winters. Holidays by car are best undertaken between April and October.

Car theft is a major problem in all parts of Bulgaria, particularly Sofia, and all possible anti-theft devices should be fitted. Petrol stations are sometimes distant from one another, and tanks should be filled up in the countryside whenever the opportunity arises. Stereos and all personal belongings must be removed from the car when parked.

Unleaded petrol is becoming more widely available, but can be very difficult to find in some places. Diesel is cheap and plentiful. Basic supplies of other necessities are reasonable, but many makes of vehicle do not have efficient spares supply networks in Bulgaria, and a very full spares kit and tools should be carried. A tyre inner tube and foot pump are useful. Spare wiper blades must be carried as they are often a target for petty thieves. Generally speaking, it is not too difficult to find spares and service facilities for Lada, Fiat, VW, Mercedes Benz and Land Rover, and some Japanese makes.

Anyone considering travel on dirt tracks or off-road should consider seriously buying or hiring a **four-wheel-drive vehicle**. Given the condition of some urban roads, they are often bought by expatriates resident in Bulgaria, although they are expensive to buy, insure and run, and are a priority target for thieves.

Driving in Bulgaria is on the right-hand side of the road. Speed limits are 60kph within cities and urban areas, 80kph outside them, and 120kph on motorways. Radar traps are common. Traffic regulations are generally the same as elsewhere in Europe, although drivers should bear in mind that driving under the influence of alcohol is taken very seriously in Bulgaria, with the official limit only equivalent to about two glasses of wine before it is exceeded. **Penalties** are severe; take care to observe the law.

The police operate a system of waving down motorists to check documents as a method of crime control, and sometimes you will be waved down to a layby by police holding a small red and white baton. **Stop at all times if required to do so**; failure results in pursuit, embarrassment and a small fine. The checks on foreigners are nearly always courteous and good humoured, but be careful to carry car documents, driving licence and passport with you. Sometimes car luggage compartments are searched. **Bandit gangs** sometimes steal police uniforms and impersonate police, before robbing drivers. If is doubt, ask to see police ID cards before opening a car door or stopping the engine.

Road signs in big towns are in both Latin and Cyrillic alphabet, but in Cyrillic only over the whole country generally. If intending to drive in Bulgaria it is advisable to learn the Cyrillic letters if at all possible.

Car hire

The car rental industry is well established in Bulgaria, with both international operators, such as **Hertz** and **Avis**, and local companies. Car hire is not cheap, allow at least £60 a day for a small vehicle, and unless on company expenses, it is best considered as a fairly short-term option. Mileage charges and insurance are often particularly expensive, scrutinise agreements carefully before signature. Cars are often much cheaper if booked and paid for in the UK before leaving, rather than in Bulgaria. For local transport around Sofia and vicinity, it is cheaper and much less stressful to retain a friendly taxi driver for a few hours. Negotiate a price in hard currency beforehand to get a good deal.

Minimum age for commercial car hire is 21 years. Some companies allow their cars to be used in FYROM as well for a small extra charge. Sofia airport is the best place to hire a car in the capital. It is essential to book in advance if using one of the big international operators.

Avis: **Sofia Airport**, ☎ 273 8023; **Sofia City**, ☎ 813 569; **Varna Airport**, ☎ 524 40793.
EuropCar: **Sofia City**, ☎ 835 049, fax 883593.
Hertz: **UK**, ☎ 0181 679 1799; **Sofia Airport**, ☎ 796 041; **Sofia City**, ☎ 814 042.
Intercar: **Sofia City**, ☎ 791477, fax 880648.

American Express and **Visa** cards can usually be used to settle bills; other credit cards are often less welcome.

By air

The only really useful and timesaving internal flights worth considering in Bulgaria are those that link Sofia with the Black Sea coast at Varna and Burgas. A guide to what is available can be found in the Balkan Airlines flight directory. It is worth checking on the up-to-date position at the last minute before booking, as there have been some recent cutbacks in schedules. Aircraft are generally old Soviet models which are noisy and basic. Prices are at about the level of the cheaper Western countries for internal air travel, although tickets are charged in hard currency for foreigners and rates have increased recently. Hemus Air also run a number of services, as indicated above. They have a reliable reputation, generally, although some flights are basically charters that only go when enough passangers have been assembled.

Local ticket sales for **Balkan** in Sofia are at 12 Narodno Sobraine Square, ☎ 880663, general information, ☎ 884 433, 884 493. In Varna the office is at 10 Alexander Battenburg Square, ☎ 884 436, in Plovdiv at 4 Gladstone Square, ☎ 222 003 or 233 081.

Hemus Air Sofia office is at 157 Rakovski Street, ☎ 881 154, 801 630.

Local charter operators include **Air Via** (☎ 521 460), **Air Link** (☎ 871 114) and **Antonov Airlines** (☎ 522 649). Air Via is part of the Multigroup conglomerate. It is best to seek local recommendations on these companies before making a business commitment.

By bicycle

The Bulgarian countryside is very pleasant for cycle touring, but Sofia and big towns are dangerous and unpleasant environments for the cyclist, and are only for the very brave. Cycling is popular in Bulgaria and there are cycle shops selling tyres and other spare parts in all the main towns and cities, but a good supply of all specialised spares should be carried as availability of particular makes is unpredictable. Cycles can be taken on most trains. If you really must have a cycle in a large town, it is worth considering buying a heavy traditional roadster model to cope with *pave* and potholes. Imported Chinese roadsters are quite cheap in Bulgaria.

By motorcycle
Motorcycling is popular in Bulgaria and spares and equipment for the main mass-market makes are generally available, if sometimes at high prices. Many of the same safety problems affect motorcyclists as pedal cyclists, especially in the winter with wet and icy badly maintained *pave* roads. A motorcycle should be registered on arrival in Bulgaria in the same way as a car. A strong anti-theft device is essential.

Taxis
Taxis are one of the minor blessings of Sofia life, being cheap, plentiful and usually helpful and knowledgeable about at least the main streets and institutions in the city. Cars are often very old and cannot carry heavy loads. Journeys are metered. Drivers usually only understand Bulgarian and if the destination is not well known, or if you have problems pronouncing the name of the destination in Bulgarian, you should get a friend to write it down on a piece of paper beforehand.

It is usually cheaper to wave a taxi down than to use a radio taxi service or to take one from a cab rank near a big hotel. The latter are the only significantly dishonest group, in most people's experience. **Avoid if possible**. It is not unknown for meters to be 'clocked' a few hundred leva, if the unwary traveller is not watching the taximeter. Taxi drivers at the Sofia railway station also have a very bad reputation for overcharging.

NB. If taking a taxi from Sofia airport to Sofia, on arrival go to the official taxi desk and buy a taxi voucher for the journey, currently $US18. **Do not have any dealings whatsoever with unofficial airport taxis**.

General information

Foreign embassies and missions in Bulgaria
Albania: 10 Krakra Street, Sofia, ☎ 441140, 443349.
Austria: 13 Tsar Osvoboditel Blvd, Sofia, ☎ 803572-3.
Belgium: 1 Velchova Street, Sofia, ☎ 651062.
EU, 36 Blvd Dragan Tsankov, Sofia, ☎ 739841/5.
FR Yugoslavia: 3 Veliko Turnovo Street, Sofia ☎ 443237, 442777.
Germany: 25 Curle Street, Sofia, ☎ 650451-55.
Greece: 68 Blvd Evlogi Georgiev, Sofia, ☎ 443770, 443765 (Consular department, ☎ 444282); 10 Preslav Street, Plovdiv, ☎ 232003.
Russia: 28 Blvd Dragan Tsankov, Sofia ☎ 668819; 53 Macedonia Street, Varna, ☎ 223546.
Switzerland: 33 Shipka Street, Sofia ☎ 443198.
Turkey: 23 Blvd Vasil Levski, Sofia ☎ 872306; Burgas, ☎ 42718, 40192, 47010; 10 Philip of Macedon Street, Plovdiv, ☎ 232309, 239010.
UK: 56 Blvd Vasil Levski, Sofia, ☎ 9801220, fax 9801229.
   The interests of Australian, New Zealand and Canadian and Irish nationals are looked after by the British Embassy.

Emergency telephone numbers
Police: 166; **Ambulance**: 150; **Traffic Police**: 165; **Fire Brigade**: 160; **Telephone enquiries**: 144 and 145; **International telephone enquiries**: 124.

Health and health insurance
Generally Bulgaria has a healthy climate and general environment, and nothing more than normal travel vaccinations are required, such as up-to-date tetanus and polio jabs. **An anti-hepatitis vaccination is vital**.
   A small medical and practical **first aid kit** including supplies of a basic antibiotic, stomach bug medicine and basic hygiene equipment is a good idea. If motoring, a comprehensive first aid kit is recommended. To date, there is a very low incidence of HIV and AIDS in Bulgaria, but the traveller may consider carrying a few plastic syringes in the medical kit to give to a local doctor in the event of an accident. If a particular vital drug such as insulin is required a spare supply should be carried, as medical goods are a frequent target for thieves.
   Condoms and **female contraceptive devices** are available, but supplies are often arbitrary and sometimes expensive and may be non-existent outside main cities. Condoms are known in Bulgarian slang as 'galoshes'. It is best to bring whatever is needed with you. The same applies to feminine hygiene requisites. Baby goods such as disposable nappies are generally widely available.
   There are one or two **minor local health hazards** in Bulgaria linked to wildlife, such as ticks which are common on dogs and sheep, and can be picked up directly, or from vegetation in the countryside if you are very unlucky. Rabies is present in the fox population, and very, very occasionally is contracted by dogs. Any bite requires immediate professional medical attention. Bulgarians are keen on dogs, and many are used for guard purposes on farms and in urban buildings. Some are semi-wild and can be dangerous. **Avoid**.
   Mosquitos are often a nuisance in the summer, and other biting insects in the

forests, and appropriate devices to plug into electric sockets and insect repellents should be carried. In remote areas mammalian wildlife itself can be a problem, with **bears**, **deer** and **wild boar** prone to interfere with campers' tents and equipment. If camping in forests, do not leave food outside at night. **Snakes** can be common is some drier rocky areas, most are harmless but the Balkan adder is very poisionous although rarely encountered. **Seek immediate medical help if bitten**. **Scorpions** are found, but are not poisonous although they have a painful bite.

Bulgarian budget hotels have all the predictable insect fauna, such as fleas, beetles, silverfish and cockroaches, and bedbugs are not unknown. If it is necessary to stay in the cheapest places, a sheet sleeping bag for the summer and a full sleeping bag for the autumn and winter is advisable. The latter is a good idea in any event, as parts of Bulgaria can become very cold indeed then. Sleeping bags are unnecessary in the skiing resorts, where hotels are well heated.

NB. Foreigners receive free treatment in Bulgarian hospitals, in theory, but in practice some payment is often necessary, especially for medicines. These can be very expensive indeed, and **full medical insurance** for all travellers is essential. This is absolutely vital on a skiing holiday. Insurance policies offered as part of the cost of package holidays should be checked for comprehensiveness of cover. If in any doubt, take out a personal travel policy before departure.

If taken ill in Sofia there is a resident British Embassy doctor who may be prepared to treat some British visitors, in utter emergency. The Institute for the Treatment of Foreign Citizens, 1 Eugeni Pavlovski Street, ☎ 75361, can offer help and advice, with a clinic with English-speaking doctors. The information number for **pharmacies** is 178. **General medical information** is on 155. **Denta** is a 24-hour dental service in 4 Dobroudja Street, ☎ 888 209.

In Sofia the are 24-hour **pharmacies** at 5 Sveta Nedelya Street; 42 Tsar Asen Street and 35 Hristo Botev Blvd.

Crime and personal security

In the communist era there was supposed to be very little overt crime in Bulgaria, although historians are continually discovering instances of corruption among the ruling elite. With the end of the one party state, **serious crime** has increased, and has been linked to the metamorphosis of parts of the the *nomenklatura* into private businessmen (the *Mafiya*). It has become a subject of obsessive interest among most Bulgarians.

Fact and political mythology in this field are closely linked and all visitors are recommended to disregard alarmist propaganda from official and semi-official Western sources that seems largely designed to discredit the elected governments of Bulgaria. All statistics show that the incidence of serious crimes such as murder and rape are far higher in the United States than in Bulgaria.

At a practical level, all that is required in Bulgaria on the part of the tourist visitor are the commonsense precautions for any large city—in avoiding doubtful areas, taking care to use well-lit streets at night and taking extra care at places such as railway stations, bus stations, shopping malls and markets. Avoid very ostentatious Western clothes and display of expensive electronic items such as video cameras and, above all, lap-top computers. Valuables should never be left in cars and stereos and CD players must be removed when the car is parked. At night secure parking is vital in Sofia and major towns.

The business visitor, on the other hand, is subject to more serious risks, and definitely needs professional security advice (see p 28).

It is worth carrying the telephone number of the British Embassy (Sofia, ☎ 885 361) with you at all times in case difficulties are encountered, although unlike other British embassies in the Balkans, the Sofia Embassy does not currently have a very good reputation among British travellers and businessmen in the region.

Anyone unlucky enough to encounter thieves or muggers should bear in mind that it is usual to be armed in the Bulgarian underworld and resistance is very unwise indeed.

Self defence and weapons

Residents in Bulgaria who wish to buy a **weapon** can do so quite legally at any of the gunshops found in all large towns and cities, providing it is licenced with the police. A Bulgarian-manufactured weapon is recommended as foreign ammunition is often very expensive, especially for Smith and Wesson. Various security devices, such as electronic stun guns, pistols, flick knives, ammonia sprays, CS gas and similar items are widely available.

There are numerous gun clubs, hunting associations, weightlifting, wrestling, bodybuilding and karate societies and women's self defence clubs in Sofia and all major towns. Although many are quite legitimate, with high quality instruction, some are thinly disguised centres for criminals and Mafiya activities and it is a good idea to be cautious and make background enquiries before joining anything. The same applies to the various 'business clubs' which are to be found in most cities, often in favoured suburban districts.

NB. Residents should only employ local security firms to fit burglar alarms to houses, cars and apartments on the basis of personal recommendation from a trusted friend. It is risky to admit anyone unknown to you to a hotel room at night, especially in cheaper places in Sofia. Visitors who come into social contact with prostitutes in bars and hotels should be aware that women in the sex industry are often used as decoys for muggers, drug dealers and thieves. 'Spiked' drinks are a common device in these circumstances.

Women travelling in Bulgaria

Under communism, Bulgarian women achieved a considerable degree of theoretical emancipation, as elsewhere in Eastern Europe. There has been some movement towards more traditional family roles in the last five years, as job guarantees have disappeared.

Foreign women travelling in Bulgaria may arouse some curiosity, but on the whole have little to worry about in terms of personal security, although there are doubtful areas of Bulgarian life, particularly in Sofia and on the Black Sea coast that both sexes should definitely avoid. See also Crime section above, p 28.

Pregnant women should bear in mind that outside Sofia and the bigger towns maternity and gynaecological facilities may not be very good.

Disabled travellers

Although the vast majority of Bulgarians are very kind people and sympathetic to disabled travellers, there are very few facilities indeed for the disabled, except at health spas, which do cater for people with wheelchairs and mobility problems. Lifts are unreliable or non-existent in many Sofia buildings. Public transport does not have facilities or special schemes for the disabled.

Public holidays and festivals

The traditional religious and national holidays were abolished under communism and the festivals of the international working-class movement were substituted. Some of these, such as May Day, were times of large officially sponsored military and political jamborees, although these days were previously the times of genuine popular festivities. The official paraphenalia has now ended, but some of the days concerned have carried on as normal public holidays, although the dates are subject to change. The main Orthodox Christian festivals are seriously observed, particularly Easter and Christmas, and it is a good idea to avoid business in Bulgaria at those times.

The very rich folk culture of Bulgaria has preserved many local feast and festival days, and do not be surprised to encounter local holidays connected with them. Orthodox saints days are also being revived. In areas occupied by the ethnic Turkish and Pomak minorities, Muslim festivals are observed, particularly the feast of Bajram the Great in spring. Ramadan is observed, but does not affect business unduly in most places.

Some of the most important of the traditional holidays are:

3 January, Day of liberation from Ottoman rule.
1 March, Baba Marta, celebrating the end of winter, holiday taken on 3 March.
27/28 April, Day of Liberation from Ottoman Rule.
1 May, Labour Day.
6 May, Gergiovden, St George's Day.
24 May, Day of the Cyrillic Alphabet.
20 July, St Elijah's Day.
6 December, Nikoulden, celebrating St Nicholas, patron saint of rivers.
20 December, Ignazhden, 'Young Year' day.
25/26 December, Christmas.
(See also section Social customs and etiquette below, p 42.)

Opening hours

In the spring, autumn and winter, shop and business hours are essentially the same as in Western Europe, but in the summer a much more Mediterranean pattern of life is followed, particularly in Plovdiv and the south. Premises frequently close in the afternoons in June, July and August.

Bulgarian shops usually open Monday to Friday from 08.00 until 17.00, and on Saturdays until 14.00. Banks are open Monday to Friday from 08.00 until 15.00, with a short opening period on Saturday mornings. Some exchange offices in Sofia and the larger cities are open for much longer hours in the evenings. Many shops in Sofia and large towns also open for a time in the evenings. If you are intending to stay for more than a day or two anywhere, it is always worth trying to find out the location and opening hours of open street and covered markets, as they are the best place to buy most fresh fruit and vegetables, and many other goods.

Visiting archaeological sites and museums

Bulgaria has a very large number of historical monuments and archaeological sites, many of which are of outstanding interest and quality; there are also numerous museums. Many of the finest are little known outside Bulgaria. In the last five years, since communism ended, the Bulgarian Institute of Archaeology (149 Rakovski St, Sofia, ☎ 880505) and many local authorities have been very short of resources, and access to many sites and museums has been restricted. Problems have been worsened by the fact that the emphasis put on mass tourist development in the communist period meant that this great heritage was never very well developed, or publicised properly abroad, and some aspects of it, such as the rich Ottoman Turkish past, and the Greek Orthodox heritage, were subject to considerable distortion and misrepresentation for political reasons. Some museums that were set up in the communist period have been closed for political reasons.

Sites fall into two main categories: those that are open all the time, and have free access, such as ancient *Nicopolis*, near Svishtov, and those that have controlled access and where tickets are required. In addition there are those that by their nature are always visible, if not fully approachable, such as the Madara Horseman, and many remote castles and fortresses.

Many less popular sites can be extremely difficult to find, and it is wise to allow plenty of time on expeditions if local help is not available. Do not expect signs to be in anything other than Bulgarian, if there are any signs at all. Local guide books and leaflets may be available for the more important sites, but this cannot be relied on. There are no safety precautions for visitors in most places. Castles and fortresses can be particularly dangerous, with loose masonry on walls, unpredictable drops and cisterns hidden by grass and undergrowth.

Telephone and postal services

The telephone and postal systems in Bulgaria both leave much to be desired in terms of being modern or efficient systems, although the telephone system in Sofia is improving. Domestic letters do usually get delivered, eventually, but foreign mail often goes adrift. Do not use the post to send goods or money to Bulgaria from abroad.

Allow at least a week for internal mail, at least three weeks for foreign mail. It helps if the address is written clearly in the Bulgarian alphabet; avoid Latin letters. If something is urgent, the only quick and reliable way of getting it to Bulgaria is by an international courier firm such as DHL. Rates start at about £25 for a small packet. Correspondence for the British Embassy, British Council and Know How Fund can be posted to or handed in at the Foreign Office in King Charles Street, London SW1 2AH. It usually takes about a week to get guaranteed delivery by the diplomatic bag.

The telephones can be very bad during the working day, when it is often difficult to get a line from abroad at all. Internal calls are marred by arbitrary disconnections and frequent wrong numbers. Matters improve late at night. Use of fax is essential for those with regular contact needs with Bulgaria.

E-mail and the Internet are also becoming more widely used in Bulgaria, but connections are often difficult because of problems with the telephone lines themselves. It is generally possible, with patience and often quite a lot of expenditure, to use E-mail to send messages to Bulgaria, but it is more difficult to access local Websites, in many people's experience. Fax is much cheaper and more reliable.

A complete modernisation of the telephone system which will install digital exchanges is planned, but it is not known when it will be undertaken. Some large hotels have their own exchanges which offer a better service than the normal phone booths. In Sofia, it is well worth paying the extra fee for telephone and fax at bureaus such as the Sheraton Hotel Business Centre, in the basement of the hotel (opening hours 08.00–20.00).

Telephone codes from Bulgaria to foreign countries

Australia 0061	**Holland** 0031
Austria 0043	**Hungary** 0036
Belgium 0043	**Italy** 0039
Canada 001	**New Zealand** 0064
Cyprus 00357	**Russia** 0070
Denmark 0045	**Switzerland** 0031
France 0033	**FR Yugoslavia** 0038
Germany 0049	**United Kingdom** 0044
Greece 0030	**USA** 001

Useful official addresses in Sofia
Presidency: 2 Knyaz Dondukov Blvd, ☎ 83839.
National Assembly: Narodno Subraine Square, ☎ 8401.
Council of Ministers: 1 Knyaz Dondukov Blvd, ☎ 8501.
Ministry of Trade: 12 A. Battenberg Square, ☎ 822 011.
Ministry of Finance: 102 G. Radovski Street, ☎ 8691.

Newspapers, magazines and the media
There are about 300 newspapers and magazines currently produced in the Bulgarian language. Many newspapers are linked to particular parties or interest groups, such as *Duma*, to the Socialist party, and *Makedonia*, to the Internal Macedonian Revolutionary Organisation. *24 Hours* and *Trud* are both influential mass circulation dailies. Newspapers are produced in the Turkish language for the minority.

Reuters in Sofia publish a very useful English-language daily news-sheet *Bulgarian Daily News*, which can be found in the kiosks and receptions at the big hotels. There is also a similar English-language economic publication *Bulgarian Economic Digest*. The *Sofia Independent* is a good weekly English language newspaper (editor Philip Bey, ☎ 871 115/981 3959). The Greek-produced, but English-language, *New Europe* weekly newspaper has good regular coverage of Bulgaria, with a business emphasis. *Sofia Western News* is an English language magazine. German, Russian and Greek newspapers are also widely available.

Imported English language newspapers and magazines are reasonably easy to find in Sofia, and on the Black Sea coast, from kiosks within the big hotels, but are almost totally unobtainable in provincial Bulgaria. It is useful to bring a small short wave radio to keep up with the BBC World Service, which many Bulgarians regard as a prime source of objective news and commentary. It is broadcast on 91.0 MHz FM, 24 hours a day.

A very few shops in Sofia sell new English- and other foreign-language books, but choice is fairly limited and it is best to bring reading matter with you. In provincial towns it is very difficult indeed to find non-Bulgarian material.

Most bigger hotels have satellite television where it is possible to watch CNN and BBC World Service TV.

Bulgarian radio broadcasts daily in English on 9700 short wave channel, and also in Greek, Serbo-Croat, Albanian, Arabic, German, Turkish and a number of other languages. Fax Radio Bulgaria on 00 359 2 650 560 or 871 061 for frequencies.

Antiques and memorabilia

Book and magazine collectors can find second-hand and antiquarian volumes, maps and share certificates in the shops around Rakovski Street, and on Sofia street stalls near the university. Plovdiv also has one or two good antique shops and second-hand bookshops. These are well worth perusal as real book bargains can sometimes be found, although in general prices match Western levels. Be very careful to obtain a receipt with the name of the shop on it for any valuable items. Other bargains can be found by the discriminating collector.

NB. Avoid purchase of anything that could contravene the art export regulations. Take great care if you are a camera collector, as fake Rollei, Nikon and Leica are common.

Old Russian cameras and antique watches and typewriters can be bargains. Ex-Soviet military equipment such as nightsights, binoculars and telescopic sights for sniper rifles are outstanding buys. It is still possible to buy English-language publications on Bulgaria produced by the communist authorities very cheaply. In view of the quantities produced, they unlikely to have investment potential.

Academic institutions

Academy of Agriculture, 12 Mendelev Street, Plovdiv.
Bulgarian Academy of Sciences, 15 November Street, Sofia 1.
Bulgarian State Conservatoire, 11 Blvd. Evlogi Georgiev, Sofia 1.
High Institute of Medicine, G. Sofiliski Street, Sofia 1.
Institute of Balkan Studies, Moskovska Street, Sofia 1.
Institute of Drama, 108A Rakovski Street, Sofia 1
Institute of Economics, Students Village, Sofia.
Institute of Forestry, 10 Kl. Ochrid Street, Sofia 10.
Institute of Geology and Mining, Student Village, Sofia.
Military Academy 'G. Rakovski', 23 Blvd Evlogi Georgiev, Sofia 1.
New Bulgarian University, 45 Blvd Vasil Levski, Sofia.
University of Saint Klement of Ochrid, 15 Blvd Tsar Osvoboditel, Sofia 1.

Religion

Catholic Church of the Eastern Rite, 10/B Sv. Ivan Riliski Street, Sofia, ☎ 520297
Central Jewish Spiritual Council, 16, Ekhzarch Josif Street, Sofia ☎ 831273
Eparchial Council of the Armenian Apostolic Church in Bulgaria, 31 Naicho Tsanov Street, Sofia, ☎880208
High Mufti of the Muslims of Bulgaria, 27 Br. Miladininovi Street, Sofia, ☎873816, 877320

The Holy Synod of the Bulgarian Eastern Orthodox Church, Sofia Sveta Mitropolia, 7 Kaloyan Street, Sofia, ☎ 872682
Methodist Church in Bulgaria, 86 Rakovski Street, Sofia, ☎ 873358

Public toilets

Public toilets in major cities usually have an attendant; all female and sedentary male needs require a small payment. Conditions vary from the adequate to the truly Ottoman. It is a good idea to carry some toilet tissue on all journeys and expeditions.

Narcotics

Both soft and hard **drugs** are illegal in Bulgaria, but there is a good deal of both around. Cannabis is widely grown and used privately. The Turkish communities in the south are active growers, and the plants are then sold to *Mafiya* interests in the cities. Heroin is imported from Turkey, and Bulgaria is an important transit route to Western Europe. Opium poppies are grown in some places, particularly in the extreme southwest of the country.

Electricity

Voltage is 220–240 AC. A two pin adaptor for British plugs is needed. Wiring in hotels and public buildings is not always in good condition, and care needs to be taken with travel irons, electric shavers and similar appliances. Do not try to use anything that is not properly earthed and/or fused. If renting an old apartment or house, it is a good idea to have a small fire extinguisher handy, especially in the country.

Drinking water

Tapwater in Bulgaria is quite drinkable, although as in the UK and many other places, there are problems with nitrate pollution. Mineral water is often very good indeed, naturally carbonated waters from Mount Vitosha and the Stara Planina in particular. In times of drought tapwater supplies can be restricted somewhat.

Time

Bulgarian time is two hours ahead of Greenwich Mean Time, the same as in Greece, one hour behind Serbia and FYROM.

Naturism

Nudist and topless bathing began to emerge under communism, but is now widespread on the Black Sea coast. There is usually a separate naturist beach at most major resorts. It is worth bearing in mind that many older Bulgarians are culturally conservative, and tact should be exercised in some places.

Sport

Spectator sport is very popular in Bulgaria. Attention nowadays is focussed on **association football**, where Bulgaria has a world class team. The standard of the Bulgarian league is high and matches are well worth watching. Sports where Bulgarians excel include weightlifting, wrestling, swimming and shooting. Some traditional festivals include sport, such as grease wrestling in the south east among the ethnic Turkish minority.

Hunting and fishing. Bulgaria is a heavily forested country that is rich in **game**. Random hunting by foreigners is not allowed, but there is good quality organised sport available through specialist companies. Facilities are expensive. Contact SOKOL, the Bulgarian Union of Hunters and Fisherman, 12 Christo Bochev Street, Sofia, ☎ 880373. Companies which specialise in international hunting tourism are MURGASH, 17 Antim I Street, Sofia, ☎ 802707 and LONGOSA in Varna, ☎ 052-225605. Most of your companions are likely to be German.

The hunting season dates are: for deer,1 September 31 January (weekends only); for pheasant and duck, hare and wild boar, 1 October–31 January; for bears and mouflon, 1 October–1 April. Funds are set aside to reward hunters who kill predators such as **wolves** and **jackal**. The population of both species is steadily increasing. A fee is charged for hunting certain species, ie, a fallow deer with antlers weighing more than 4.5kg will cost the hunter 4600 Deutschmarks. Wild boar trophies are charged on the basis of tusk length—4400 Deutschmarks for each 24cm.

Bulgaria has the largest population of **bears** in Europe—about 800. They breed mainly in the areas of Blagoevgrad, the Central Balkan range, the Rhodope Mountains, and the north slopes of the Rila mountains. Hunting is strictly controlled and is restricted to omniverous bears. Trophies are charged a minimum of 17,000 Deutschmarks per bear. A wounded bear costs the hunter a fine of 3000 Deutschmarks. A new law was proposed in 1996 that will synchronise Bulgarian hunting laws with the rest of Europe, which is likely to result in a slightly longer hunting season.

Many Bulgarian mountain streams offer good **trout fishing**, particularly in the Rhodopes where there are large hatcheries for trout fry and a fish farming industry. Permits are not required. Lake fishing is available in some places, where coarse fish such as perch and carp predominate. The Black Sea used to offer good basic sea fishing, and still does in some places, but has been seriously affected by overfishing and pollution near cities such as Burgas. Avoid eating shellfish here completely.

Social customs and etiquette

In general Bulgarian culture, customs and cultural traditions are little known in the West. The reasons for this are complex, and go back a long way into 19C cultural history. Bulgaria was not a subject of interest to Lord Byron, or other prominent members of the Romantic Movement, and the Gladstonian campaigns for Bulgaria in the 1870s onwards in Britain have been largely forgotten. The Bulgarian language was, and is, hardly studied in the USA or the UK. In the 20C, Bulgaria was allied to Germany in both world wars, and then was cut off from contact with most of the non-socialist world by the close links of the Bulgarian communist government with the Soviet Union and the Warsaw Pact countries.

In the post-communist period, in the Balkans, Bulgarian compliance with United Nations and Western policies has led to almost total media neglect of the country and its culture. Serbia, Albania and Croatia are much better known as a result of their involvement in the Balkan conflict.

The heart of the Bulgarian nation has always been in the central mountains and in the traditional small towns, and this has in essence been that of a peasant culture. As a capital, Sofia was very much a 19C creation. Large towns under the Ottoman Turks were cosmopolitan and mixed, and often dominated by Muslims or minority nationalities, such as the Greeks in parts of Plovdiv or Turks in Ruse. The essential Bulgarian identity lay in the countryside, and in a deeply traditional, in some senses archaic peasant culture. Peasant society and its values continued to dominate Bulgaria until the 1940s, with Sofia being a very provincial town open to foreign influences.

Industrialism began relatively early in Bulgaria, in Balkan terms, and a socialist and trade union movements soon grew up, but working-class hegemony was not achieved until the communist period after the Second World War. Despite the immense emphasis put on industrialism and heavy industry in the last 50 years, rural values have remained very important in Bulgarian society, along with immense respect for the family as a social unit and the preservation of the very rich rural culture and folklore of Bulgaria.

In general, **social life** is Mediterranean and informal, with close economic and practical links being maintained between family members. This has often been necessary for survival in many times in the recent history of Bulgaria. Produce from rural plots worked by a family member is a vital part of the economy of many urban families. There is a fairly clear social stratification in most Bulgarian towns and cities between the elite, in the old days the communists and their entourage, now the new business class, and the vast majority of the people. Real poverty and material deprivation still exists on a wide scale among them, and Western visitors should try to understand the economic pressures many families face before jumping to conclusions about aspects of Bulgarian life they may dislike.

Dress and social culture among the elite imitates Western models, with a great fondness for large expensive cars, Mercedes Benz in particular. Housing is an important part of personal wealth, and many less privileged families nevertheless own impressive properties. Generally speaking, for business purposes, dress is as in the rest of Europe, but informality is very common and widespread. Women's dress is conservative among the middle-aged and older generation, but completely Westernised in younger age groups. Traditional costume is still worn in some areas for weddings and some festivals. Family relationships are still firmly patriarchal in the countryside and smaller towns, but in Sofia and the Black Sea coast women have more independence.

Bulgaria is very much a gift-giving culture and it is polite to bring something for the hostess if invited out. Flowers are very popular in this respect, and every Bulgarian town has numerous flower stalls. Scotch whisky is very popular with nearly all Bulgarian men, *Bells* and *Johnny Walker* in particular. Gin is not drunk very much.

Bulgaria is a tobacco-growing country with many smokers, and is free from politically correct anti-smoking restrictions, except on public transport coaches and some trains. Western cigarettes, especially *Rothmans* and *Camel* make good presents. Cannabis is becoming quite widely smoked by young people, and is easy to buy in most towns.

Night life and relationships

Bulgarian nightlife has benefited considerably from the end of communism, where a heavy puritanical ethos dominated society. All kinds of pubs, clubs and restaurants have opened catering for different tastes and age groups, particularly in Sofia. Traditional restaurants with their folk-dancing displays continue to be popular, alongside discos and clubs. Economic difficulties still affect many establishments, which tend to shut early outside the summer months. Casinos and gambling halls are widespread. Stud poker is a favourite game.

In family and heterosexual relationships, Bulgarians are generally broad-minded, moderately hedonistic and tolerant. Within marriages, lovers and mistresses are common in the towns. Divorce is not particularly encouraged. Homosexuality exists, but is strongly disapproved of by most Bulgarians, and discretion is required. Public parks in Sofia are conventional evening meeting places. Prostitution is not legal, but is a fact of life in Sofia and Black Sea coast nightlife. The popular districts for street prostitutes in the big cities, such as around the Hotel Pliska and the Lion's Bridge in Sofia are dangerous, in every sense. **Avoid**.

Under communism the divorce rate was quite high, family sizes were small, and abortion was common. The Bulgarian birthrate has been low for many generations in any case, although this is not the case among the Muslim minorities. Rural familes were highly traditional and patriarchal, but a different world existed in Sofia and the Black Sea cities. In a different guise, much of this has remained the case after five years of pluralism. Sofia has comfortably adapted to Western *mores*, while much of the rest of the country stoutly resists change.

Intermarriage between Orthodox Bulgarians and members of ethnic minorities is very unusual and is generally not encouraged. In the case of Turkish minority Muslims and Roma, it is virtually unknown in most communities. The Rhodope Pomaks have widely intermarried with Christian Bulgarians since the 1970s.

Language

Alphabet

А	а	as	-a-	in calm	/a/
Б	б	as	-b-	in back	/b/
В	в	as	-v-	in view	/v/
Г	г	as	-g-	in glass	/g/
Д	д	as	-d-	in die	/d/
Е	е	as	-e-	in bed	/e/
Ж	ж	as	-s-	in measure	/j/
З	з	as	-z-	in zoo	/z/
И	и	as	-i-	in ship	/i/
Й	й	as	-y-	in yet	/y/
К	к	as	-c-	in class	/k/
Л	л	as	-l-	in lot	/l/
М	м	as	-m-	in mother	/m/
Н	н	as	-n-	in not	/n/
О	о	as	-o-	in pot	/o/
П	п	as	-p-	in pack	/p/
Р	р	as	-r-	in rod	/r/
С	с	as	-s-	in soon	/s/
Т	т	as	-t-	in tie	/t/
У	у	as	-u-	in put	/u/
Ф	ф	as	-f-	in fool	/f/
Х	х	as	-h-	in hot	/h/
Ц	ц		ts		/ts/
Ч	ч	as	-ch-	in church	/ch/
Ш	ш	as	-sh-	in shoe	/sh/
Щ	щ		sht		
Ъ	ъ	as	-e-	in hotter	/â/
	ь	as	-y-	in yet	/y/
Ю	ю	as	-u-	in tube	/yu/
Я	я	as	-ya-	in yard	/ya/

Vowels
Open   Narrow

Open		Narrow	
a	A	â	Ъ
o	O	u	У
e	E	ɪ	И

Note: when the open vowels are not under stress or are at the end of a word they are usually pronounced like the corresponding narrow vowels.

Consonants
Voiced Voiceless

Voiced		Voiceless	
b	Б	p	П
v	В	f	Ф
g	Г	k	К

D	Д	T	Т
J	Ж	SH	Ш
Z	З	S	С

Note: when the voiced consonants are at the end of a word or after a voiceless consonant they are usually pronounced like the corresponding voiceless consonants.

Й й put in the beginning, in the end of a word or after a vowel. ь put after a consonant.

Greetings

Hello	Zdravèy (te)	Здравей/те/
Good morning	Dobrò ùtro	Добро утро
Good afternoon	Dòbâr dèn	Добър ден
Good evening	Dòbâr vècher	Добър вечер
Good night	Lèka nòsht	Лека нощ
Good-bye	Dovìjdane	Довиждане

Useful expressions

Yes	Da	Да
Please	Mòlya	Моля
Great!	Chudèsno!	Чудесно!
Thank you	Blagodaryà	Благодаря
Thank you very much	Mnògo Vi blagodaryà	Много Ви благодаря
Not at all	Nyàma zashtò	Няма защо
That's right	Tòchno takà	Точно така
No	Ne	Не
No, thank you	Ne, blagodaryà	Не, благодаря
Excuse me; sorry	Izvinète	Извинете
That's OK	Nyàma nìshto	Няма нищо
All right	Dobrè	Добре
I know	Znam	Знам
I don't know	Ne znàm	Не знам
How much is that	Kòlko strùva tovà	Колко струва това
Please can you	Mòlya Vi, mòjete li dà	Моля Ви, можете ли да
repeat	povtòrite	повторите
speak more slowly	govòrite pò-bàvno	говорите по-бавно
write it down	gonapìshete	го напишете
Sir/Mr ...	Gospodìn/Gospòdine ...	Господин/Господине…
Madam/Mrs ...	Gospojà/Gospòjo ...	Госпожа/Госпожо…
Miss/Miss ...	Gospòjitsa/Gospòjitse ...	Госпожица/Госпожице…

Name

What's your name?	Kàk se kàzvate?	Как се казвате?
My name is ...	Kàzvam se ...	Казвам се…
How are you?	Kàk ste?	Как сте?
Very well, thank you	Mnògo dobrè, blagodaryà	Много добре, благодаря
I am here	Tùk sâm	Тук съм
on business	po ràbota	цо работа

on holiday	na pochìvka	на почивка
I am a journalist	Àz sâm journalìst	Аз съм журналист
I am from ...	Àz sâm òt ...	Аз съм от
I have an appointment with...	Imam srèshta s...	Имам среща с…
May I speak to...	Mòga li da govòrya s...	Мога ли да говоря с…
I am staying	Otsèdnal sâm	Отседнал съм
at a/the hotel...	v hotèl...	в хотел…
in ... Road/Street	na ùlitsa...	на улица…

On the street

I've lost my way	Izgùbih se	Изгубих се
Where is...?	Kâdè e...?	Къде е…
How di I get to...?	Kàk da stìgna dò...?	Как да стигна до…?
bus station	àvtogàrata	автогарата
railway station	gàrata	гарата
the airport	letìshteto	летището
the market	pazàra	цазара
...Square	Ploshtàd...	Площад…
...Street	Ulitsa...	Улица…
the post office	pòshtata	пощата
the police station	politsèyskiya uchàstâk	полицейския участък
the town centre	tsèntâea na gradà	центъра на града
Is there near here...?	Ima li nablìzo...?	Има ли наблизо…
a bus stop	avtobùsna spìrka	автобусна спирка
a chemist's	aptèka	аптека
a petrol station	benzinostàntsiya	бензиностанция
a hospital	bòlnitsa	болница
a museum	muzèy	музей
a church	tsârkva	църква
a telephone box	telefònna kagìna	телефонна кабина
a restaurant	restorànt	ресторант
a shop	magazìn	магазин
a theatre	teàtâr	театър
Which way is	Nakâdè e	Накъде е
the museum	muzèyat	музеят
the church	tsârkvata	църквата
the archeological site	arheologìcheskiyat obèkt	археологическият обект
the mosque	djamìyata	джамията

Possible answers

Left	Lyàvo	Ляво
Right	Dyàsno	Лясно
Straight on	Napràvo	Направо
Turn	Zavìyte	Завийте
Over there	Tàm	Там
First one on the left	Pârvata vlyàvo	Първата вляво
First one on the right	Pârvata vydàsno	Първата вдясно
Second one on the left	Vtòrata vlyàvo	Вторато вляво

Second one on the right	Vtòrata vdyàsno	Втората вдясно
At the crossroads	Na krâstòvishteto	На кръстовището
After the traffice lights	Slèd svetoràfa	След светофара
It's (Is it) near/far?	Blìzo/delèch (li) e?	Близо (ли) е/Дадеч(ли)е

A little grammar

To be			It		To	To
I	Az	Аз	It is		Tò e	То е
I am	Az sâm	Аз съм	We		Nìe	Ние
You	Ti	Ти	We are		Nìe sme	Ние сме
You are	Ti si	Ти си	You		Vìe	Вие
He	Tòy	Той	You are		Vìoe ste	Вие сте
He is	Tòy e	Той е	They		Te	Те
She	Tyà	Тя	They are		Tè sa	Те са
She is	Tyà e	Тя е				

Food and drink

pub	krâchma	кръчма
brandy	rakìya	ракия
chilli peppers	lyùti chùshki	люти чушки
Shopska (salad)	Shòpska (salàta)	Шопска (салата)

Breakfast / **Zakùska** / **Закуска**

I would like...	Bìh ìskal...	Бих искал…
coffee	kafè	кафе
with sugar	sâs zàhar	със захар
without sugar	bez zàhar	без захар
white	s mlyàko	с мляко
with cream	sâs smetàna	със сметана
tea	chày	чай
milk	mlyàko	мляко
bread	hlyàb	хляб
butter	maslò	масло
jam	slàdko	слацко
boiled egg	varèno yaytsè	варено яйце
ham-and-eggs	hèm-end-egs	хем-енд-егс
cheese	sìrene	сирене
yellow cheese	kashkavàl	кашкавал
mineral water	mineràlna vodà	минерална вода
juice	naturàlen sòk	натурална сок
hot chocolate	gorèshto kakào	горещо какао

Possible answer

We don't have	Nyàma(me)	Няма/ме/

Drinks

Drinks	Napitki	Напитки
A bottle of...please	Butìlka...ako obìchate	Бутилка…ако обичате
A glass of...	Chàsha...	Чаша…
red wine	chervèno vìno	червено вино
white wine	byàlo vìno	бяло вино
rosé wine	rozè	розе
dry	sùho	сухо
sweet	slàdko	сладко
champagne	shampànsko	шампанско
A (double) whisky	Ednò (dvòyno) uìski	Едно (двойно) уиски
on the rocks	s lèd	с лед
with water	s vodà	с вода
with soda	sâs sòda	със сода
Gin	Djìn	Джин
and tonic	i tònik	и тоник
with lemon	s linòn	с лимон
Waiter!	Kèlner!	Келнер!
The bill, please!	Smètkata, mòlya!	Сметката, моля!
I think you've made a mistake	Mìslya, che ìma grèshka	Мисля, че има грешка
Where is the toilet, please?	Kâdè e toalètnata, mòlya?	Къде е тоалетната?

Snacks

Snacks		
Sandwich	Sàndvich	Сандвич
with cheese	sâs sìrene	със сирене
with ham	s shùnka	с шунка
with/without meat	s/bez méso	с/без месо
with salad	sâs salàta	със салата
Hot dog	Hòt-dog	Хдт-дог
Hamburger	Hàmburger	Хомбургер
Pizza with mushrooms	Pìtsa s gâbi	Пица с гъби
Chips	Pârjeni kartòfi	Пържени картофи

In the restaurant

In the restaurant		
Restaurant	Restorànt	Ресторант
Is this table occupied?	Tàzi màsa zaèta li è?	Таеи маса заета ли е?
Is the seat occupied?	Myàstoto zaèto li è?	Мястото заето ли е?
A table for	Màsa za	Маса за
one	edìn chovèk	един човек
two	dvàma	двама
three	trìma	трима
four	chetirìma	четирима
The menu, please	Menyùto, mòlya	Меиюто, моля

The menu	Menyù	Меню
Starters	Ordyòvri	Ордьоври
cheese	sìrene	сирене
ham	shùnka	шунка
salami	salàm	салам
salads	Salàti	Салати
tomatoes and cucumbers	domàti i kràstavitsi (mèshana)	домати и краставици
with cheese	Shòpska (mèshana)	Шопска /мешана+сирене/
Russian salad	Rùska salàta	Руска салата
filtered yoghourt and cucumbers	Snejànka	Снежанка
seafood salad	salàta s mòrski delikatèsi	Салата с морски деликатеси
prawn cocktail	koktèyl ot skarìdi	салата от скариди
olives	maslìni	маслини
Soups	**Sùpi**	**Супи**
cream soup	krèm sùpa	крем супа
chicken soup	pìleshka sùpa	пилешка супа
bean soup	bòb chorbà	боб чорбоа
pea soup (lentils)	gràhova sùpa (lèshta)	грахова супа/леща/
oxtail soup/stock	bulyòn	бульон
vegetable soup	zelenchùkova sùpa	зеленчукова супа
tripe soup	shkembé chorbà	шкембе чорба
Egg dishes	**Yàstiya s yaytsà**	**Ястия с яйца**
scrambled eggs	bârkani yaytsà	бъркаяи яйца
fried eggs	pârjeni yaytsà	пържени яйца
eggs sunny side up	yaytsà na ochì	яйца на очи
omelette	omlèt	омлет
Fish	**Rìba**	**Риба**
trout	pâstârva	пъстърва
salmon	syòmga	сьомга
carp	sharàn	шаран
anchovy	anshuà	аншуа
turbot	kalkàn	калкан
scad	safrìd	сафрид
mackerel	skumrìya	скумрия
tuna	rìba tòn	риба тон
cod	treskà	треска
octopus	oktopòd	октопод
squid	kalmàri	калмари
prawns	skarìdi	скариди
oysters	strìdi	стриди

mussels	mìdi	миди

Meat — **Mesò** — **Месо**

beef	govèjdo	говеждо
lamb	àgneshko	агнешко
pork	svìnsko	свинско
veal	tèleshko	телышко
mutton	òvneshko	овнешко
rib	rebrò	ребро
joint	bùt/plèshka	бут/плешкѣ
steak	biftèk	бифтек
chop	pârjòla	пържола
sausage	nàdenitsa	наденица
minced meat	kaymà	кайма

Game — **Divech** — **Дивеч**

quail	pâdpâdâk	пъдпъдък
pheasant	fazàn	фазан
rabbit	zàek	заек
boar	gligàn	глиган
venison	elènsko mesò	еленско месо

Poultry — **Ptìtsi** — **Птици**

| chicken | pìle | пиле |
| turkey | pùyka | пуйка |

Offal — **Drebolìi** — **Дреболии**

kidneys	bâbrecheta	бъбречета
gizzard	vodenìchka	воденичка
head	glavà	глава
tongue	ezìk	език
brains	mòzâk	мозък
liver	dròb	дроб
tripe	shkembè	шкембе

Vegetables — **Zelenchùtsi** — **Зеленчуци**

cabbage	zèle	зеле
potato	kartòf	картоф
onion	lùk	лук
lettuce	marùlya	маруля
carrot	mòrkov	морков

Dessert — **Desèrt** — **Десерт**

| ice-cream | sladolèd | сладолед |
| cream pastries | pàsti | пасти |

Fruits — **Plodovè** — **Плодове**

| banana | banàn | банан |
| orange | portokàl | портокал |

apple	yàbâlka	ябълка
pear	krùsha	круша
grapefruit	grèypfrut	грейпфрут

Preparation

baked or roast	pechen	печен
boiled	varen	варен
broiled	na skara	на скара
fried	pârjen	пържен
grilled	na gril	на грил
stewed	zadushen	задушен
stuffed	pâlnen	пълнен

oil	olio	олио
vinegar	otset	оцет
salt	sol	сол
pepper	piper	пипер

History of Bulgaria

Eurasian pastoral nomads and the origins of Bulgaria

Professor Sir Dimitri Obolensky FBA

Pastoral nomadism

The raison d'être of pastoral nomadism was defined by Arnold Toynbee as follows: 'The opening for pastoral nomadism is in country that is too dry for raising crops but is not too dry for pasturing sheep and cattle if the flocks and herds are kept constantly on the move, in an annual circuit, from one pasture to another in time with the seasons at which each successive pasture is ripe for grazing' (*Constantine Porphyzogenitus and his World*, London, 1973, p 412).

From time immemorial the **open steppe** has offered pasture lands to the sheep rearing, horse-riding nomads moving westward from their homes in central Asia, through the funnel-shaped corridor between the Black Sea coast and the wooded steppe further north, towards the Carpathians and the middle Danube. Some were content to remain close to the warm and fertile plains by the sea and to the coastal cities which offered prospect of trade or plunder. Others, driven by economic necessity, by bottlenecks of fresh invaders further east, or by military ambition, followed the 'steppe corridor' to its end, through the narrow passage between the Danube delta and the arc of the Transylvanian Alps, into the Romanian plain of Wallachia: from there they could either press on across the passes on the Banat mountains into the plain of Hungary, or else cross the Lower Danube into the Balkans.

On the western fringes of the steppe the more abundant rainfall made agriculture possible. This caused the **Eurasian nomad** to rely for his subsistence not only on pasture land, but also on ready supplies of agricultural produce: these he could obtain both from the farming population of the wooded steppe and from the coastal cities; these cities also provided him with fixed bases for empire building. The tendency of the nomad to shift towards an agricultural mode of life brought the steppe of Eurasia into an intimate relationship with the wooded steppe and the Black Sea coast, comparable to that which prevailed between nomad and farmer in the Sahara and the Syrian desert. And the resultant interest, compounded of envy and contempt, which the Eurasian nomad showed for the farmer and the merchant, underlies much of the human drama in the medieval history of Eastern Europe. The origins of the Bulgarian nation lie in this world.

Asparuch and the Onogurs

In the scattering of Central Asian tribes that was taking place in the mid-7C, one of the branches of the **Onogur** people suddenly emerged as a menacing cloud on Byzantium's northern horizon. Led by Kovrat's son Asparuch, a horde of considerable size moved westward across the steppe and, probably soon after 670, arrived on the delta of the **Danube**. Like so many of their predecessors who had reached this terminal point on the historic highway of Eurasia—most recently the Avars—the Onogurs longed to cross the Danube, partly to escape from the hazards of the steppe, partly, no doubt, because, being then in a transitional stage between pastoral nomadism and an agricultural economy, they sought for lands to colonise and cultivate. And so, from their grazing grounds in southern Bessarabia and from the natural stronghold they had occupied probably to the north of the Danube delta, Asparuch's hordes began, in the 670s, to push southward into the Dobrudzha.

It was the traditional policy of **Byzantium** to welcome potential allies on the northern bank of the Danube, but to oppose by every means their attempts to cross the river: so in 680 a large squadron of Byzantine warships, under the personal command of the emperor Constantine IV, sailed up the Black Sea coast and disembarked north of the Danube estuary; simultaneously a detachment of cavalry was rushed across Thrace to the river. But the **Bulgars**—as the Balkan Onogurs were to be known henceforth to the Byzantines—taking advantage of the terrain, avoided battle and retired behind the swamps and lagoons of the delta. The emperor, stricken by gout, retired to Mesembria, and his forces, having achieved nothing, were obliged to withdraw. While they were crossing the Danube they were attacked by the Bulgars and driven back, suffering many losses. The victorious Bulgars advanced to the neighbourhood of Varna and occupied the Dobrudzha.

The empire was in no position to expel the invaders: the Bulgars had come to stay. In 681 Constantine IV concluded peace with Asparuch and undertook to pay an annual tribute to his people. Thus was Byzantium forced to acknowledge the existence of an independent 'barbarian' state on imperial territory. The extent of this disaster may not have been immediately apparent to the Byzantines: for the area occupied by the Bulgars south of the Danube had to all intents and purposes been lost to the empire after the Slav invasions. Yet the *Sklaviniae*, here as elsewhere in the Balkan peninsula, were loose tribal associations, lacking any clearly defined political structure, and over them the fiction of Byzantine sovereignty could still be maintained. The Bulgars, whose political institutions and military organisation had developed long before they came to the Balkans, were a different matter. Asparuch had carved himself a powerful kingdom on Byzantine soil. For the first time in its history the empire was compelled formally to relinquish sovereignty over a significant fragment of the Balkan peninsula. The peace treaty of 681 was indeed, in the words of a medieval Byzantine chronicler, 'a disgrace to the Romans'.

Asparuch's realm extended on both sides of the lower Danube, from the mouth of the Dniester to the Balkan Mountains. It comprised Southern Bessarabia, some of the Wallachian plan, the whole of the Dobrudzha, and the province of Lower Moesia between the Black Sea coast and the Timok river. The latter region became the political and economic kernel of the country henceforth to be known as **Bulgaria**. It was in Eastern Moesia that Asparuch established his capital, Pliska, a fortress which inherited the strategic position of the Roman Marcianopolis, guarded the southern approaches to the Dobrudzha, and controlled the northern sector of the road linking the Danube, across one of the Balkan passes, with Anchialus and Constantinople.

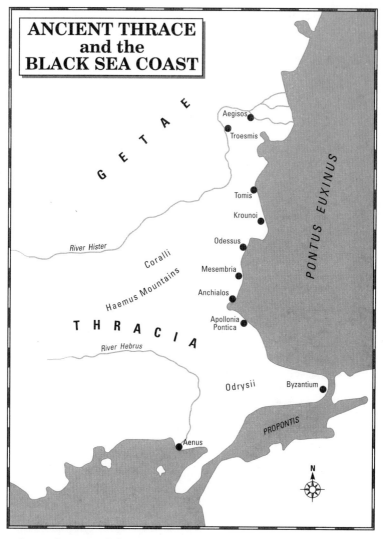

The Bulgars and the Slavs

The Bulgars' new home in the Balkans had, during the past 80 years or so, been colonised by the **Slavs**. There is no doubt that the Moesian Slavs were subjugated by Asparuch's horde. However, in his subsequent treatment of his Slavonic subjects Asparuch showed himself a statesman as well as a conqueror. He first settled them on the periphery of his kingdom, as guardians of its military frontiers: thus the tribe of the Severi was transferred from its home by the Veregava pass in the Balkan Mountains to the eastern borders of Bulgaria, which it was expected to defend against the attacks launched by the Byzantines from the cities they still held on the Black Sea coast; while another group of Slavs, collectively known as 'the Seven Tribes', was established by Asparuch along the southern frontier and also on the western borders, where his realm abutted on the lands of the Avars. Gradually some of the Moesian Slavs appear to have agreed to collaborate politically with the Bulgars, whose growing hegemony in the north eastern Balkans promised their subjects a permanent relief from Avar attacks and the prospect of further territorial aggrandisement at the expense of Byzantium.

This symbiosis probably saved the Slavs in this area from losing their ethnic identity: for, had they not been incorporated into the Bulgar kingdom, they would doubtless have been as thoroughly Hellenised in the course of time as the Slavs in Greece. In fact, during the next two centuries, they became an increasingly important partner, and eventually the dominant element, in the medieval Bulgarian state. For some time to come Byzantine writers continued to differentiate between Bulgar and Slav inhabitants of this realm. But the assimilation of the Turkic Bulgars by the far more numerous Slavonic population gathered momentum; recent archaeological discoveries suggest that this fusion had advanced considerably by the 9C; and by the 10C Bulgaria was to all intents and purposes a Slav country.

The Bulgars and Byzantium

Tervel

The Bulgars had not long been established in the Balkans before their realm began to play a significant role in Byzantine politics. The Emperor Justinian II, as the result of a revolution in Constantinople, had been deposed and exiled to Cherson in 695. Pursued by the vengeance of his enemies in the capital, he fled from the Crimea to the Khazar-controlled city of Phanagoria, at the mouth of the Kuban, and thence to the estuary of the Danube. There he appealed for help to the Khagan **Tervel**, Asparuch's successor. The Bulgar ruler seized this golden opportunity to intervene in the internal affairs of the empire: in 705 his army of Bulgars and Slavs appeared before the walls of Constantinople. The fortifications once again proved impregnable, but Justinian crawled through a pipe of the aqueduct into the city during the night, and in the ensuing panic regained his throne.

The timely, if hardly disinterested, services of the Bulgar *khagan* were duly rewarded. Tervel was invested by the emperor with the dignity of Caesar. Like Asparuch, Tervel was a pagan; yet he could now glory in a title more resounding than the one which his Christian ancestor Kovrat had obtained from the empire: for the rank of Caesar was, next to the imperial dignity, the highest in the hierarchy of Byzantium. No barbarian ruler had ever risen so high, and the Bulgarians were not soon to forget that their khagan had received, as an associate of the emperor, the homage of the people of East Rome. The Byzantines, however, viewed the ceremony of 705 with different eyes: Tervel's title, which carried no power, could be regarded as a sign of his recognition of the emperor's supreme authority.

The treaty of 705, even more than that of 681, ensured Bulgaria's position as a rising power in the Balkans. The Byzantine authorities had every reason to feel alarmed by the presence of this vigorous alien body on a territory which, despite the treaties signed with Asparuch and Tervel, they persisted in regarding as belonging by right to the empire. The Bulgars had in 705 their first taste of the riches of Constantinople: it was a heady experience; and Tervel showed no signs of behaving as a vassal of the empire. In 712, a year after the death of Justinian II, he invaded Thrace, marched unopposed to the walls of Constantinople and devastated the surrounding country.

In 716, as the Arabs were preparing to lay siege to Constantinople, the Emperor Theodosius III concluded a treaty with the Bulgarians. Two of its clauses are of special importance. The frontier between the empire and Bulgaria was fixed along a line running through Northern Thrace, probably from the Gulf of Burgas to a point on the Maritsa about half-way between Philippopolis and Adrianople: this shows that the Bulgarian realm had started to expand into the plain of Thrace, had advanced its frontier to within striking distance of the Byzantine ports of Mesembria and Anchialus, and had reached at one point the Belgrade–Constantinople highway.

The ports and the highway had a commercial as well as a strategic importance, and it is noteworthy that another clause of the treaty provided for regular state-controlled trade between the two countries. It was probably in 716 that the Bulgarians began to play an active part in the export of Thracian corn to the Byzantine cities on the Black Sea coast and in the import of manufactured goods from Constantinople and the Mediterranean world through these same towns into the interior of the Balkans. Thus, through trade, diplomacy and military expansion, the young Bulgarian state was gradually anchored in the Balkans and brought into closer relationship with the cities of the Byzantine Empire.

The three peace treaties which Byzantium had concluded with the Bulgars were little more than desperate expedients, devised by the imperial diplomats to confine the invaders to the area north of the Balkan Mountains. The territorial arrangements of 716 showed, however, that this policy of containment could not be successful for long. The Bulgarian *khagans* and many of their boyars, the Turkic warrior aristocracy, were consistently hostile to the empire, and could be expected to pursue a policy of further expansion into Thrace. Only a determined attempt to stamp out the parasitical kingdom and to throw the Bulgars back beyond the Danube could, in the view of the Byzantine government, bring permanent relief to the northern frontier. Yet, as the campaigns of the emperor Maurice had so clearly demonstrated, only when the seasoned imperial troops were transferred from the eastern front to Europe could Byzantium hope to conduct a successful offensive in the Balkans.

By the mid 8C the victories of Constantine V in Syria, Armenia and Mesopotamia had temporarily removed the Arab menace in the east, and the emperor could turn to what he regarded as the main military and political task of his life—the annihilation of Bulgaria. For some 20 years (756–75) Constantine V devoted his considerable talents as a soldier and diplomatist to this objective. He very nearly succeeded. He took advantage of the political instability which overcame Bulgaria in the third quarter of the 8C by kindling the latent antagonism between the Bulgar aristocracy and the Slavs; and in a series of nine campaigns, mostly successful, which usually combined—in what was now traditional Byzantine strategy—land attacks across Thrace with naval expeditions to the Danube estuary, he routed the Bulgarian armies again and again. But even his victory by Anchialus in 763, the greatest of his reign, did not subdue the country. Constantine's death on his last campaign (775) left the empire stronger in the northern Balkans than it had been since the reign of Maurice. But Bulgaria, though exhausted and crippled, was still on the map, its ruling classes more united than ever in their hatred of Byzantium.

Krum

The vitality of the Bulgarian state, and the danger which its military recovery could present to the empire, were dramatically demonstrated when **Krum**, the mightiest of its early rulers, became Sublime Khagan in the early years of the 9C. The destruction of the Avar Empire by Charlemagne had enabled the Bulgarians to annex Transylvania and the eastern part of present-day Hungary, where many Bulgars lived, thereby vastly increasing the territory, the economic resources and the military potential of their state; and Krum became the sovereign of a kingdom which stretched from Northern Thrace to the Carpathians and from the lower Sava to the Dniester, and adjoined the Frankish Empire on the Tisza. He was soon to prove as great a scourge to the Byzantines as Constantine V had been to the Bulgars. A strong line of imperial fortresses, which had probably been restored by Constantine, extended in a semi-circle south of the Balkan Mountains, barring the Bulgarian advance on central Thrace and Macedonia; its key points were Serdica, Philippopolis, Adrianople and Develtus.

During the five years that followed Krum's first major onslaught on Byzantine territory (809), every one of these cities was captured by the Bulgars. Even Mesembria, whose position on a small peninsula at the northern end of the Gulf of Burgas, joined to the mainland by a narrow isthmus, made it almost impregnable, was stormed by Krum after a two weeks' siege (812). Apart from large hoards of gold and silver, the Bulgars gained possession in that city of a supply of Greek fire, the celebrated secret weapon of the Byzantines; and, a fact which illustrates even more clearly the military expertise the Bulgars had acquired, Krum could now rely, when he besieged imperial cities, on the technical advice of the distinguished engineer Eumathius, who had deserted from Byzantine service after the fall of Serdica (809). Despite occasional Byzantine successes, such as the capture and sack of the Bulgar capital of Pliska by the Emperor Nicephorus I, the war was disastrous for the empire. In July 811 Krum gained his most celebrated triumph: a Byzantine army was trapped by the Bulgars in a defile of the Balkan Mountains and slaughtered almost to a man. Nicephorus himself perished in the fray; and from his skull Krum made a goblet, encrusted with silver, out of which he made his boyars drink.

This was a terrible blow to the empire's prestige: not since the death of Valens on the field of Adrianople (378) had an emperor fallen in battle against the barbarians. Equally dramatic was the appearance in July 813 of Krum's army at the gates of Constantinople. But the land walls proved too strong even for him, and the Bulgars had no fleet: so the khagan offered peace terms. In the meeting which followed with the emperor Leo V on the shore of the Golden Horn, Krum barely escaped a Byzantine plot to murder him; breathing vengeance, he laid waste the environs of the city, and stormed Adrianople. But the following spring, as he was preparing a huge assault on the Byzantine capital, Krum suddenly died (April 814).

Krum's death removed from Constantinople a danger as acute as that which had faced it during the Avaro–Slav siege of 626. But the balance of power in the

Balkans had radically altered. Bulgaria, a country which 50 years before had seemed on the verge of extinction, was now one of the great military powers of Europe. About 816 the Khagan Omurtag made a peace treaty with Byzantium; the frontier between the two realms was to run along the so-called 'Great Fence', cutting across Northern Thrace from Develtus by the Gulf of Burgas to Makrolivada near the Maritsa, and thence northward to the Balkan Mountains: it thus coincided with the boundary of 716. The peace between **Byzantium** and **Bulgaria** was not to be seriously disturbed until the end of the century. But, although the great fortresses captured by Krum were returned to the empire, the stabilisation of its frontier in the Northern Balkans was more apparent than real: Adrianople and Mesembria, it is true, were heavily fortified after 815; but Serdica and Philippopolis, whose fortifications had been dismantled by Krum, were left undefended—a constant encouragement for the Bulgarian state to expand towards the south.

Elsewhere in the **Balkans**, the situation in the early years of the 9C was still far from favourable to **Byzantium**: in the northwest its authority was confined to the main cities on the Adriatic; in the interior, the Serbs had shaken off the shadowy dependence imposed upon them by Heraclius; the Croats in Dalmatia and north of the Sava were subjects of the Frankish Empire; the central and southern regions of the Balkans were studded with independent *Sklaviniae*, over which the Byzantine administration, operating from the few coastal cities which had escaped the Slavonic occupation, had as yet little or no control. But the ethnic and political map of the Balkans, so fluid and confused during the period of the barbarian invasions and settlements, was gradually becoming stable; and in the course of the 9C, during which Byzantium made a determined and largely successful effort to regain its power and influence over southeastern Europe, the Balkan peninsula began to emerge from its Dark Ages and to assume, in broad outline, the features it was to retain during much of its medieval history.

Bulgaria after the end of Ottoman rule

Professor Richard Crampton

Ottoman rule

Bulgaria was in almost constant conflict with its mighty neighbour, **Byzantium**, until the battle of Belasitsa in 1014 after which a victorious Byzantine emperor blinded 99 out of every 100 Bulgarian soldiers and left the hundredth with one eye to guide his stricken comrades home. The Bulgarian state could not survive the destruction of its army. A second Bulgarian empire appeared in the late 12C. It was enfeebled, however, by constant wars and by a rapacious nobility. It fell relatively easy prey to the Ottomans who captured the capital of the Second Bulgarian Kingdom, Turnovo, in 1393.

Ottoman rule was to last for almost 500 years. The Ottomans destroyed the existing political elite and allowed Islam a privileged status, but by and large the Christians were left to regulate their own cultural affairs. This meant the survival of the Bulgarian church which was the main factor in keeping alive the language and a sense of cultural identity. But if a sense of cultural separateness survived there was little in the way of a national revival.

The first signs of this revival came in the 18C and were to a large extent a reaction to increasing Greek domination of the church. A Bulgarian monk, Paisii of Hilendar, wrote a history of his people in which he enjoined them not to adopt foreign tongues or to be ashamed of their own national past; though written in the 18C, Paisii's work was not printed until 1845.

By then the national revival had quickened considerably. After some 40 years of turmoil the Ottoman empire, in the 1820s, achieved internal stability. This new peace enabled Bulgaria's home-based textile producers to flourish and much of the wealth thus created went to finance homes, churches and education. In 1860 the Bulgarian church seceded from the Greek, though not until 1870 did the Ottoman authorities recognise the **Exarch**, as the head of the Bulgarian church was known. By this time Bulgarian schools had multiplied, literacy was spreading rapidly, Bulgarian newspapers and journals were being published, and every large village had its cultural centre, or *chitalishte*.

Political activity was always less apparent than cultural. There were a number of political organisations in the 1860s and early 1870s but it was the failure rather than the success of an attempted rising in 1876 which brought about Bulgaria's political separation from the Ottoman Empire. So brutal was the suppression of the rising that Russia intervened militarily. At the preliminary **peace of San Stefano** (March 1878) a huge new Bulgarian state was created—but this frightened Britain and Austria-Hungary who saw it as a means of Russia gaining control of the Balkans. At their insistence the new Bulgaria was drastically reduced in size by the **Treaty of Berlin** (July 1878).

The Bulgarian state

In 1879 an assembly in Turnovo produced a constitution for the new state. A single chamber parliament, the sûbranie, elected by universal adult male suffrage was to be the prime legislative body; the head of state, who was to remain a vassal of the **Ottoman sultan**, was to be a prince elected by the assembly. Sofia was chosen as the capital.

The first prince was Alexander of Battenberg, a young officer who had fought with the Russians in the recent war and who enjoyed the confidence of Queen Victoria. Alexander soon found that he could not work with the constitution, Bulgaria's politicians, or Russia's representatives. In 1881 he suspended the constitution but two years later was forced to reinstate it in order to save himself from the overbearing Russian officers on whom he had come to rely.

He faced further problems in 1885. The Treaty of Berlin had separated northern from southern Bulgaria, the latter forming the autonomous Ottoman province of Eastern Rumelia. In September 1885 pro-Bulgarian elements in Rumelia declared for union with Bulgaria. Alexander could not reject so popular a move but it was one much resented by Russia and Serbia. The latter invaded Bulgaria, only to suffer crushing defeat at Slivnitsa, despite the fact that Russia had withdrawn all its military advisers from Bulgaria. The Tsar never forgave Battenberg and in 1886 sanctioned his deposition.

Ferdinand

For over a year Bulgaria was without a prince until **Ferdinand of Saxe-Coburg Gotha** accepted the post. He faced intense opposition from the Russians and their Bulgarian allies against whom he was vigorously defended by Stafan Stambolov, a young but tough-minded liberal who had dominated the regency. The intrigues of Ferdinand's opponents forced Stambolov to take uncompromising action and in so doing he stimulated opposition. Ferdinand, as soon as he was secure on his throne, dropped his increasingly unpopular pilot. A year later, in 1895, **Stambolov** was brutally murdered. After Stambolov's death Ferdinand constructed a complicated but effective mechanism of political control based on clientism and corruption. By 1900 Ferdinand's 'personal regime' had given him complete mastery over Bulgaria's foreign policy and a decisive influence in internal affairs.

By the turn of the century foreign policy was a critical issue. **Macedonia**, another part of San Stefano Bulgaria lost at Berlin, was falling into increasing disorder from which Bulgaria, Greece and Serbia hoped to profit. Secret societies promoted the interests of each country and financed guerilla bands, *cheti*, which operated in Macedonia itself. One Bulgarian group which advocated autonomy for Macedonia, the **Internal Macedonian Revolutionary Organisation** (IMRO), was to remain a feature of Balkan politics for decades. Ferdinand allowed the Bulgarian army to establish secret ties with the pro-Bulgarian *cheti* but the Bulgarian cause in Macedonia received a severe setback with the ill-fated **Ilinden rising** in August 1903. Its failure meant the imposition of effective reforms in Macedonia which remained in force until the Young Turk revolution of 1908. In October of that year Bulgaria took advantage of a diplomatic crisis to declare itself completely independent and thus end its vassal status. Ferdinand was declared King of the Bulgarians.

The Balkan Wars

By 1912 **Macedonia** was once more on the path towards chaos. The Balkan states, fearing an independent Albania or great power intervention to prop up Turkey-in-Europe, concluded a series of alliances and in October 1912 invaded the Ottoman Empire. They enjoyed brilliant military success but suffered abject diplomatic failure. Ottoman Europe had been conquered by the spring of 1913 but the great powers had insisted upon the creation of an independent Albania; this deprived Serbia of areas it had earmarked for itself and it demanded compensation from the gains Bulgaria expected in Macedonia. Bulgaria refused and in June launched an attack on its former allies. The latter were joined by Romania and Turkey, thus placing the Bulgarians in a hopeless position. In August they signed the treaty of Bucharest by which they lost the rich lands of the southern Dobrudzha and most of their recent gains in Macedonia.

The bitter experience of the **Balkan wars** of 1912–13 meant that Bulgaria would take the first opportunity to regain its lost Macedonian lands. That opportunity came, it appeared, with the First World War. In 1915 the central powers secured a number of victories and in October of that year Bulgaria therefore entered the fray on the German side, occupying much of Macedonia as its reward. By the late summer of 1918, however, allied blockades had reduced much of the Bulgarian population to the verge of starvation and the army, with its morale broken, collapsed. Bulgaria was the first state to leave the German side in 1918. Ferdinand abdicated a few days later to be succeeded by his son, Boris III.

The Bulgarian economy

When Bulgaria separated from the Ottoman empire in 1878 it was predominantly a land of the small peasant farmer who relied upon his own family for labour. Few needed to seek even part-time employment outside their property, and there were few items which they could not produce themselves; an enquiry in the 1880s in a village in the Rusé region showed that nails and window-frames were the only shop-bought items used in the construction of a new house. There were some centres of manufacturing, most of which still relied upon home or workshop production, and which were organised into guilds. It was the guilds which financed the church and school building of the national revival, and which built many of the fine houses of the same period which are still to be enjoyed by the visitor to Plovdiv, Koprivshtitsa and other centres.

The traditional manufacturing towns, however, declined after 1878. Many of them in the textile sector had relied heavily on providing cloth and braid for the Ottoman army, a market closed after political separation. Furthermore, the growing town population of reborn Bulgaria sought new, or as they would call them 'European', modes of dress; the coarse cloth of the old manufacturers and the traditional styles which went with them held no attractions for the young belles and beaux of Sofia, Plovdiv and the other cities. And as demand for imported goods rose, supply became easier. Bulgaria's increasing integration with the markets of central Europe, symbolised by the connection of the country's railways to the main European network in 1888, facilitated the import of fashionable items together with a whole range of other more mundane articles which were cheaper, more modern and of higher quality than the local product. The old manufacturing industries were gradually replaced by new centres of production in Sofia and elsewhere.

After the liberation the **Turkish population**, which in 1875 had probably accounted for one-third of the total, declined. Many Turks found the atmosphere of a Christian state uncongenial and left; a few did so to escape the understandable vengeance of the Bulgarians. The lands of the departing Turks were eventually granted to Bulgarians and this, together with the taking over of unused village lands and forests, prevented any serious rural over-population until after the First World War.

Taxation, however, could not be avoided. The new state apparatus was larger and more expensive than the Ottoman, and foreign loans needed to be serviced. As one of its revenue-raising schemes the government in 1899 replaced the land tax with a tithe in kind. The ensuing fury produced Bulgaria's most original political organisation: the Bulgarian Agrarian National Union (BANU), which soon found a natural leader in Aleksandûr Stamboliiksi. The late 1890s also saw the emergence of a small socialist movement.

BANU and Stamboliiski

The First World War discredited the old political parties. The two main forces competing to replace them were the radical **Agrarians** of BANU and the **Bulgarian Communist Party** (BCP) formed in 1919 from the left wing of the socialist movement. BANU emerged the winner. Stamboliiski had been made prime minister in 1919 and in the following year he secured, by somewhat questionable means, an absolute majority in the sûbranie.

One of his first tasks had been to sign the **Treaty of Neuilly-sur-Seine** in November 1919. The victorious allies deprived Bulgaria of four small enclaves on its western border, Aegean Thrace imposed strict limitations upon the Bulgarian armed forces and exacted heavy reparations. They also promised that Bulgaria would be granted economic access to the Aegean Sea, a promise which was not kept.

At home the BANU government produced many reforms. A compulsory labour service was introduced for all Bulgarian youths; restrictions were placed on the amount of land any individual could own, and these restrictions applied also to urban property; the alphabet was reformed; the Church's role in education was reduced; and there was action to limit the power of the monarchy, the lawyers and the usurers, all of whom the Agrarians regarded as parasites. There were attempts to prevent the progressive splintering of land-holdings through divided inheritance, as well as efforts to bring together in one compact holding the many strips which frequently constituted a peasant's property. In its grand design of redistributing property, however, the Stamboliiski regime made little progress, not least because there were few large estates available for redistribution.

In **foreign policy** Stamboliiski's administration abjured the territorial nationalism of previous governments and sought friendship with Yugoslavia and the other Balkan states. This angered many Bulgarian nationalists, not least because friendship with Yugoslavia seemed to condone that state's centralising policies in Macedonia. The disaffected nationalists' feelings were shared by the Macedonian organisations, including one IMRO faction which had established a virtual state within the state at Petrich from where it launched raids into Yugoslav and Greek Macedonia. To these disaffected elements were added unemployed former army officers, the thousands of refugees who had fled from Macedonia, and supporters of the old political parties who feared, not without evidence, that Stamboliiski was intending to declare a republic and establish a one-party state. On 9 June 1923 a conspiracy in which most of these disaffected elements were represented deposed the BANU government. In so doing the conspirators indulged in shamefully violent retribution, the most prominent victim being Stamboliiski himself; his captors tortured and dismembered him, sending his severed head to Sofia in a biscuit tin.

1923 to the Second World War

Violence dominated Bulgarian public life for the next three years. In September 1923 the BCP, which had remained docile in June, was ordered by Moscow to redeem its honour by staging a rising. It was a farce which achieved little beyond affording the new government under Aleksandûr Tsankov an excuse for further restrictions on political and trade union activity. In April 1925 he was able to go further after the communists killed over 130 Bulgarian *prominenti* by exploding a bomb in the roof of Sofia's Sveta Nedelya cathedral during a funeral service. Thousands were arrested as a result, some of them being executed in public. Many more disappeared; according to rumour some of them had been fed into the central heating furnaces of Sofia's police headquarters.

International distaste at such excesses eventually forced Tsankov out of office in 1926, his departure being made a condition for a loan to help support Macedonian refugees. Tsankov's successor, Andrei Liapchev, himself a Macedonian, allowed political relaxation but did nothing to check the activities of the Macedonian organisations in Petrich and elsewhere. Nor could he prevent the progressive splintering of Bulgaria's political parties, a process which reduced the sûbranie to little more than a farce.

In the elections of 1931 the Bulgarian electorate registered its disapproval of this drift by returning to power the opposition People's Bloc, which included representatives from some factions of the now disastrously split BANU. A further indication of considerable popular dissatisfaction came in 1932 when the electors of Sofia returned a communist majority to the city council. The council was dissolved the following year.

The People's Bloc had created many expectations, not least amongst the peasants who were stricken by the world economic crisis. Almost none of these expectations were fulfilled. By 1934 the government was a depressing spectacle of incompetence and corruption. On 19 May 1934 it was overthrown by a small band of disgruntled army officers led by colonels Damian Velchev and Kimon Georgiev, acting in association with the intelligentsia group Zveno (Link).

King Boris

The men of 19 May wanted to cleanse, rationalise and centralise Bulgarian political life. To this end they abolished the parties, which they regarded as the fount of all political evil, fused the trade unions into one government-dominated organisation, reformed local government and merged a number of central ministries and banks. The architects of the 19 May coup were better at seizing power than keeping it. In January 1935 King Boris removed the prime minister and appointed someone more to his own taste; by April civilians well disposed to the King had replaced all the pro-republican army officers in the administration. Boris had established his own personal regime.

The King's first priority was to neutralise the army. In October 1935 Damian Velchev had returned clandestinely from exile and had been apprehended at the border. He was tried and sentenced to death in February 1936, though the sentence was commuted to life imprisonment. Boris used the trial to emphasise the dangers of military interference in politics and dissolved the powerful Military League. With the army no longer a danger Boris and his prime minister, the bridge-playing Georgi Kioseivanov, set about redefining the constitution to conform with the authoritarian, though not totalitarian, ideas which they espoused. They introduced limitations to the franchise but they did not replace the Tûrnovo system nor did they establish an official, mass political party such as that set up by the King of Romania.

As the 1930s drew to a close the Bulgarian government, like all others in Europe, was preoccupied with foreign affairs. Boris did not want to be drawn into the gathering storm despite the virtual stranglehold which Germany had established on Bulgaria's foreign trade, and despite the fact that after the Munich settlement Bulgaria was the only state defeated in 1918 not to have profited from German-sponsored territorial changes. When the European war began in September 1939 Boris declared neutrality but in February 1940 he hedged his bets by replacing the pro-Western Kioseivanov with the pro-German Bogdan Filov. After the defeat of France in May–June 1940 and the secession to Bulgaria of the southern Dobrudzha in September, German pressure became intense and eventually, in March 1941, Boris bowed and Bulgaria joined the Axis powers. As a reward it was allowed to occupy most of Macedonia and Thrace.

In the **Second World War** Bulgaria assumed a unique stance. It declared war on Britain and the USA but not on the Soviet Union. Boris insisted his people were too pro-Russian and his army insufficiently well equipped to fight the Red Army; better, he argued, that his forces be kept in the Balkans where they could guard against an allied landing or a Turkish invasion. Hitler accepted this argument though he did later insist that Bulgarian troops be used to help garrison areas of occupied Yugoslavia. Hitler did not succeed, however, in forcing the Bulgarians to deport their Jews to the death camps in Poland. Legislation had been passed requiring Jews to wear the Yellow Star, and their entry to universities and the professions had been restricted, but when plans for the deportations became known a wave of angry revulsion swept the country. The plan was pilloried in public, in the press, in parliament, in the pulpits and in the palace. Laws were passed requiring the Jews to leave the cities and many of them were interned in camps, but almost all of the pre-war 50,000 survived. Nothing, however, could save the Jews in the territories occupied by Bulgaria.

In August 1943 Boris died aged only 48, probably of natural causes. As his son, Simeon II, was a minor, a regency was established with Filov as its dominant figure. Already some circles in Bulgaria were pressing for escape from the war and their public support increased early in 1944 after heavy allied air raids on Sofia. By May the Soviet Union was demanding that Bulgaria declare war on the Third Reich. Filov refused but pressure was mounting externally from the allies and internally from the resistance forces of the communist-dominated Fatherland Front. In late August, when Romania switched sides, the Red Army was brought to the Danube. A series of changes of prime minister could not assuage Soviet pressure and on 5 September Stalin declared war on Bulgaria. Three days later the Red Army passed unopposed into Bulgaria, and on the same night, 8–9 September, the Fatherland Front staged a bloodless coup in Sofia.

The Republic of Bulgaria

The government established on 9 September was dominated by **the communists**. They soon extended their control over the police force and the army and, thus equipped, set about destroying all actual and potential political opposition. The first to be subdued was the old establishment, most of whose leaders were tried and executed in January 1945. The Agrarians were now the chief threat. By mid-1945 their undisputed leader was Nikola Petkov, a courageous and skilful politician who ridiculed the communists' huge expenditure on the police and later railed against the way in which the communists rigged the elections of November 1946. In June 1947 he was arrested in the sûbranie, subjected to a grotesque show trial and executed on 23 September. Although BANU remained in existence and even joined the government in coalition with the BCP, the latter was recognised as the leading force in society.

Bulgaria had become a republic in September 1946 and in December 1947 a new constitution was adopted. The 'Dimitrov constitution' was based on the Soviet model and was named after Georgi Dimitrov, the former secretary of the Comintern, who had returned to Bulgaria to lead the communist party in November 1945.

Under the Dimitrov constitution the BCP set about reshaping Bulgaria after the Soviet fashion. Private enterprise was squeezed out of the economy which was subjected to central planning under a series of five-year plans. Investment was concentrated on heavy rather than light industry or the consumer sector, urbanisation proceeded apace, and agriculture was collectivised, Bulgaria in 1957 becoming the first East European state to declare that it had completed the collectivisation process. During that process many Turks had been allowed to emigrate, particularly from the rich lands of the Dobrudzha which were high on the BCP's list for collectivisation.

The early years of complete communist domination saw continuing political persecution. Any religious organisation with foreign connections, including the Roman Catholics, suffered, as did former members of non-communist political parties. The BCP, too, was purged of its allegedly careerist elements, and after the Hungarian revolution of 1956, thousands of reformist communists were sent to the concentration camp at Belene on the Danube.

This was despite the fact that in 1954 de-Stalinisation had begun and in 1956 the BCP had adopted the more relaxed 'April Line' which was to remain the basis of party policy until 1987.

In 1954 **Todor Zhivkov** became leader of the BCP and in the mid-1960s the neutralisation of an army plot established him unassailably as the dominant figure in Bulgarian politics. Zhivkov remained in office until 1989, the chief feature of his rule being his obedience to Moscow; he even suggested on two occasions that Bulgaria be incorporated into the USSR. This close relationship provided Bulgaria with a dependable market and also allowed it to buy Soviet oil cheaply and sell it on at world prices. Yet this subservience was irksome to many Bulgarians who therefore welcomed the reassertion of Bulgaria's cultural identity by Ludmila Zhivkova, Zhivkov's daughter who rose to dominate cultural policy in the late 1970s. Zhivkova died in 1981 aged 39.

By that time the whole Soviet system was heading for crisis. It was unable to switch from extensive to intensive economic growth and, particularly disorientating for Zhivkov, the gerontocracy in Moscow was incapable of consistent leadership. Gorbachev's advocacy of 'perestroika and glasnost' was hardly an improvement for Zhivkov; he had no desire to see glasnost imported into Bulgaria and therefore argued that glasnost was only necessary for those systems which had not yet embarked upon perestroika; Bulgaria, he maintained, had set out on that course. In fact perestroika in Bulgaria was little more than a succession of reforms in economic administration whose main effect was to dislocate production.

An even greater problem was Zhivkov's disastrous attempt in the mid 1980s to coerce Bulgaria's remaining Turkish population, about a tenth of the total, into jettisoning the Muslim religion and adopting the Bulgarian language and Bulgarian names. The name changes enforced on the Turks disgusted many Bulgarian intellectuals who had already been affronted by their country's implication in scandals such as the murder in London of exiled journalist Georgi Markov. Many more were seriously disturbed by the ecological disaster BCP policies were inflicting on the country.

By the spring of 1989 organised opposition was appearing and the BCP hierarchy was mobilising to ditch its leader. In May, in a fit of hubris, Zhivkov offered the Turks the chance to leave, little expecting that many of them would do so.

Over a quarter of a million fled, disrupting the economy and further discrediting Bulgaria in the international arena. Zhivkov could not survive. He was deposed in a palace coup on 10 November 1989.

Bulgaria and the end of Communism

James Pettifer

The great changes that overtook Eastern Europe in 1989 had clearly not been anticipated by the Bulgarian communist party leadership any more than among communist leaderships elsewhere. Nevertheless, the country was in some ways in a little stronger position to cope with them than totally impoverished neighbours such as Romania and Albania. There had been a degree of economic liberalisation for many years, numerous business relationships existed with foreign interests in particular fields such as the wine industry and tourism, and Bulgaria and Bulgarians had been used to contact with the West for much longer than some communist states and peoples.

In the early days the central feature of political development was the relatively peaceful and orderly nature of the transition, with the overthrow of the sclerotic Zhukov leadership group by a younger reformist element led by **Petar Mladenov**, who became president. This group had a new programme for Gorbachev-type political reforms, with the beginning of genuine Press freedom, freedom of movement, a multi-party system, economic reform and the end of anti-Turkish policies. The progress of reforms was slow, in practice, and it was not until 1990 that mass demonstrations and strikes led to the first serious reforms of the political system.

Mladenov soon disappeared from the centre of power and gave way to **Andrei Lukanov**, who became Prime Minister. An able man, he was later the victim of an assassination attempt in November 1996, but at this time led the reformist wing of the renamed Bulgarian Socialist Party. This party was victorious in the first multi-party elections in June 1990, against the opposition SDS, the Union of Democratic Forces. The Turkish minority had formed their own party, the Movement for Rights and Freedom. A pattern of voting was established in this election that has dominated post-communist Bulgarian politics, of great urban support for the SDS opposition, but strong residual support for socialism in the small towns and the countryside.

After the elections, public order was seriously threatened by clashes in the streets, and the newly elected President **Zhelyu Zhelev**, of the SDS, brought order back to the capital only with difficulty. A notable event was the attack by anti-communist demonstrators on the party headquarters in Sofia which was set on fire.

In 1991 the socialist government was narrowly displaced in the general election by the Opposition SDS but by now the downward spiral in the Bulgarian economy had begun which has not ceased to date. Profitable parts of the old state industries were appropriated by groups from within the old nomenklatura, and many industries collapsed into dereliction and chaos. Food supplies to many cities were very uncertain in the winter, power cuts were widespread and the whole population became involved in a battle for survival. As a result the weak SDS government was immediately challenged, and in 1992, in the January Presidential elections, President Zhelev only just won the contest against the Socialist Party candidate, Velko Valkanov.

The country staggered on during the next 18 months, in a climate of increasingly serious difficulties. The war in ex-Yugoslavia and United Nations economic sanctions against Serbia seriously affected Bulgarian trade patterns, adding to the damage caused by existing sanctions against Iraq, a hitherto important trading partner. Capital resources and hard currency were still being exported from the country, and there was a noticeable and serious growth in the influence of the *mafiya* over national life. The general election of December 1994 was won convincingly by the Socialist Party, under a new young leader **Zhan Videnov**, and the body politic was split between the government and the Presidency.

Although the socialist government was elected on a programme promising accelerated privatisation and much more rapid economic reform, to help the country out of stagnation, in practice little was achieved in the first year of government. In 1996 the economy began to decline even more rapidly, with a major run on the bank and collapse in the value of the leva in the spring. The dissatisfied electorate rejected the Socialists in the Presidential election in autumn 1996, choosing lawyer **Peter Stoyanov** for the post. After violent street protests, parliamentary elections in spring 1997 brought the SDS to power under premier Ivan Kostov.

Greek influences in Bulgarian life and history

James Pettifer

As a country on one of the great crossroads between Europe, the Middle East, the Balkans and Asia, Bulgaria has been exposed to many external cultural influences in its long history, from the original world of the **Eurasian steppe** where the proto-Bulgars originated, through the **ancient Greek** and **Roman** civilisations, to the **Byzantine** world and the **Ottoman Empire**.

In the process of civilisation, by far the most powerful influence was **Greek**, from the time of the colonisation of the Black Sea coast by ancient Greek merchants through the Greek-speaking Byzantine world to the common struggle for the survival of both communities and the Orthodox Church under the Ottoman Turks. Some Greeks have always lived in Bulgaria, and that remains the case today. Some knowledge of the complex and often politically sensitive interaction between the two peoples and cultures is useful in understanding many aspects of Bulgarian life, Christian monuments in particular.

In the ancient world, Greek traders and explorers began to push north through the Bosphorus and into the Black Sea as early as the 7C BC. Remains on the coast dating from as early as this time have been found, but the quantity is small, and indicates occasional northern ventures by ships from the Mediterranean along the Black Sea littoral. The voyage of Jason and the Argonauts dates from this early period, and indicates, in the mythological sphere, the Greek desire for conquest and settlement in the Black Sea region. Colchis, the place of the mythological Golden Fleece, was known for its mineral wealth.

More systematic and planned exploration and colonisation began in the next 200–300 years. In the territory covered by most of modern Bulgaria, the Greeks found a thickly forested wilderness inhabited by fierce Thracian tribes, and made no attempt to conquer or civilise them in their interior mountain fastnesses, but set up trading posts on the coast. The Thracians had some mining skills, and were already exploiting deposits of copper and gold that lay near the surface in the mountains. These metals were eagerly sought by the Greeks. Salting and exporting the rich reserves of coastal fisheries was also an important activity. In time independent city states were established, such as *Apollonia*, modern **Sozopol**, and *Mesembria*, modern **Nesebur**. These retained close links with the mother cities in Greece, for whom they generated considerable new wealth. Writers such as **Herodotus** and **Strabo** described the coastal areas.

After the Roman conquest of the Black Sea coast that culminated with the fall of Mesembria in 76 BC, Greek culture survived in the coastal towns, although generally at a lower level of prosperity than had existed before. The main Roman trade centre was at *Odessus*, modern **Varna**, where Greek remained the language of most educated people. The great expansion of Greek cultural influence that followed in the next centuries was inextricably linked to the rise of Christianity within the later Roman Empire, and the adoption of Greek as the official language of the Eastern Empire. In central and western Bulgaria, there had been a marked differentiation in the Roman period between towns which were fully Romanised, and Latinate in their culture, such as *Serdica*, modern **Sofia**, while *Philippopolis*, modern **Plovdiv**, or *Pataunia*, modern **Kjustendil**, were essentially Hellenic, and used Greek as the language of law and administration. The spread of Christianity and the adoption of the new religion as the official religion of the Empire greatly assisted the spread of Greek in Bulgaria where it became the language of culture, art and government.

This situation changed rapidly under the influence of the barbarian invasions in most of Bulgaria, although some Black Sea coastal towns fared better, such as *Mesembria*, which remained under Byzantine control for centuries. This established a regional pattern for the influence of Greek, which has remained a living language on parts of the Black Sea coast up until the present day, but has never had a significant presence in most parts of the interior, the central mountains in particular. In this sense, elements of the cultural patterns of antiquity are relevant to understanding growing Greek influence in contemporary Bulgaria.

The struggles between Greek-speaking Byzantium and Bulgaria provided a focus for the development of a new Bulgarian culture, linked to the beginnings of Slav-Christianity and the adoption of Christianity by the Bulgarian rulers. Bulgaria in this process adopted the Cyrillic alphabet and on the surface the culture began to diverge more and more from the heritage of the Hellenic Byzantine world. Nevertheless close links remained, in trade and religion, and in the Bulgarian language, which includes many words of Greek origin. From the time of Khan Asparuch to 893, the official language of the Bulgarian state, for home and international affairs, was Greek. Long after the introduction of Cyrillic in that year, all diplomatic correspondence of the state continued to be conducted in Greek. Some Greek names are considered by contemporary

Bulgarians as old Bulgarian names, despite their clear Greek origin (eg, *sevastokratoritsa* that appears on 20 Leva banknotes). Cities such as *Philippopolis*, modern Plovdiv, were deeply Hellenised in their origins and later development in the Byzantine and Ottoman world, and even the most energetic protagonists of Slav and Bulgarian culture and language have recognised this.

Under the **Ottoman Turks**, the Orthodox Church survived under the *milet* system of self-governing religious communities, and what remained of both Greek and Bulgarian culture was first linked with the Church. This remained the case until the later Empire, when in 17C and 18C Bulgaria, ethnic Greeks in towns such as Philippopolis and Melnik began to dominate local trade, and became Bulgaria's first effective capitalists. Although Bulgaria did not have a formal *Phanariot* system, as neighbouring Romania had, with Greeks forming a clear governing elite with authority derived from the Sultan, rich individual families had enormous local power. They were valued intermediaries for the Ottoman imperial administration between the local peasants and the Porte.

In the time of emerging capitalism in the 19C, Greeks were also strongly represented among the new and emerging class of local level tradesmen and small entrepreneurs, a status that did not always endear them to the Bulgarian peasants who had to purchase their goods at often highly inflated prices. Greek traders in Bulgaria, then and now, have always had the inestimable advantage of close links with the great port of Thessaloniki and its economic centrality in the life of the southern Balkans.

In the struggle against the Ottoman Turks in the 19C, Greeks and Bulgarians often collaborated at a practical level in the early years, although this happy relationship changed rapidly after the establishment of the Bulgarian Exarchate which led to the modern national church, and the late 19C evolution of the **'Macedonian Question'** dating from the decisions taken by the Congress of Berlin in July 1878. The struggle for Macedonia, and a 'Greater Greece', and a 'Greater Bulgaria' incorporating Macedonian land put the two emerging Balkan nations at loggerheads and established a pattern of territorial conflict that in many aspects continued until the end of the Greek civil war in 1949. Greek culture in Bulgaria was eroded, substantial ethnic Greek populations in towns such as Haskovo and Melnik had to leave the country or agree to assimilate totally. A pogrom against Greeks in Varna took place in 1906, and various Greek Church property was attacked throughout Bulgaria. This year can be seen as a turning point in Greek-Bulgarian relations, with the expulsion of Greek monks from Bachkovo monastery, and widespread anti-Greek campaigns throughout the country. In July 1906 Anchialos (Pomorie) was burnt down by anti-Greek irregulars. Repression intensified after the Second Balkan War, in 1913–14, when all Greek schools were closed.

Bulgarian speakers in Greece were equally marginalised and were regarded as potentially subversive by all Greek governments. Education in the Bulgarian language in Greece was not allowed. An exchange of populations was agreed, after the **Treaty of Neuilly**, in 1919, which ended 'Greater Bulgaria', and deprived the country of its access to the Aegean. A number of Greek mayors were assassinated by IMRO in the 1923-24 period, and use of the Greek language was discouraged. There was a trickle of further emigration to Greece throughout these years. Under communism there was no open persecution of ethnic Greeks, although certain professions, such as the army, were not in practice open to them.

The **Greek refugees** from the repression and witch hunts organised by the Greek right after the civil war ended in 1949 quickly made a mark in Bulgaria, and Greeks under the communist regime were prominent in the usual professions, such as the law and medicine, and in trading relationships with foreign countries. The Nedelya area near the railway station in Sofia was a centre of Greek society and culture in the city, with flourishing schools and cultural societies. In the late Zhivkov period Greece was seen as a friend and a possible trade partner for Bulgaria, compared to Turkey which in the Cold War period was little more than an American satrapy. This remained the case in the post-communist transition period, with many family links providing the seed from which wider business relationships grew. Greece has been seen by many Bulgarian entrepreneurs as a useful and sympathetic link to the capitalist world, offering indirect EU market access, and hard currency working capital, by comparison with instinctively pro-Turkish members of the EU such as Germany and Britain. Many Bulgarian businesses have Greek joint-venture partners, and use Greek links as a route to foreign business activities. Organised crime often uses Greek banks for money laundering. There are about 2500 students from Greece in Plovdiv and other universities in Bulgaria, and the church is reviving, with about 200 usable churches remaining from the 300 used by local Greeks in 1945, and about 100 Greek-speaking priests in the country. The Bishop of Sliven is responsible for this diocese. Greeks are not recognised as an ethnic minority in Bulgaria, largely through an informal agreement between the Sofia and Athens governments. The Greek government has found this arrangement to be convenient as it prevents Bulgarian demands for the recognition of Slav-speakers in Greece as an ethnic minority.

The Turkish minority in Bulgaria

Dr Hugh Poulton

Turks began to settle in Bulgaria towards the end of the 14C with the establishment of Ottoman rule. Other smaller Islamic Ottoman groups, such as Circassians and Tatars, also came and have tended to be assimilated into the Turkish mass. A number of Bulgarians living mostly in the central Rhodope Mountains Islamicised in the 15C–19C. Known as the **Pomaks**, and numbering some 220,000, they have often been confused, deliberately or otherwise, with the Turks who live mostly in the Arda river basin in the south of the country centred around Kardzhali (bordering and overlapping with the Pomaks), and in the northeast. In both regions the Turks make up majority communities, especially in the countryside.

The Turks and other Muslims were seen as essentially alien to the new Bulgarian state when it emerged from the Ottoman Empire in the 1870s and large-scale emigration was encouraged by the authorities from the outset. During the 1920s and 1930s, Turkish schools, especially primary schools, were closed and the advent of dictatorship in 1934 saw a further deterioration with bans on the use of the new Latin script and the reinstatement of the Arabic script for all Turkish publications. This was mainly to hinder links with Ataturk's Turkey. Emigration of Turks to Turkey has—despite some pauses (most notably the banning of freedom of movement by the communist regime)—remained a constant feature. However, the high birth rate of Turks and other Muslims has compensated for this and the emigration has not in this century substantially changed the percentage of the Muslim population, remaining at 10–12 per cent of the population with the Turks numbering some 10 per cent of the total population. The last census (1992) recorded 822,000 Turks (9.8 per cent).

The post-war communist authorities began under the slogan of 'socialist modernisation' by attempting to undermine the traditional religious attitudes of the Muslims. This saw a further **mass emigration** of Turks to Turkey in 1950–51. Beginning in the mid 1950s, the Zhivkov regime pursued a repressive forced assimilatory policy which was progressively applied to all the country's major minority populations with the exceptions, for propaganda reasons, of the small Jewish and Armenian ones. The policy began with the problem of those in the southwest who espoused a Macedonian consciousness separate from a Bulgarian one. It continued with the closing of the Turkish educational establishments and repressive campaigns against the **Pomaks** and the Muslim **Roma** (Gypsies) in the 1970s. The policy came to a head with the massive violent campaign against the ethnic Turkish minority beginning in late 1984. All names were compulsorily changed to 'Bulgarian' forms, mosques were shut and religious practices such as circumcision were banned, as was the speaking of Turkish and the playing Turkish music.

This campaign was justified by the authorities with the claim that the ethnic Turks were in fact descendants of those forcibly Islamicised Bulgarians (i.e. they were all Pomaks) and they were now 'voluntarily' and 'spontaneously' reclaiming their heritage and becoming equal first-class citizens of the 'unified Bulgarian socialist nation'. The campaign was met with resistance with many killed and hundreds imprisoned. In 1989, taking advantage of leeway afforded by *glasnost*, mass hunger strikes and protest marches by ethnic Turks occurred in a number of places. The authorities panicked and allowed those who wanted to, to leave for Turkey. Within a few months some 370,000 had fled (half of these later returned after finding life in Turkey was not as idyllic as they thought). The ensuing economic collapse caused by this mass exodus was one factor in Zhivkov's downfall.

In **post-Zhivkov Bulgaria** the Turks quickly organised themselves and were led by the Movement for Rights and Freedoms (DPS) which has, despite a backlash from Bulgarian nationalists, secured a reversal of the repressive features of the Zhivkov assimilation policy. In the October 1991 elections the DPS gained 24 members of parliament, over 650 village mayors, 1000 councillors and 20 municipal mayors—and held the balance of power between the former communists and the Union of Democratic Forces (UDF). Despite the constitutional ban on ethnic-based parties (the DPS despite having non-Turkish members remains a predominately ethnic Turkish party), the Constitutional Court narrowly ruled that it was legal. The DPS did not formally enter government but instead embarked on a de facto coalition whereby the parliamentary commissions were shared by the UDF and the DPS keeping the ex-communist Bulgarian Socialist Party (BSP) firmly out in the cold.

However, this unofficial coalition broke down over the economic policies of

Filip Dimitrov's government which was causing a new mass exodus of ethnic Turks in the south around Kardzhali. The price of tobacco, a staple crop in the south, halved and unemployment has soared—it was 40 per cent for ethnic Turks in July 1992 with some settlements experiencing 80 per cent. This combined with the government's policies on land privatisation which meant that the ethnic Turks who until then had worked the land would be unable to become owners. The DPS, faced with the severe erosion of its electoral base, began to distance itself from the government and called for UDF Prime Minister Filip Dimitrov's removal. In October, Turkey announced tougher immigration measures to try to stem the continuing flood of Turkish immigrants from Bulgaria. It seems that the ethnic Turks are experiencing a country to town shift similarly to the Slav Bulgarians in the 1950s and 1960s. However now, with the greater freedom of movement internationally, they are choosing to move to Turkish (i.e. in Turkey itself) rather than to Bulgarian cities such as Sofia. The education programme for ethnic Turks remains woefully inadequate and this tendency of emigration will continue unless things change. (It must also be noted that, in common with other former communist Balkan states, there is also a massive outflux of the majority population's young intelligentsia, so much so that some see this as a veritable demographic disaster.)

The ensuing stalemate in forming a government was eventually broken by the formation of a 'cabinet of experts' under the DPS mandate, led by Professor Lyuben Berov with non-Turkish DPS member Evgeni Matinchev as a deputy prime minister and also minister for labour and social welfare. The leadership of the DPS has played a constructive role in making Bulgaria something of an exception in Balkan nationalist politics. The DPS, however, is faced with serious problems of splits and erosion of support due in part to emigration and in part to supporting unpopular economic policies in the last coalition government. The first challenger was the more radical Turkish Democratic Party (so far officially unrecognised), headed by expelled DPS member Adem Kenan. Another was the Muslim Party of Justice headed by the former (under the Zhivkov regime) and somewhat discredited Chief Mufti Nedim Genzhev. A more serious rival appeared in 1994 in Kardzhali led by Mehmed Hodzha—a former DPS leader whose power base was among the more religiously conservative Turks in the south. The DPS leadership led by Ahmed Dogan, whose playboy life-style antagonises some Turks, has its powerbase in the northeastern Turkish mass.

In the elections in late 1994 however, the DPS retained the bulk of the ethnic Turkish vote winning 5.4 per cent of the total vote which translated into 15 seats in parliament. Despite their past record of being partners in coalition governments, their possible participation in the BSP-led cabinet of Zhan Videnov was ruled out due to the nomination of Ilcho Dimitrov as minister of education, science and technology. He was minister of education and chair of the co-ordinating committee on the 'regeneration process'—the official euphemism for the brutal forced assimilation of the ethnic Turks by the Zhivkov regime—operating with the Bulgarian Academy of Sciences in 1986–89.

Bulgaria and the Macedonian Question

James Pettifer

Some knowledge of what is known to students of Balkan politics as the **'Macedonian Question'** is important in understanding many aspects of modern Bulgarian history and culture, and visitors to Bulgaria will find that without it, it will be difficult to appreciate the full significance of some important monuments. There is a complex, profound, and often uncertain relationship between the Bulgarians, and the 'Macedonian' element in their history and identity that goes to the heart of contemporary Bulgarian society.

In the immediate past, the Macedonian issue was very troublesome in inter-war Bulgaria, centred on the activities of the ultra-nationalist **Internal Macedonian Revolutionary Organisation** (IMRO) which was in many respects the first modern terrorist organisation. It was a highly organised and effective secret society that became a 'state within a state'. IMRO brought political turmoil in its wake throughout the southern Balkans and elsewhere, with frequent shootings and bombings of public figures and ordinary Bulgarians alike. The best known IMRO killing in the inter-war era was the assassination of King Alexander of Yugoslavia at Marseilles in 1934. The first Yugoslavia, the Kingdom of Serbs, Croats and Slovenes, did not include a 'Macedonian' state at all, but regarded most of geographic Macedonia as part of south Serbia.

The Macedonian Question in the southern Balkans is a very complex issue, originating in the declining Ottoman Empire in the 19C, but was at the heart of many 20C conflicts, from the time of the Balkan Wars in 1912–13 to the 'Third Round' of the Greek Civil War, ending in 1949. It has re-emerged in the crisis of ex-Yugoslavia, where FYROM, a new state, has been formed, based on the territory of the old Socialist Republic of Macedonia, within the second, and now defunct, Yugoslavia. FYROM did not join the third Yugoslavia (FRY), now comprising Serbia and Montenegro, and became independent in a referendum in September 1991. The history of FYROM has been controversial to date, with only Serbia, of the surrounding states, giving full diplomatic and *de facto* recognition under its preferred name of the '*Republic of Macedonia*', while Greece and Albania have used the accepted United Nations terminology of 'Former Yugoslav Macedonia (FYROM)', and Bulgaria has only recognised FYROM as a 'state', not as a 'nation' and does not recognise the 'Macedonian' language.

The origin of the Macedonian Question lies in the attempts of different new nations, principally Bulgaria, Greece and Serbia, in the 19C to lay claim to parts of the territory of what was then known as **'Turkey-in-Europe'**, the portion of the southern Balkans that remained under Ottoman control. It includes parts of modern Greece, Bulgaria, Serbia and Albania. The population of Macedonia has always been very ethnically mixed, giving the origin of the name 'Salade Macedoine' in cuisine, and today the state has a Slav-speaking majority, but a large minority of Albanians (at least 24%), and smaller numbers of Turks, Vlachs, Roma and Serbs. Prior to World War II, the part of Macedonia that lies within the boundary of modern Greece also had a large Jewish population. The Slav-speaking majority contains groups whose primary identity is 'Macedonian',

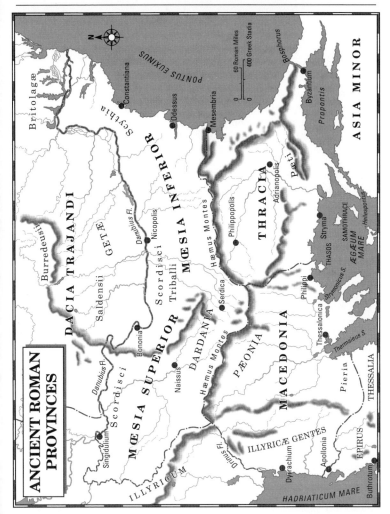

but with some more pro-Yugoslav or pro-Serb in orientation, while others look more towards Bulgaria. These people generally support a Skopje-based IMRO, VMRO-DPMNE.

As a small, landlocked country, Macedonians have traditionally had a poor relationship with their neighbours, seeing them as the 'Four Wolves' who have designs on their territory. Although Greek, Bulgarian and Serbian states already existed in the late 19C, they were all smaller than they are now, and all had claims on the land in Turkey-in-Europe known from ancient times as Macedonia. **Albania** did not achieve independence from Constantinople until 1913, and has only become interested in the fate of the Albanian inhabited parts of Macedonia much more recently. **Greece** has always seen Macedonia as Greek, based on the fact that in antiquity Alexander the Great was a Macedonian, and that Greeks have always lived there since the earliest times. In recent years, Greece has sought to prevent international recognition of FYROM under its preferred name of '*Republic of Macedonia*', and Greeks call citizens of FYROM, '*Skopjeans*'. Some Greeks will also claim that the monasteries of Macedonia, including some that are now in Bulgaria, such as Bachkovo, were of Greek origin.

The Bulgarian interest in Macedonia dates primarily from the decisions of the 1878 Russo-Turkish preliminary peace treaty of San Stefano which awarded very large new territories to Bulgaria, including much of modern FYROM and modern northern Greece, including part of the Aegean coast. A 'Greater Bulgaria' was created that would have dominated the southern Balkans with a much larger territory and a Mediterranean port. The Western Powers, particularly Britain and France, revised this at the Congress of Berlin soon afterwards, fearing Russian domination of the region via Bulgaria, and Bulgaria lost most of this Macedonian territory. The fundemental impulse behind the foundation of the **Internal Macedonian Revolutionary Organisation** in 1893 was to recover these 'lost' lands and people.

Bulgarians have always seen the Berlin decision as a fundemental national injustice, based on their view that the majority of the population of the Macedonian geographical region has always been Bulgarian speaking. This is linked, in IMRO's eyes, to the further injustice of the 1919 Treaty of Neuilly, which gave back most of Macedonia to Greece, including Thessaloniki, which IMRO still regards as a Bulgarian city, and calls *Solun*. The concept of a 'Macedonian' language is not accepted in Bulgaria, as Bulgarians see the inhabitants of FYROM as speaking a dialect of Bulgarian. This has been a major difficulty in relations with FYROM since 1991, in that it has not been possible to agree on the language that FYROM-Bulgarian treaties should be written in.

The region of Bulgaria that is 'Macedonian' in its interests and identity is the west and south west, with Blageovgrad the main town. The south west has a very strong IMRO tradition indeed, in towns such as Sandanski and Petrich. Under communism IMRO was not allowed to function as a political movement, but certain Macedonian cultural and regional associations were allowed, under the general auspices of the 'Macedonian Scientific Institute 'in Sofia (see p 92).

After 1990, IMRO—as a mainstream political movement which had cast off its terrorist past—was legalised in Bulgaria, and has grown as a political force in the country, with influence in the new Kostov government elected in 1997. In Sofia society it is now fashionable to have Macedonian roots and family connections, whereas under communism this was something many people tended to conceal if they were socially or politically ambitious. Relations between the Sofia-based IMRO and Skopje VMRO are complex, reflecting the traditional split between those Slav-speakers in FYROM who see themselves as wholly Bulgarian, and those who affirm the more seperate 'Macedonian' identity and consciousness that has developed since Tito set up the first 'Macedonian' state within the second Yugoslavia. The Titoist regime also set up the new 'Macedonian Orthodox Church' in Skopje, the only time in history that a communist government has founded a new Christian Church. This Church is offensive to Serbia, Bulgaria and Greece, and is unrecognised in all three countries.

Useful works for those wishing to study this important topic include *Macedonia—its Races and their Future* (London, 1906) by the Edwardian authority H.N. Brailsford, while for study of contemporary issues, *Who are the*

Macedonians? by Hugh Poulton (London, 1995) and *The New Macedonian Question* (ed. James Pettifer, London 1998) are useful. IMRO in Sofia has some publications which are in English, and a newspaper *Makedonia* (see p 92). A very good analysis of the key post World War II period written from a Greek point of view is *Nationalism and Communism in Macedonia* by Evangelos Kofos (Thessaloniki, 1964). An important Bulgarian volume (in English) is *Macedonia: Documents and Material* (Sofia, 1979).

The views of the current Skopje government on events can be found, in English, in *Macedonian Times* magazine, 39 Vasil Georgiev Street, Baraka 7, 91000 Skopje, ☎ and fax 00 389 91 121 182.

Bulgarian culture and folklore

Although most Balkan countries have very rich independent popular cultures and folklore, Bulgaria is outstanding in this respect. The ethnic and cultural composition of the Bulgarian people is complex. Bulgarians have assimilated many Greek, Roman and Ottoman Turkish influences. This has left a complex and many sided **popular tradition** of beliefs, festivals, literature, song and dance. These traditional cultural manifestations have been based in peasant and rural society, on the whole, but have survived in many towns.

The long centuries of Byzantine and Ottoman domination meant that Bulgarians preserved their identity in these popular and usually oral traditions, which have survived under all governments. The different ethnic and religous groups in Bulgaria, such as the Pomaks, have also kept their own local traditions, rituals and festivals. Under communism new popular festivals with a mass-participation character were introduced, such as May Day marches, although there was usually some antecedent for them. The end of communism has meant the revival of many religious festivals that had been discouraged under the one-party state, and Moslem festivals and holidays that had fallen victim to the persecution of the ethnic Turkish minority in the 1980's are being celebrated again. The same applies to liturgical music, which has benefited from the considerable revival in Orthodoxy since 1989. Liturgical music is often sold on the same street stalls as western rock music and Bulgarian pop songs.

Bulgarian music has a particularly famous vocal tradition, in both sacred and secular music, with large choirs of international reputation. Many traditions coexist, from the more Slavonic music and songs of the north-west, akin to Serbian models, the purely Bulgarian modes of the Central Mountains, the Russian and Tartar influenced music of the north-east, the Turkish traditions of the minority community, and the music of the Rhodope mountains in the south, which shows Greek and Georgian influences.

Street musicians in Sofia

There are also strong local repertoires in regions such as the Pirin Mountains. Western rock songs are of course popular with the young, but on the whole Bulgaria has thankfully been spared the wholesale rejection of traditional inherited national culture which has disoriented some countries in eastern Europe. Bulgarian pop music often shows an interesting interaction of traditional and western modes.

The vast network of **folklore** has been extensively chronicled by the Institute of Folklore in Sofia, and ethnography was a favoured academic subject under communism, so there is an Ethnographic Museum of high quality in most towns. There is a huge variety of traditional costumes, which have been studied and preserved in collections since National Revival times. Generally speaking, the most primitive dances and festivals have died out, which were often based on fertility rituals, but many others are still performed as part of local festivals, and folkdancing and singing still plays a part in Bulgarian education. Bulgarian **Roma** are often accomplished musicians, and have their own styles of music, often based on the violin and a bass drum. Weddings are often a good place for the visitor to hear traditional music and songs if he or she is fortunate enough to come across one.

There is also a multiplicity of local crafts and practical art traditions. Woodcarving is a Bulgarian speciality, along with traditional ceramics, lace-making, rugweaving and ironwork.

Bulgarian literature is little known in the West, and it is unfortunate that the state publishing house which, under communism, had begun to translate and publish some of the more important authors is no longer functioning. In that respect, communism was beneficial to international knowledge of Bulgarian literature, and the market economy has brought Bulgaria real cultural isolation. The work of classic nineteenth century authors in English and other foreign language translations such as Hristo Botev and Ivan Vasov can still be found on second-hand bookstalls fairly easily in Sofia and other big towns. The situation with music and video is much better, as there is a very large pirate CD, video and casette tape industry in Bulgaria which brings everything available on the music scene to the public very efficently.

Bulgarian ecology and wildlife

Bulgaria has a very interesting **wildlife** which is primarily based in the very large areas of mountain and forest throughout the country, some of which has remained largely untouched by man since antiquity. The population density is low, and many large mammals and birds of prey which are extinct or threatened elsewhere in Europe have found at least relative security in these vast forests. Hunting was promoted as an up-market tourist pursuit under communism, which had the benefit of establishing some reasonable level of game management and putting shooting quotas on the most vulnerable animals, such as brown bears (see p 42). The large mammals, such as bear, deer and the wolf are the glory of the Bulgarian forests, and much more could be done to promote **ecotourism** in the country, although there are some promising early steps being taken in some places. Bulgaria has a very rich birdlife, and specialist tourism is well established in this field (see p 17).

In the uplands and mountains, the ecological situation is best, in the lowlands there are major problems of pollution and environmental damage in many areas, although not generally on the scale and severity of neighbouring countries such as Romania. The most serious problems are with the Danube and the Black Sea, which are well known and have been widely publicised internationally. Chemical pollution from riparian industry, sewage pollution and new dams have caused very serious damage to the great river, and despite various international efforts to improve the condition of the water, little has been achieved to date except in the delta. Black Sea pollution is local and bathing is safe away from the estuaries and industrial areas.

Pollution of the Danube has nevertheless affected the Black Sea ecology, which has also experienced overfishing in recent years. The communist regime had a particularly bad record, even establishing a dolphin fishery and dolphin oil factory at Burgas which caused a decimation in the dolphin population. Communist period industrial development was also very bad for the environment in many places, such as the establishment of the chemical and petrochemical industry in the Burgas lagoons and near Varna.

Agriculture is less destructive than in the European Union countries, with many Bulgarian farmers unable to afford much in the way of nitrate fertilisers. Local water supplies are generally safe and may be of a very high standard in the mountains. Air quality is generally good away from the main industrial installations, although Sofia can have problems at all times of year if weather conditions encourage smog. Acid rain is not a serious problem in Bulgaria outside a few small localities. Drought has been a major issue in recent years, seriously affecting agriculture in the west and northwest, and producing water shortages for Sofia and other cities, although recently the situation has improved.

Select Bibliography

Bulgaria has a long and interesting history but most of it is little known or studied in Western Europe and the United States. There are fewer books on Bulgarian subjects in English or other Western European languages than any comparable Balkan country.

In the **ancient world**, the region known as **Thrace**, which covers most of modern Bulgaria, was important, and was often mentioned in the works of ancient Greek historians and geographers. **Herodotus** and **Strabo** wrote extensively about ancient Thrace, and about events along the Black Sea coast where Greek colonial cities had been established. Seminal works in ancient literature, such as Euripides' play *The Bacchae*, have links with Thrace, and well-known figures such as the Roman slave leader **Spartacus**, and a number of **emperors**, were Thracians.

After the barbarian invasions, the genesis of the **first Bulgarian kingdom** was mentioned in Byzantine chronicles, and in the Ottoman period the region was part of the wider empire and is often discussed as an imperial province. In the later medieval era, Bulgaria more or less disappeared from the wider

European consciousness. During the **Renaissance** and **Enlightenment** in northern Europe, there is little Bulgarian literary presence, and later on less sense of an emerging nation, compared to the public perceptions of other Balkan nationalities such as Greece and Serbia.

In the **Romantic period** the country sufferred the key handicap of a lack of knowledge and interest by **Lord Byron**, who effectively determined the consciousness of more than one generation of European intellectuals on the anti-Ottoman struggles in the Balkans. In France, there was a little more knowledge, exemplified by descriptions of parts of Bulgaria in works such as Lamartine's *Voyage en Orient*. The close cultural links with Imperial Germany that developed in Bulgaria in the 19C were unhelpful to sympathetic interest in many Western circles in the later Ottoman period, as was the later pro-German involvement in the Second World War.

Apart from a very small number of specialised works, Bulgaria only came to popular attention and consciousness in the later part of the 19C when the developing national struggle against Ottoman domination brought it to the forefront of anti-Ottoman political campaigns by liberal politicians. The British Prime Minister W.E. Gladstone had a key role in this process. Journalists such as W.C. Stillman and James Bourchier, the great *Times* Balkan correspondent, played an important part, as well as books by British Bulgarophiles such as Noel Buxton MP. In this period Bulgarian life and culture entered the knowledge of the wider educated public for the first time.

In the period up to the First World War, there is an extensive English-language literature on Bulgaria, but almost exclusively concerned with the role of the country in the **Balkan wars** (1912–13), and then recording the fighting on the Macedonian front in the First World War. Many of the best sources for this period of Bulgarian life are actually in books about the **Macedonian Question**.

In the inter-war period a number of travel books of varying quality were published, but in general the country re-entered a period of obscurity. This was reinforced in the communist period post-war, when the official publications in English about the country became a byword for dogmatic propaganda and obfuscation. There was some improvement in the 1980s, mainly linked to the interest that the British millionaire publisher Robert Maxwell took in Bulgaria which resulted in the publication of an English-language encyclopedia on Bulgaria, as well as a number of highly sycophantic books about the Bulgarian political leadership. Although a product of the communist regime, the encyclopedia has some value as an independent reference book if read critically. There was also an improvement in native Bulgarian publications in some fields then, particularly archaeology, although in general literature about the country was dominated by propaganda. Material produced in the Zhivkov era particularly distorts the Ottoman contribution to the heritage of the country. In the field of literature, there were some useful translations into English of classic Bulgarian authors in this period, such as the novels of Ivan Vasov and the poetry of Hristo Botev.

In the post-communist period, there has been a great increase in the variety of books published in Bulgaria and works translated from other languages, but very little of this output has been translated into English, or other foreign languages. There was much more foreign-language publication in Bulgaria in the communist period than there is now. The serious student of Bulgaria in the United Kingdom will need to cultivate connections with second-hand book dealers in order to find volumes. Specialists include: **M. Dworski Books**, 37 Lion Street, Hay-on-Wye HR3 5AA, **Eastern Books**, 125A Astonville Street, London SW18, **Zeno Bookshop**, 6 Denmark Street, London WC2, **Beaumont Travel Bookshop**, 31 Museum Street, London WC1A 1LH.

Bulgarian museum guides should be read critically; there are common distortions in ancient history, particularly in descriptions of the Hellenistic period when ancient Thrace was a part of the Greek world. Material about the origins and history of the Bulgarian Orthodox Church can be highly speculative, to say the least, as well as material about the ethnic Turkish and other Islamic minorities. The Ottoman conquest can be a particularly difficult period in Bulgarian material; anyone seriously studying this period should read the relevant sections in Lord Kinross's monumental work *The Ottoman Centuries*.

Old guide books can be useful sources of information. *A Guide Book to Bulgaria* (Sofia,1957) gives the regime's often unintentionally amusing view of itself as the country first began to open to Westerners. The Nagels *Guide Bulgaria* (Geneva, 1968) gives a very informative, if very rose-tinted, picture of 1960s communist Bulgaria, and the first edition of the *Rough Guide to Bulgaria* (1993) is strong on the atmosphere of the transition from communism, and IMRO. Isambert's masterly 1881 survey (see below) is indispensable on the late Ottoman and National Revival periods. The 1933 *Guide Bleu Romanie-Bulgarie-Turquie* published by Hachette in Paris is unique in giving an objective picture of the interwar period, although many important regions of the country are omitted.

There is a growing literature on the hitherto neglected ethnic minorities and their cultures. A very valuable series on the Roma (Gypsies) is *Studii Romanii*, in Bulgarian, Rom and English, published in Sofia and financed by the Soros Foundation. A number of specialised reference works contain information on Bulgarian Jewry.

There are various Bulgarian language courses on sale, of which *Teach Yourself Bulgarian* is perhaps the most widely used.

Archaeology

There are a number of Bulgarian archaeological publications, most of which are not available in foreign languages. The Institute of Underwater Archaeology at Sozopol publish a very interesting learned journal *Thracia Pontica* which is usually partly in English. There is some useful regional material in *Thrace* (ed. Selemis) Athens, 1994, a large volume of essays translated from Greek.

Ancient World

Epic of Jason and the Argonauts
Herodotus, *Histories*
Strabo, *Geography*
Ovid, *Tristia*
Ovid, *Epistulae ex Ponto*
Arrian, *Anabasis*
Euripides, *Bacchae*
D.P. Dimitrov, *Bulgaria, land of ancient civilisation*
Tim Severin, *The Jason Voyage*
Neal Acherson, *Black Sea*

Panorama Society of Athens, *The Greeks in the Black Sea*
R.F. Hoddinott, *Bulgaria in Antiquity*
S. Casson, *Macedonia, Thrace and Illyria*
Nicholas Hammond, *The Origins of the Macedonian State*
Georgi Mihailov, *Inscriptiones graecae in Bulgaria repetae*
Ludmila Zhivkov, *The Kazanluk Tomb*
British Museum, *Thracian Treasures from Bulgaria*

Byzantine and Medieval

Sir Dimitri Obolensky, *The Byzantine Commonwealth*
Sir Dimitri Obolensky, *The Bogomils*
Lyuben Prashkov and others, *Monasteries in Bulgaria*
Atanas Bozhkov, *Bulgarian Contributions to European Civilisation*
Magdalina Stancheva, *Veliki Preslav*

Robert Browning, *Byzantium and Bulgaria*
Cyril Mango, *Byzantium*
George Ostrogorsky, *The Origins of the Byzantine State*
Mercia MacDermott, *A History of Bulgaria 1393–1885*
Antony Handjiyski, *Rock Monasteries*

Ottoman period and the Twentieth century

Lamartine, *Voyage en Orient (1832–33)*
M. Blanqui, *Voyage en Bulgarie*
Rev. W. Denton, *The Christians of Turkey*
John Mason, *Three Years in Turkey*
Karl Marx, *The Eastern Question (1853–56)*
R T. Shannon, *Gladstone and the Bulgarian Agitation 1876*
Robert Wagner, *With the Victorious Bulgarians*
Noel Buxton, *With the Bulgarian General Staff*
Mercia MacDermott, *Apostle of Freedom*
Mercia MacDermott, *For Freedom and Perfection*
Frank Fox, *Bulgaria*
F.W. Herbert, *The Defence of Plevna, 1877*
Lady Grogan, *The Life of J. D. Bourchier*
James Bourchier, *The Times Correspondent Reporting from Sofia*
R. Ward Price, *Balkan Cockpit*
W.E.Curtis, *The Turk and his Lost Provinces*
J.A.R. Marriott, *The Eastern Question*
W. Crawfurd Price, *Balkan Cockpit*
L. Villari (ed.), *The Balkan Question*
Harry Gregson, *Buffer States of the Balkans*
Sir Reginald Rankin, *The Inner History of the Balkan War*
K. A. Vacalapoulos, *Modern History of Macedonia 1830–1912*
R. H. Markham, *Meet Bulgaria*
A. Hulme Beaman, *Stambuloff*
Graham Hutton, *Danubian Destiny*
Nigel Clive (trans.), *Koromila-In the Trail of Odysseus*
Georgi Markov, *The Truth That Killed*

M. Padev, *Escape from the Balkans*
Elizabeth Barker, *British Policy in South East Europe during the Second World War*
Bernard Newman, *Bulgarian Backdoor*
Bernard Newman, *Balkan Background*
Eric Williams, *Dragoman Pass*
Ali Eminov, *Turkish and Muslim Minorities of Bulgaria*
Anton Zischa, *The Other Europeans*
Lesley Branch, *Under a Lilac-bleeding Star*
Harold Rose, *Your Guide to Bulgaria*
Georgi Dimitrov, *Works* (3 vols)
A Short History of the Bulgarian Communist Party
A.L. Haskell, *Heroes and Roses*
Claudio Magris, *Danube*
Albert Londres, *Terror in the Balkans*
Nadejda Muir, *Dimitri Stancioff Patriot and Cosmopolitan 1864–1940*
Stella Blagoeva, *Georgi Dimitrov*
Philip Thornton, *Ikons and Oxen*
Joseph Swire, *Bulgarian Conspiracy*
Anna Stancioff, *Recollections of a Bulgarian Diplomatist's Wife*
Richard Crampton, *A Short History of Modern Bulgaria*
Edouard Calic, *Life in Bulgaria*
Rev. Stanley Evans, *History of Bulgaria*
H.T. Norris, *Islam in the Balkans*
Philip Ward, *Sofia*
Mercia MacDermott, *Bulgarian Folkcustoms*
John R. Lampe, *The Bulgarian Economy in the 20th Century*

THE GUIDE

Sofia

Sofia (pop. 1,082,315) is the capital of Bulgaria and the centre of the political, cultural and administrative life of the country. It also has some important economic and industrial installations within the city and on the outskirts. Sofia is built on an ancient site below the slopes of **Mount Vitosha**, a beautiful pine-covered range to the south of the city. The suburbs resemble those of some German and Austrian cities, with dense woods and old houses and some large middle-class mansions. The population has grown considerably since the Second World War and the rapid industrialisation of Bulgaria under the communists, and there are many depressing inner city areas dominated by very large monolithic apartment blocks designed on Soviet lines. They do not, however, detract from the remarkable **historic centre** with its buildings from the ancient, Byzantine, Ottoman and National Revival periods.

The visitor is likely to stay in or near to this old historic centre, whose *Quartiers* seem to most people to be those of a typical old Balkan capital, with rattling trams, *pave* streets, ill-lit alleyways and grandiose public buildings in a state of minor or major decay. The survival of this very attractive late 19C ambience is due, in a large part, to the course of modern Bulgarian history when the alliance Sofia governments adopted in World War II, as an ally of Germany, meant that the historic centre avoided the Nazi Blitzkrieg that so devasted the great historic centre of Belgrade and so many other Balkan towns and cities. The ambience has often been matched by the political reality. Bulgaria has rejected many aspects of Europeanist modernisation in the post-communist period.

Sofia in the recent past has been the quintessential Balkan city of intrigue, assassination and conspiracy, an atmosphere that in some aspects continues today, with the hand-forged guns of the Macedonian revolutionaries being replaced by the Beretas and huge black Mercedes cars of the often highly politicised *Mafiya*. Although the gangsters' often lethal quarrels should not deter or touch the holiday visitor, it is a good idea to have some awareness of the power of these forces in Bulgarian society.

Until the 1880s the city had an almost wholly **Ottoman Turkish** character, with winding narrow streets and tortuous alleyways until most of it was razed to the ground under the direction of the new monarchy. King Ferdinand in the 1880s and 1890s built a new city in the 19C style of urban planning, *après* Baron Haussmann, with wide boulevards, parks and other amenities. The wooded recreation grounds and gardens in many places evoke a small German provincial capital. Parts of central Sofia underwent redevelopment under communism, and there had been some war damage, but on the whole the main historic buildings have survived, if often used for inappropriate purposes. There are also many inner city streets which lack outstanding individual buildings but which are nevertheless full of character and interest.

Although the area covered by the historic centre of the city has been inhabited from early times, Sofia only became an important urban centre under the Roman Empire, when it was known as *Serdica*. It developed rapidly as a military depot on the crossroads of the roads linking Constantinople with the great legionary garrison at *Naissus* (modern Nis, in Serbia). It has remained a vital transport locus in the Balkans ever since, and became an important administrative centre for the Byzantines and the Ottoman Turks. In the 19C the line of the Orient Express railway was routed through the city.

At least two days are needed to see the main sights in Sofia, and a week is needed for a thorough exploration that includes important buildings and sites nearby (see Environs of Sofia, p 111), but if on a business trip, it is possible to make quick visits to at least some of the most rewarding places. Visitors in the winter months should bear in mind that the city has a continental climate, and can become very cold indeed on occasion. In these months Doc Martens boots, or similar footwear, are very strongly recommended, as pavements and drains are not all they might be, and roads can often be ankle deep in slush, snow and mud. In the spring and autumn the climate is generally very pleasant, but mid-summer can be very humid. Heavy rainfall is possible at almost any time of year.

Sofia is at the centre of the national transport system, and most travellers to provincial Bulgaria will find themselves starting their journey there, except for those travelling directly to the Black Sea coast.

Getting to and from the airport

The airport is about 10km to the east of the city. It was opened in 1939, and is scheduled for modernisation. It is on the fringe of the Iztok (east) area of Sofia. It is usually easy to reach without traffic problems—allow about 20 minutes by taxi from the city centre, longer during the rush hour. There is an intermittent bus service, from the central office of Balkan Airlines, but it can be unreliable. **Not recommended**, use taxis.

NB. Airport security is not all it might be. Take care with baggage and offers of help from people you do not know, and beware pickpockets.

If travelling by any other airline than British Airways and Swissair, it is definitely a good idea to **reconfirm flights** within 72 hours of departure. On busy summer weekends this is really essential. Be sure to check in in good time.

Car hire

Most easily organised from Sofia airport on arrival where all the main operators have offices, although they also have city centre offices. In general, the latter offices do not have cars on hand and more time should be allowed if you are dealing with them. The Hotel InterContinental also has a number of car hire offices in the interior reception. See p 109 for details. **Europcar**, 8 Positano Street (☎ 835049, fax 883593), where most of the company staff are well trained and helpful, is particularly recommended. So is **Avis**, the office at the Intercontinental Hotel is efficient and helpful. **NB**. **Full insurance is expensive but essential**.

Emergency telephone numbers

These numbers should operate throughout the country. Police ☎ 166, Ambulance ☎ 150, Fire brigade ☎ 160.

Hotels

Sofia has a large number of hotels, but the larger hotels are expensive, for what is offered, and very tuned to the international business traveller. A Hilton is planned in the Lozenets quarter of the city.

The **Sheraton** is generally regarded as the best hotel, though it is very expensive; see below p 96. It is at 5 Sveta Nedelya Square, Sofia 1000 (☎ 981 6541, fax 980 6464, telex 2 30 30 Shera BG; manager: Mr Even Frydenberg).

In the medium price range the three star **Grand**, opposite the Parliament building in Narodno Subraine Square (☎ 878821, telex 23405) is a safe choice. The **Hotel Rila** in Tsar Kaloyan Street (☎ 881861, fax 650106, telex 24058) is also three stars but slightly cheaper.

It is difficult to find good cheap hotel accommodation in Sofia. The **Slavyanska Besseda** in Rakovski Street (☎ 880441, fax 872123) is clean and central, for about $US30 a night (see below p 107).

See also p 109ff below for information on other hotels.

Taxis

Taxis are everywhere in Sofia and are generally cheap and efficient. They can be waved down or found in taxi ranks. If possible, avoid those from ranks near big hotels or the main railway station where there is a minor *Mafiya* problem. Fares are metered but drivers try to charge foreigners above the official rate.

If coming from the airport, buy a ticket (currently $US18) from the official taxi kiosk in the arrival lounge for the journey into Sofia. **Do not use unofficial taxis**.

Trams and trolleybuses

As in other Bulgarian cities, these follow set routes and are a reliable and very cheap means of transport, if grubby and very old fashioned. Tickets are purchased from kiosks and validated on the vehicle.

Underground railway

An attempt to build the beginnings of a Metro system foundered in the 1970s, but has been revived recently. As yet, the line is not complete or in operation.

History of Sofia

Sofia was founded by the *Serdii* tribe in prehistoric times, when Thracian village settlements were established on and around the slopes of Mount Vitosha. The little town became known as *Serdica*, and was laid waste by Philip II of Macedon in 339 on his Scythian expedition.

Serdica nevertheless survived but only grew to be a place of any significance in the 1C AD, when the Roman road networks in the Balkans were being established, and numerous landless ex-Roman army veterans were being settled by the early Emperors. After further growth under Trajan (98–117) *Serdica* became the capital of the Imperial province of Dacia, and was renamed *Ulpia Serdica*. It became a prosperous trading centre, and in

347 an Ecumenical Council was held in the town. In 447 it was ravaged by **Attila the Hun**, then rebuilt by Justinian (527–65).

In the 6C and 7C the town was attacked by the Slavs, and most of the population fled. It was renamed *Sredec*. In 809 Khan Krum and his Bulgarian tribesmen occupied Sredec, and it became part of the Bulgarian Kingdom for 300 years. In 1078 the town, now called *Triadica*, was destroyed by the Pecheneg horde. In 1096 the First Crusade passed through, after which, in 1183, it was attacked by the Serbs and Magyars, and by the Crusaders in 1189. In 1194 it joined the Second Bulgarian Kingdom, under Turnovo.

The town was first known as *Sofia* in the 14C, when in 1382 it was pillaged by the Turks. After 1396 it became an Ottoman administrative centre, which it remained for hundreds of years. It was particularly prosperous in the 18C, but did not maintain this position so that by the Liberation in 1876 only about 20,000 people lived in it. In the 20C it grew rapidly from the influx of peasants from the surrounding countryside. Under communism this process accelerated, with over a quarter of the entire Bulgarian working population resident in it. In the post-communist period, this has resulted in acute problems of unemployment and social dislocation, with the closure of many old enterprises in the city and the decline of rural life outside it.

Central Sofia and ancient Serdica

Many of the most important buildings in modern Sofia, particularly government ministries, churches and museums, are built very near the centre of the **ancient settlement of Serdica**, and it is possible to gain a good impression of the nature of the heart of the ancient and modern city on the same walk. The outstanding Roman and Byzantine churches here are some of the most important historic buildings in Bulgaria and should be included in any visit to the city. The area they occupy is compact and all these buildings can be reached on foot, without the use of a car.

The **Sheraton Hotel** on Sveta Nedelya Square makes a good starting point, a solid and characterful edifice that was built as a communist VIP hotel at the same time as the monumental complex of party and government buildings nearby. In those days it was known as the Balkan Hotel, and the general vicinity Lenin Square. Pre-war, the site was occupied by a mixture of Ottoman and 19C Revival buildings, and was subject to some damage in the RAF bombing of Sofia in 1944. In 1956 the architect T. Zlatev redesigned the whole area—all existing buildings apart from the ancient monuments were demolished—and the locality is a classic surviving example of 1950s Stalinist urban planning in Eastern Europe. All the buildings are constructed in the same grey granite blocks, conveying an impression of authoritarian rule in a neo-classic dimension.

The Sheraton Hotel is well-managed, relaxed and an essential meeting place for almost everybody who visits Sofia, although it is rather expensive to stay here. The hotel generally has been brought up to date in a sympathetic way by the Sheraton management. The interior is mostly beige marble, in Renaissance style, agreeably serious and monumental without being grandiose. It has happily avoided the aggressive and unpleasant 'business culture' that permeates some similar establishments in Eastern Europe, and is welcoming to everybody providing the dress code is observed. Uniformed bodyguards and personal weapons are not allowed on the premises. The management has an enlightened policy of promoting the work of Bulgarian contemporary artists, and exhibitions are frequently held in the rear lounge.

The **restaurant** and **bars**, though, are good if not cheap, with generally excellent local wines, and some traditional Bulgarian dishes. CNN television is available in the bedrooms, which are wonderfully large and old fashioned, and evoke perfectly the ambience of the old *nomenclatura*. The public rooms are often used for diplomatic corps functions.

There are some useful shops inside the hotel, along with the British Airways and Austrian Air offices, a barber, and a very helpful travel agency in the basement, along with the Sheraton Business Centre and a night club.

The newspaper shop has the widest range of foreign newspapers and magazines available in the city, and there is an interesting shop next to it selling high quality modern ikons by Bulgarian artists.

The **Sheraton Business Centre**, in the basement, offers very useful and efficient facilities for foreign telephone calls, telex and fax messages. It is open to non-residents.

To the rear of the Wiener Bar is the **Casino** (open 20.00–04.00), under separate management, where roulette and blackjack are the most popular games. The roulette tables are large and well run. Stakes are not high, by Western standards, and it is generally free from the worst excesses of *Mafiya* and underworld activity that permeate some similar Sofia establishments. Western visitors are welcome. If you plan to stay until the early hours it is a good idea to go with a Bulgarian companion. Personal weapons are banned.

Opposite the Casino entrance, across a grassy oblong area known as the **Largo**, is the **TSUM** department store, with several floors, a very close copy in design and social fuction of the old GUM store in Moscow. It embodied the consumerist ethos of Bulgarian communism, that of an orderly and egalitarian showcase for the products of the country that were meant to be available equally to all Bulgarians. The exterior is heavy and dominating, redolent of the atmosphere of late Stalinism, with a grim façade, and rows of neo-Florentine arches on the ground floor.

Nowadays TSUM has become rather redundant, in terms of its original function, although it still has links with some state factories, and can be a good place to buy a cheap hat or scarf. Most consumer goods are imported now, and are as expensive as in the West. It nevertheless has one or two specialist counters which are very useful, such as the wine and spirit shop on the ground floor, which sells a range of high quality wine and *rakia* at much keener prices and with a much wider choice than most hotel shops. As the airport duty free shop does not sell much in the way of wine at all and nothing of *rakia*, it can be a good place for a quick last-minute shopping trip before leaving Bulgaria. Good traditional musicians sometimes play in the arcades outside.

Backing directly onto TSUM on the Largo are government office buildings currently used by the Foreign Ministry, opposite which at the far (eastern) end of the square, is the old **Party House**. This is an imposing building, which covers

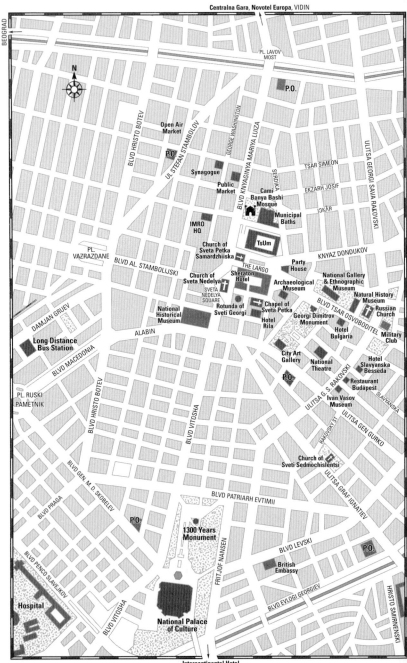

BEOGRAD

Centralna Gara, Novotel Europa, VIDIN

PL. LAVOV MOST

N

P.O.

BLVD HRISTO BOTEV

Open Air Market

UL. STEFAN STAMBOLOV

GEORGE WASHINGTON

BLVD KNYAGINYA MARIYA LUIZA

SERDIKA

TSAR SIMEON

ULITSA GEORGI SAVA RAKOVSKI

P.O.

Synagogue

Public Market

Cami
Banya Bashi Mosque

EKZARH JOSIF

IGKAR

IMRO HQ

Municipal Baths

PL. VAZRAZDANE

Church of Sveta Petka Samardzhiiska

TsUm

BLVD AL. STAMBOLIJSKI

THE LARGO

Party House

KNYAZ DONDUKOV

Church of Sveta Nedelya

Sheraton Hotel

SVETA NEDELYA SQUARE

Archaeological Museum

National Gallery & Ethnographic Museum

Natural History Museum

BLVD TSAR OSVOBODITEL

Russian Church

DAMJAN GRUEV

National Historical Museum

Rotunda of Sveti Georgi

Chapel of Sveta Petka

Hotel Rila

Georgi Dimitrov Monument

Hotel Bulgaria

Military Club

Long Distance Bus Station

ALABIN

City Art Gallery

National Theatre

Hotel Slavyanska Besseda

SLAVYANSKA

BLVD MACEDONIA

P.O.

Restaurant Budapest

PL. RUSKI PAMETNIK

BLVD HRISTO BOTEV

BLVD VITOSHA

ULITSA G. S. RAKOVSKI

Ivan Vasov Museum

ULITSA GEN GURKO

RAKOVSKY ST

Church of Sveti Sedmochislentsi

ULITSA GRAF IGNATIEV

BLVD GEN. M.D. SKOBELEV

BLVD PRAGA

BLVD PATRIARH EVTIMII

BLVD PENCO SLAVEJKOV

P.O.

1300 Years Monument

FRITJOF NANSEN

BLVD LEVSKI

P.O.

British Embassy

HRISTO SMIRNENSKI

Hospital

BLVD VITOSHA

National Palace of Culture

BLVD EVLOGI GEORGIEV

Intercontinental Hotel

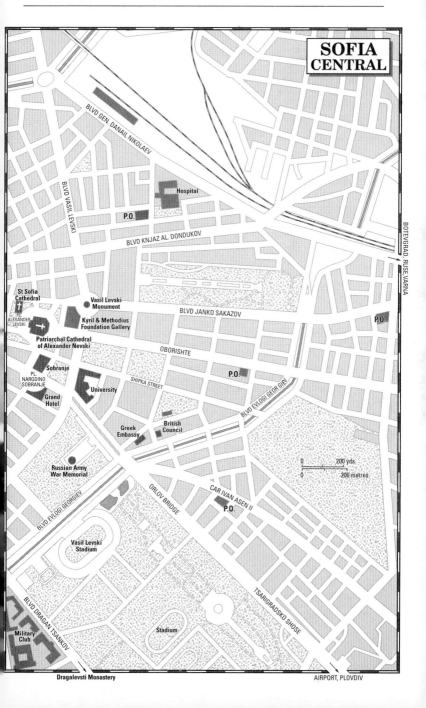

SOFIA CENTRAL

BLVD GEN. DANAIL NIKOLAEV

BLVD VASIL LEVSKI

Hospital

P.O.

BLVD KNJAZ AL. DONDUKOV

BOTEVGRAD, RUSE, VARNA

St Sofia Cathedral

PL ALEXANDER LEVSKI

Vasil Levski Monument

Kyril & Methodius Foundation Gallery

BLVD JANKO SAKAZOV

P.O.

Patriarchal Cathedral of Alexander Nevski

OBORISHTE

Sobranje

PL NARODINO SOBRANJE

SHIPKA STREET

P.O.

BLVD EVLOGI GEOR GIEV

University

Grand Hotel

Greek Embassy

British Council

Russian Army War Memorial

0   200 yds
0   200 metres

BLVD EVLOGI GEORGIEV

ORLOV BRIDGE

CAR IVAN ASEN II

P.O.

Vasil Levski Stadium

BLVD DRAGAN TSANKOV

TSARIGRADSKO SHOSE

Military Club

Stadium

Dragalevsti Monastery

AIRPORT, PLOVDIV

The Party House

a largely triangular central site on the traffic island, the central entrance of which dominates the whole open square. Above the central entrance, the façade is dominated by a row of huge concrete Ionic colums, surmounted by a central tower and spire. The design of the top of the building seems to have been copied from the dramatic series of Stalinist skyscrapers that ring central Moscow. The general impression is of pretentious and severe monumentality—architecture to celebrate a new power elite; enclosed, ruthless and dictatorial. The building has remained largely empty and boarded up since 1990, when the old communist apparat was dispossessed. At the rear and side windows, it is possible to see signs of flame marks on the walls after it was set on fire by anti-communist demonstrators in August 1990.

This building was intended by the original architects to have a symbolic value and importance, and that has remained the case, even a number of years after the demise of communism. The inability of the country to decide on a suitable public use for the premises illustrates the difficulty many sections of Bulgarian society have had in coming to terms with the communist past.

Rotunda of Sveti Georgi

Across the road from the front of the party building, back towards the Sheraton is the rear entrance to a block of government offices, currently used by parts of the **Foreign Ministry and Office of the Presidency**. Through a series of open arches 100m to the left of this entrance you can reach the **Rotunda of Sveti Georgi**.

History of the Rotunda

This outstanding Roman building, universally known as the Rotunda, was constructed in the 2C and 3C BC. Scholars disagree over the original purpose of the building, but it seems most likely it was a pagan temple, dedicated to the Imperial cult. In the time of Constantine it was made into a church. In the 5C, probably 447, it was seriously damaged in the Hunnic invasions, then rebuilt in the 6C by Justinian. It was decorated with frescoes in the 11C, 13C and 14–15C, and made into a mosque by the Turkish invaders in the 16C, when it was known as the **Rose Mosque**.

The Rotunda is one of the most important churches in Bulgaria. It stands as part of an excavated complex of Roman *Serdica*, including the foundations of associated buildings and a stretch of **Roman pavement**. At the extreme east end of the site is the foundation of an ancient church of octagonal shape, dating from the time of Constantine which may also have originally been part of a pagan Roman temple complex. Three sacrificial altars were found in rescue archaeological work 40 years ago. The great interest and distinction of the buildings, however, is markedly diminished by the almost total enclosure of the complex within the high walls of the surrounding buildings from the communist redevelopment. It is as if the early communist leaders were afraid of their Classical and Christian heritage and sought to enclose it, like a dangerous animal in a zoo.

The difficulties for the visitor are increased by the fact that the Rotunda church is very often completely closed, allegedly for redecoration and restoration, although it is difficult to find evidence of any recent activity. The most that can currently be expected is the chance to examine the exterior and the Roman precinct, although this is certainly very rewarding, unless the visitor is lucky enough to encounter a VIP party at the site.

Walking back to the street past the rear entrance of the Sheraton Hotel, and turning left back towards the Casino entrance, you come to the corner of the street by the entrance to the Weiner Bar. Turn right here and walk down into the underpass (**NB**. Use in daylight hours only) that crosses the main road to TSUM. Here on the Largo is a **craft market**, with lace, ikons, musical instruments and wood carvings on sale. Although quality varies, on the whole it is quite high and it is possible to find really interesting and authentic souvenirs, although anyone wishing to buy lace, particularly table cloths, may do better in terms of price and range of choice at the open air lace and embroidery stalls near the Institute of Balkan Studies (see p 101). Black market moneychangers also haunt this area.

In an open area in the middle of the underpass complex is the **Church of Sveta Petka Samardzhiiska**, *St Petka of the Saddlers*. This is a small medieval building that has been preserved as an historic monument in rather incongruous surroundings as part of the 1950s communist redevelopment of the area. It has a single nave and vaulted roof with a semicircular apse. Part of the interior is painted with very good 16C **frescoes** but the

Church of Sveta Petka Samardzhiiska

building is usually closed and it is very difficult to get access to see them. Church holidays and festivals are the best chance to see the interior.

History of the church
This church was the church of the Saddlers' Guild in old Sofia, hence its name (*samar* means 'saddle'). It is believed to date from the 14C, but the saint was an 11C figure from the Sea of Marmara, suggesting possible Byzantine links and an earlier building on the site.

Walking through the underpass and up the steps by TSUM, if you continue past the main entrance of TSUM, the **Cami Banya Bashi** (Mosque of the Baths) is in front of you. This is the only functioning mosque left in central Sofia and is an evocative, attractive building designed by the greatest Ottoman architect, Sinan, and opened in 1576. It was admired by the Turkish traveller Celebi in the 17C. In its time it has often been the subject of much controversy. It stands in a small enclosed garden and paved area, surrounded by railings, and it is generally only possible to see the interior on Fridays. There are stalls selling Islamic literature outside on most days of the week, and a stall with the best selection of second-hand historic maps in the city.

The **interior** of the mosque is very beautiful, with a single whitewashed dome and walls above a square prayer room, and a finely painted, decorated tracery of plants and flowers upon the walls. There are some good rugs on the floor, and a wooden women's gallery showing fine craftsmanship. It is a pity that the building is not more generally accessible, its circumstances at the moment seem to express in physical terms the slightly beleaguered and uncertain atmosphere of Islam in Bulgaria. Most of those attending Friday prayers nowadays do not seem to be Bulgarian, with a preponderance of Arab world students from Sofia University.

Turning right by the mosque, you come to the front of the **Municipal Baths**, a very fine public building that was opened in 1913 but is unfortunately now in a very poor state, with a partially collapsed roof, and trees and shrubs growing in the interior. It is to be hoped that it will soon receive the attention it deserves, as the façade is very fine, with inlaid mosaic decoration. It is built on the site of the old Ottoman *hammam*, and Roman baths before them. The constant hot water has a temperature of 46 degrees. The building has never really recovered from the destruction of a similar building next to it in an Allied air raid in 1944.

Crossing the wide boulevard here, you come to the old **Public Market**, the *Hali*, an impressive but semi-ruined edifice that was reconstructed in communist times on the foundations of earlier buildings opened in 1911. It is currently under reconstruction and it should before long be returned to its original use, which will be a distinct asset to this part of the city. In recent years the building has become an eyesore and a refuge for unpleasant stray dogs. The market occupies a large square site, with rows of external arches and an arcaded interior. There is a small clock tower above the entrance.

Behind the market in Tsar Boris I Street is the **Headquarters of the Internal Macedonian Revolutionary Organisation** (IMRO), a large oblong grey office block, with the often notorious black and red flag of IMRO flying outside. In communist times it was known as the 'Macedonian Scientific Institute', before IMRO was legalised again in 1990. It is used as the headquarters of the movement and the editorial offices for a newspaper. English language speaking members of staff are available to brief callers; contact Mr Dimitar Dereliev on the fourth floor. Some knowledge of the history of IMRO is an essential part of understanding modern Bulgarian and southern Balkan history and society.

For the history of **IMRO**, in its time the most feared secret society and terrorist organisation in Europe, see p 74. Modern IMRO is primarily a cultural and regional lobby, although it has considerable political influence in the west and southwest of the country. A branch of VMRO, VMRO-Ilinden, is currently banned by the Bulgarian government. There are IMRO-influenced members of the current government.

On the west side of the market, in Ekzarh Josif Street, is the **Sofia Synagogue**. This is an outstanding, dramatic building, the largest synagogue in the Balkans. It was seriously damaged by RAF bombing in 1944, and was never restored properly under communism. At the moment work is in progress on a complete renovation, financed primarily by Bulgarian Jews who have emigrated to Israel in the past, and Israeli foundations. In the last two years work has been completed on the dome, a wonderful metal-cased structure. The building generally follows the Sephardic style, fitting the origins of most of the Bulgarian Jewish community, with very fine tracery in the deep red brickwork, and imposing high walls.

The Sofia synagogue

The office of the Chairman of the Council of Jewish Organisations of Bulgaria is in the building, and he is happy to welcome visitors (Mr J. Levy; speaks German). The interior is full of scaffolding at the moment, and is difficult to appreciate, but it is worth requesting admission to have some sense of the

The Jewish community in Bulgaria

The Bulgarian Jewish community is one of the largest and most influential in the Balkans, and thanks to the protection of at least some sections of the Bulgarian people, was able to survive the Nazi period and the Second World War rather better than most communities in neighbouring countries. There were large pre-1939 Jewish settlements in Vidin, Plovdiv, Varna and Ruse, as well as in Sofia. Most Bulgarian Jews have Sephardic origins, and came to Bulgaria when it was an Ottoman province from the very large communities in Constantinople and Thessaloniki. The Ladino language of these people has died out, although it was spoken by some people in Plovdiv until the Second World War.

At the end of the Second World War there were about 45,000 Jews left in Bulgaria, after the community had on the whole avoided mass deportation to Nazi extermination camps, but had been made to do forced labour in Bulgaria. This number has shrunk to about 6000 people today, mostly through direct emigration to Israel. Nearly all contemporary Bulgarian Jewry live in Sofia or Plovdiv. Many people left Bulgaria between 1945 and 1948, then more emigrated in the 1950s, mostly elderly people, and a significant number after the end of communism in 1989/90. Bulgarian Jews in Israel have retained close links with their motherland. Jews are prominent in commerce and in the professions, such as law, the university and in medicine. The community is also well represented in parts of the civil service.

grandeur of the great central dome. Entry is through a small metal gate in the railings on the south side of the building. Donations to help with the very high cost of the building works are warmly welcomed, and a certificate of thanks is provided for larger donors.

George Washington Street continues south, with some interesting if rather dilapidated early 20C and inter-war buildings into a residential area.

Immediately in front of the Sheraton, across a paved plaza, is the **Church of Sveta Nedelya**. This is a notable Sofia landmark, and is very much a functioning community church, often used for weddings by the better-off citizens of Sofia. It also has a strong Royalist following in the congregation. In modern times it was notable for the notorious assassination attempt on the life of King Boris III in 1925 (see History below). The roof was blown off, and extensive damage caused, but the king escaped with his life. It is a warm, friendly, informal church with welcoming priests, and is a sympathetic place for non-Orthodox Christians visiting Sofia to attend a Sunday service. **Open** for Sunday services at 10.00.

History of the Church of Sveta Nedelya

The present church was built after the Liberation in 1876, and stands on the site of several earlier buildings. The site is on the junction of two ancient Roman roads. Originally the Roman *praetorium*, several small Christian churches stood here, followed by boyars chapels under the medieval Bulgarian kingdoms. This vicinity of the Ottoman town was known as *Varosh* and a church was built here called *Sveti Kral*. It was named after the tomb of the medieval Serbian king, Stefan Urosh II, who was buried here. In the 19C it became the Metropolitan church of the city.

On 16 April 1925 a bomb, planted either by IMRO or the communists, exploded in the church, intending to kill King Boris and his cabinet. It failed to do so, but there were 123 other fatalities.

Turning sharp left into Saborna Street by the side of the Sheraton, there is the office of Turkish Airlines, and the entrance to the sunken **Chapel of Sveta Petka Paraskeva**. This is a wonderful little building and a centre of the renewal of Orthodox spirituality in Bulgaria, where worship takes place in an atmosphere and surroundings that must be similar to that of Ottoman times. The entrance, by a small carved stone door in the street, leads to a small vestibule, with ikons and candle stands, then descend by steps to the nave. The interior is poetic, private, deeply Orthodox. On the corner is the **Church Historical Museum** (**open** Mon–Fri 09.00–12.00, 14.00–17.30).

National Historical Museum

Walking across the plaza from the church door to the south, you cross the road to the National Historical Museum, a dark and rather heavy neo-classical edifice that was originally built as the Palace of Justice. It contains the most important collection in the country, including the magnificent **Thracian and Hellenistic metalwork**, works of art of the highest order that should be seen on any visit to Sofia.

Entrance is through the central door after climbing the steep front steps. The collection is on two floors, with material from the Thracian, Classical, medieval Bulgarian and Byzantine world on the lower floor, and an ethnographic collection upstairs. Although well worth visiting, the latter is of more specialised interest and business visitors with little spare time can cover everything really outstanding on the lower floor. **Open** 09.30–17.30, ☎ 831555, fax 883284; information ☎ 809601. In theory, it is closed on Mondays but sometimes appears to be open seven days a week.

In the entrance hall there are two kiosks selling tickets and publications; there is a souvenir shop to the left. A good, up-to-date English language guide book is now available.

History of the museum

The present museum was established in 1973. In 1979 two floors of the old Palace of Justice were made available to the museum. The current exhibition was opened in 1984. By the middle of 1995, the collection comprised no fewer than 600,000 items, including a large amount of material taken from old pre-1989 museums such as the Museum of the Revolutionary Movement and the Rila Monastery Historical Museum. This has had the unfortunate effect of preventing many interesting items from being seen by the visitor to Bulgaria, due to lack of space.

Ground Floor

The Ground Floor covers prehistoric Bulgaria, ancient numismatics, the latter on the left of the main entrance hall in a separate room, and Classical and medieval Bulgaria.

The first rooms, all on the left, show the earliest human settlement in Bulgaria, from the **Old** and **Middle Stone Age** periods (20,000–7000 BC), with exhibits of stone and bone tools used by the hunter-gatherer people. Next there are exhibits from the **New Stone Age**, showing early farming cultures, with ceramics, leatherwork and votive objects from this period.

Room 9 is devoted to the beginnings of the **Bronze Age** in Bulgaria, the Chalcolithic period (5000–4000 BC), where the rich copper and gold deposits lying near the surface in some parts of Bulgaria were exploited. There is some very fine **metalwork** from this period, and interesting displays showing funereal customs from the Varna necropolis, and early religious practices. The material from the **Ovcharovo excavation**, showing a model stone temple dedicated to the Sun, Moon and Elements, is quite outstanding.

The next series of exhibits depicts **Orphic Thrace**, and the transition from a tribal society to a form of settled social organisation. They present an interesting picture of Thrace about the time of the Homeric poet, with very good material from the megalithic tombs and on the Orphic religion. The remarkable **goldwork** from the Valchitran excavations illustrates the main development of Thracian art, with a Geometric style based on abstraction from the animal world.

Following this, and occupying the whole of the rear of the museum on this floor, is the great exhibition of late monarchical Thrace and Hellenistic Thrace, with some of the finest examples of **ancient Hellenistic metalwork** in existence. Thrace achieved its height of independent cultural development under King Kotis I (383–359 BC), and was playing an important part in international events with the Persian invasion of the southern Balkans and Greece and the subsequent development of the Macedonian state. Treasures include the material from tribal burials of the Bessai tribe, from Douvanli, near Plovdiv and the Mogilinska burial mound near Vratsa. The greatest treasure was found at **Rogozen**, dating from the mid 4C BC, with wonderful gold and silver gilt rhytons, silver bowls and jugs.

Additional displays show the Hellenisation of Thrace at its height, with a large quantity of imported and domestically manufactured ceramics. The **Panagyurishte Treasure** is the central feature, dating from the end of the 4C and the beginning of the 3C. It was made by a Greek goldsmith in Asia Minor, probably in ancient *Lampsac* in the Dardanelles. The **deer's head rhyton and amphora** are magnificent works of the goldsmiths' art that can stand comparison with the artefacts of any historical period.

The remaining galleries on the ground floor are dedicated to the **Roman period** in Thrace and medieval Bulgaria. Although many of the exhibits are interesting, there is nothing to compare with the previous material. There is some good metalwork, marble statuary and votive reliefs, from Roman Thrace, and a fine small statuette of Zeus from Pernik. In the **Medieval rooms**, the most interesting exhibits are those from ancient *Preslav*, particularly the gold diadem of the accession of Alexander, and some very fine jewellery and illuminated manuscripts.

Upper Floor

The Upper Floor displays later material, some of it of a very high quality and general interest, such as the master-pieces of the 16C **Chiprovtzi goldsmiths**, with the remarkable 1626 monstrance and silver inlaid vessels, along with a good deal of general ethnographic material of more specialised interest.

The most interesting section, by far, is in the long oblong gallery housing the **Struggle for National Self Determination** display. A wide variety of material, including engravings, flags, books, reproductions of early photographs and paintings, show the struggle of the Bulgarian people against Ottoman rule and the convoluted and complex history of the independence movement from its early days to the Liberation. It also has a very comprehensive collection of material on the **Macedonian Question**, including Internal Macedonian Revolutionary Organisation documents, ceramics, flags, and old photographs and engravings.

Return to the Sheraton by the same route.

The city centre east of the Sheraton Hotel

The monuments so far visited belong, in general, to the world of ancient, Byzantine and Ottoman Sofia. The area of the city to the east of the Sheraton mainly comprises the parts of town which were developed in the 19C after the Liberation, and includes the old Royal Palace, the Archaeological Museum, art galleries, the Natural History Museum, the Ethnographic Museum, some remarkable churches, the Parliament, and the University of St Clement of Ochrid. The main sights can be covered on foot in half a day, although a longer period for a visit is a good idea. The outstanding Byzantine Cathedral of St Sofia is also in this part of the city.

In antiquity, much of this area was covered by important public buildings in the fortified Roman town of *Serdica*.

Walk from the Sheraton down Blvd Tsar Osvoboditel, which runs to the right of the old communist party headquarters, with the arcades leading to the Rotunda within the Sheraton complex on the right. In front of you over the road is the **Archaeological Museum**. This was closed for renovation at the time of writing, and during the period of research of this book, and it has not been possible to make an inventory of the contents. The most important part of the old collection was the ancient section with material from *Nicopolis ad Istrum* (see p 205) and the medieval section. The museum has been widely criticised ever since it opened in 1892 for the inadequacy of the displays and the fact that most of the 250,000 plus objects in the collection have never been catalogued properly or seen by anyone other than the museum staff. One can only echo the comment of Philip Ward in his book on Sofia, that the building should be restored to Islamic use, and a proper Archaeological Museum constructed that is large enough to show at last the important items in the national collection.

The museum building itself was originally an Ottoman mosque, the **Bujuk Dzamija (Great Mosque)**, which was constructed at the end of the 15C. It was a very large building, with three central domes, and a rectangular prayer room. It was of some architectural distinction, but was largely ruined in the 1930s' redevelopment of the area by the erection of the **National Bank** building which is physically linked to it by a concrete wall. The bank is a grandiose building in the 1930's fascist architectural style which most people find externally heavy and threatening, but the **Banking Hall** inside is worth visiting, a vast echoing chamber with fine polished woodwork and numerous cubby holes that hide staff performing often obscure bureaucratic functions. The atmosphere is that of the 1930s, plus a few computers. It is possible to change foreign currencies and cash travellers' cheques and Eurocheques at a small window to the right of the entrance in the main hall. Do not expect to find rapid customer service.

About 100m away from the National Bank is the **Georgi Dimitrov Mausoleum**. This used to contain the embalmed body of the famous Bulgarian communist leader, hero of the Reichstag Fire Trial in Leipzig in 1933. It was constructed along the general lines of the Lenin Mausoleum in Moscow, and served as a saluting platform for the communist leadership at rallies, in the same way that the Sheraton area urban redevelopment provided a theatre for the daily life of the party elite. The mausoleum is built of white marble, 8m long, and 6m wide, 3m high, enclosed by a low wall. It was badly vandalised in the 1992–93 period, and covered with slogans extolling sex and rock music but was restored and repainted after the election of the socialist government in 1995. In general, it is a dignified and restrained monument, compared to some of the crude excesses of much Bulgarian communist art and architecture, and seems likely to retain a place in the Sofia urban landscape. The closure of the car park in front of it would improve the general aspect. It is also strange that, given that Dimitrov is one of the few Bulgarian communists foreign visitors to Sofia may have heard of in any sympathetic context, there is no information whatsoever available to the public at this monument.

Georgi Dimitrov

Georgi Dimitrov (1882–1949) was the most prominent Bulgarian communist leader this century and the only figure in the party to achieve international recognition and some degree of approbation in the capitalist world. He was universally seen in the anti-fascist movement in the 1930s as a brave and resolute man who had been framed by the German Nazis for the Reichstag Fire but had managed to save his own life by his brilliance in the courtroom. He went on to become one of the architects of the Popular Front strategy in the Communist International, and by an adept policy of total loyalty to the Soviet Union on domestic issues and a canny understanding of actual conditions in the capitalist world, survived Stalin's purges. He spent the Second World War in Moscow. He returned to Bulgaria as head of the first communist government after the war.

Georgi Dimitrov was born in the village of Kovachevtzi, not far from modern Radomir, in the heart of the 'Red Belt' to the southwest of Sofia. His father was a craftsman, his mother a farmhand and a socialist militant. Two of his brothers were killed in the political struggle, one in Russia in 1917. He was apprenticed to a printer, and soon became general secretary of the printers' trades union, and joined the Bulgarian Social Democratic Party in 1902. After establishing his power base among the rapidly growing working class in Pernik and Sofia, he became a prominent socialist leader and trades unionist before taking part in anti-war movements between 1914 and 1919. He was a founder member of the Bulgarian Communist Party in 1920, and went underground with the rest of the party leadership in 1923 after the failure of the workers' uprising that year. He spent much of the next 10 years in exile in Berlin and Vienna.

On 9 March 1933, Dimitrov was arrested in Berlin and charged with arson of the Reichstag, the German Parliament building, along with Ernst Torgler, the leader of the German Communist party (KPD). His conduct in the trial, where he conducted his own defence, was noteworthy for his brilliant exposure of the then little known Hermann Goering, Nazi Minister of the Interior. The leading Swiss newspaper, the *Neue Zuricher Zeitung* commented at the time, 'The threats against Dimitrov which burst forth from Goering in his mad foolhardy rage, have suddenly made the whole proceedings of the court worthless'.

Although he returned to Bulgaria as head of state in 1945, after spending the war in Moscow, Dimitrov never achieved the degree of approval and recognition among his own countrymen and women that he had in progressive circles abroad. His assumption of power was marked by ruthless repression of opponents, even from within the communist party, and the imposition of a rigid and Stalinist system of government. At a deeper level, the complicity of many sections of Bulgarian society with Germany, in terms of general historic links, and collaboration with the Nazis, in very recent history, meant that Dimitrov's passionate and genuine anti-fascism never had the resonance in Bulgaria that it did abroad.

Opposite is the **Ethnographic Museum and Gallery of National Art**, in a long, low two-storey building that used to be part of the royal residence complex in the 19C. **Open** 10.30–16.40, closed Mon and Tues, ☎ 881 947.

It is a very good, well-lit collection on two floors, mostly from the rich variety of Bulgarian folk costumes, and articles from traditional peasant life. The collection on the upper floor showing a traditional rural wedding is of the greatest interest, and indicates the long survival of primitive customs in peasant society.

The Ethnographic Museum and Gallery of National Art

Even if you do not visit the museum, the excellent souvenir shop on the ground floor is worth a look, as it is one of the best places in the centre of town for quality craft work, especially rugs and jewellery.

200m across the street is the Aeroflot office on the corner. Some 30m to the right of the Aeroflot office is a small marble plaque, commemorating the fact that for many years the building contained the Sofia apartment of James Bourchier, the famous late 19C–early 20C correspondent of *The Times* in Bulgaria, who is buried at Rila Monastery (see p 218). 150m down Krystal Street on the left is the **Egyptian Embassy**.

The **Grand Hotel Bulgaria** is a rather fine gloomy old place that offers cavernous, dusty and slightly sinister rooms with vast armchairs and velvet plush curtains at a reasonable price for a prestige city centre hotel, currently about $US60 a night. There is a night club downstairs that is much used by visiting Greek businessmen. The bar is popular with ex-communist functionaries and is a place for connoisseurs of old party chic.

Opposite is the **Natural History Museum** (open 10.00–17.00 except Mon). This is a rather dull and worthy collection, with all the usual stuffed animals and birds and endless dusty glass cases, but specialists may enjoy seeing the **Mineral Collection of King Ferdinand**, on the lower floor, a tribute to the energy, public spirit and deep knowledge of Bulgarian geology of the late 19C monarch.

Russian Church of St Nicholas

One hundred metres beyond the museum, on the left, is the **Russian Church of St Nicholas**. This is a wonderful, evocative building that should be a priority on any visit to Sofia. The gold-leaf-cased roof and onion-shaped domes, recently restored by the Metropolitan of Moscow, are probably the single most beautiful sight in urban Sofia, best seen on a bright sunny winter's day with a little snow on them. There is an outstanding **choir**, in which the famous Bulgarian bass Boris Christoff used to sing. To hear the liturgy here is to share in the revival of Orthodoxy in eastern Europe that is bringing together the spirituality of the Russian, Greek, and Bulgarian peoples.

The church, consecrated in 1913, was designed by the Moscow architect M. Preobrajensky, in the traditional style of the 17C Moscow cathedrals. It was then part of the old Russian Embassy which stood on this site. Most of the construction work was done by imported Russian craftsmen, who reflected in stone and gold-leaf the perfect proportions and subtle architectural rhythms of the original design. The dark, mysterious interior was painted by Professor Perminov of the Moscow School of Ikonography, and the iconostasis is a masterpiece of rich engraved work, with images of St Nicholas, the church patron, the Holy Virgin, Alexander Nevski and Jesus the Saviour, modelled on the origins in the Cathedral of St Vladimir at Kiev, in the Ukraine.

Archbishop Seraphim of Sofia (1881–1950), who is buried in the church, was a prominent Orthodox theologian and an outstanding leader of the Bulgarian church during the difficult years of the Second World War and the subsequent advent of communism. His white marble grave in the **crypt** has become a place of pilgrimage for many Bulgarian Christians who already regard him as a saint.

In 1994 the Russian Federation Embassy in Sofia started collecting money to pay for restoration work on the golden domes, which was completed in 1996 by Russian and Bulgarian experts. Gold for the work was supplied by the Patriarchate of Moscow. The building has a small formal garden to the rear. Opposite the Russian Church is the **Danish Embassy**, the DHL offices and a good modern art gallery, and the junction with Rakovski Street.

Rakovski Street is one of the most interesting streets in Sofia, and runs right through the city centre (see p 91ff). On the corner opposite the small public park and the Kristal Café is the **Military Club**. This is a grand old late 19C building in the Habsburg style, ochre painted and with an interesting gallery above street level. It used to be a traditional venue for officers' conspiracies, and was at the height of fame and influence in the period immediately prior to the First Balkan War in 1912. It was popular with Mustafa Kemal (**Ataturk**), the founder of modern Turkey, when he was the Sultan's Military Attache in Sofia after the Second Balkan War in 1913. He used the building as a drinking den and as a base from which to chase the ladies of Sofia. They had a poor opinion of his directness, while he had an equally downbeat view of their looks.

Turn left by the side of the Military Club and walk up the slope for about 100m at the edge of a small public park. Here is the Fleamarket, in the section of the park adjoining the House of the Orthodox Patriarch of Bulgaria. On the left is the great Byzantine Cathedral of St Sophia, and the **Eternal Flame Monument** for the fallen of the wars. On the grass by it is a very fine **bronze lion**, the symbol of royal Bulgaria throughout history.

The **Fleamarket** is well worth visiting. On the whole there are more stalls at weekends; Saturday morning is often the best time. If the weather is bad, and in the winter, many stallholders do not appear at all. The market is particularly good for **communist memorabilia**, such as Red Army and Bulgarian medals, items of uniform, and statues of political leaders, but the collectors of classic cameras, watches, clocks, cigarette cases, typewriters, musical instruments, modern weapons, amber jewellery, coins, banknotes, Ottoman swords, pewter, postcards, wood carvings, and modern paintings and ikons, will find much to interest them.

Most dealers are cheerful and fairly straightforward although prices on more expensive items are very negotiable. It is usually slightly cheaper to offer to pay in Deutschmarks or dollars. Some dealers also sell black market caviare; if purchasing, check the date on the tin and also see that the lid is undamaged. The lower stalls near the back of the Military Club specialise in work by modern Bulgarian artists; while quality varies, the average standard is quite high and this is a much better place to buy an interesting memento of a Bulgarian trip than most official souvenir shops.

NB. If buying an ikon that looks at all old, even if it is quite new, it is a good idea to obtain a receipt stating exactly what it is and where it was bought, and from whom, to show the Bulgarian customs officials when you leave the country. **It is also worth bearing in mind that some of the militaria and personal weapons that may be on sale in the market, such as handguns and flick-knives, are illegal in the UK. Camera collectors should beware of fake Leicas, Rolleis and Nikons**.

On the opposite side of the road to the Fleamarket, beyond the Eternal Flame Monument, are the stalls specialising in lace and embroidery. Quality is generally high and this is the best place to buy these goods in Sofia. Prices are usually quoted in leva.

Behind the stalls, in Moskovska Street, is the **Institute of Balkan Studies**, which welcomes academic visitors (contact Dr R. Gradeva).

St Sophia Cathedral

On the opposite side of the thoroughfare from the Patriarchate, and also on Moskovska Street, is St Sophia Cathedral, in my opinion the most moving Christian monument in Bulgaria, with a very long history and deep roots in the ancient world. It is a fairly low, long building, with an unusual external appearance caused by the absence of the normal pattern of church windows, and it has a little of the atmosphere of a fortress. The church is one of the oldest buildings in Bulgaria and has a distinguished, if sometimes chequered and painful, history, mirroring that of Bulgarian Christianity and the Bulgarian nation itself. It is also an archaeological site of major importance.

After a particularly difficult period after the Second World War and in the early communist period, the situation of the building has improved recently and a very extensive overall restoration scheme has started. It is often open, and services are held on Sundays in the single aisle that is not occupied by the builders. This has a temporary floor, a low wooden screen, and temporary wood panelling up to a wall height of about 2m. Rugs are laid on the floor.

History of the cathedral

In the fortifed Roman city of *Serdica*, buildings spread over a wide area from the city centre, west of the modern Presidency to the present George Washington Street. A **theatre** existed on, or near, the present site of the cathedral, in front of the east gate in the city walls. This was constructed late in the 2C AD, probably in 192 under the dissolute Emperor Commodus. At this time the Romanised Thracian Azelius Emilianus was governor of the province of Thrace. When mass persecutions of Christians started, the theatre was used as a site for **savage human sacrifices** of believers, where Christians were thrown to hungry wild animals and eaten alive.

After the Edict of Milan in 313, persecutions stopped and local churches built **martyries** all over the Empire to commemorate the martyred Christians. A small chapel of this type was erected on this site in *Serdica* beside the wall of the old Commodian theatre, the ruins of which were excavated here in 1949, and parts of an ancient pagan necropolis which extended towards the present Sobranje building. A large number of tombs of prominent *Serdica* Christians from the late Empire were also found near the chapel. Painted decoration was found in one of the mid 4C tombs excavated, in the Pompeian style. There are indications that much of the shrine was destroyed during the persecutions of Julian the Apostate (361–63), but it was rebuilt about 20 years later under Emperor Valens.

At this time, probably about 370, the original **shrine** was transformed into a **small church** with three naves, with a narthex, and concealed apse, in the Syrian style. This church was shortlived, and was destroyed in 378 in the great assault on *Serdica* by the Goths, when Valens was killed near *Hadrianopolis*, present-day Edirne, in Turkey. In about 381 Theodosius the Great began the construction of the third church on the site, enlarged to three naves, which again lasted only a few years, until the Goths Uprising of 391, when it was damaged, then totally destroyed by the Huns in 447. The present church was built after the reign of Justinian, in the 6C, along the same lines as its predecessor, and rebuilt during the Second Bulgarian Kingdom, between 1300 and 1400, when it became the seat of a bishop.

After the Ottoman invasion it was converted into a mosque and the interior whitewashed. A *caravanserai* was built nearby, and it became a **Dervish tekke** for a time. The mosque was badly damaged by earthquakes in 1818 and 1858, and was largely abandoned. In 1910 restoration began and St Sophia was reconsecrated.

Most of the interior of the church is full of scaffolding. It is possible on request to gain access to the nave and north aisle. Excavations are currently in progress which have opened up several large holes in the concrete floor, which have revealed an early crypt, part of which can be seen through a deep hole on the south side of the nave. The walls are being completely stripped, mainly to remove accretions and Islamic decoration from the time that it was a mosque. It is a mammoth undertaking, and it is likely to be many years before it is completed.

Vasil Levski

Vasil Levski (1837–73) was one of the most important 19C revolutionaries in Bulgaria. He was born into a craftsman's family in Karlovo, and soon became active in the national struggle against the Turkish oppression, after abandoning an early vocation for the Church. He excelled in underground political organisations, and was instrumental in setting up hundreds of secret revolutionary committees throughout Bulgaria. He was captured by the Turks in 1872, and charged with plotting armed rebellion against the state. Levski was hanged at a gallows on the site of this monument on 6 February 1873.

There is an interesting book in English on Levski's life and significance in Bulgarian history by Mercia MacDermott, *The Apostle of Freedom* (Sofia Press, 1986).

Donations to assist the works are very much welcomed, in any currency—there is a large iron chest for this purpose near the west entrance doors.

Opposite the church is the **residence of the Orthodox Patriarch of Bulgaria**, a large imposing late 19C building (not open to the public). It has very fine patterned stonework, with inlaid mosaic decorations.

Immediately beyond the Patriachate is the **Sobranje**, the building of the Bulgarian Parliament. This is a pleasant unpretentious white stucco building that has something of the atmosphere of the Regency buildings in England. Construction began in 1884, of the central block, but it was not completed until 1928, when the north wing facing Alexander Nevski Square was built. Under communism it was a 'rubber stamp' institution but has now regained its former importance. The entrance is at the rear, security is stringent.

To the left of the Sobranje, across the park, is the **Monument of Vasil Levski**, on a small traffic roundabout at the junction of Vasil Levski Street and Boulevard Janko Sakazov.

Just beyond the monument, at the beginning of Boulevard Janko Sakazov, is the **Slovak Embassy**, in an ugly modern building. The **Greek Orthodox Church** is nearby, in Panaiot Volov Street, behind this embassy. Return towards the Largo.

In the centre of the great open paved area is the **Patriarchal Cathedral of St Alexander Nevski**. It was built to commemorate the 1877–78 War of Liberation and the Russian contribution to victory. It took 42 years to build and was completed in 1924, to the designs of the St Petersburg architect Pomerantsev. As many as 5000 people can be accommodated to hear the Liturgy. Opinions of non-Bulgarians tend to diverge sharply about its visual character and architectural merits. To some, it is a grandiose, heavy and rather pretentious building, with a gloomy and undistinguished

Patriarchal Cathedral of St Alexander Nevski

interior. To others, it is one of the most impressive monuments in Eastern Europe, a symphony of interlocking domes and curved surfaces that perfectly embodies the spirit of the National Revival period and the liberation of the country from the Ottoman Empire. Whatever view you take, it is certainly worth a visit to see the cavernous and dramatic interior.

In the crypt, reached by a set of marble steps through an entrance to the left of the main west door, is the **Ikon Museum. Open** 10.00–17.30 (closed Tues), ☎ 878697. There is a good souvenir shop which sells modern productions of some of the historic ikons, and new ikons, all of which may be exported without special permit.

The ikon museum is of great interest, even to those who normally do not particularly like ikons and it should be included on any visit to Sofia. It contains 200 ikons, including outstanding works of art from all historical periods. *Our Lady of Tenderness* (13C) and the 14C *Nesebur Ikon* are superb examples of Byzantine art, as are the examples of the work of the National Revival master, Zahari Zograph. The crypt has been plastered and painted to make a very fine gallery, with many gently curving arches and, unlike many Bulgarian museums, it is very well lit.

To the rear of the cathedral there is a small park, on the right of which is the **SS Kyril and Methodius Foundation Gallery**, housed in the very large and impressive buildings that were the Royal Printing House. It was completed in 1887. **Open** 10.00–17.00, closed Mon.

This contains some of the most important Western European paintings in Bulgaria, particularly a very good **French Impressionist** section and an outstanding collection of **Indian art and sculpture** on the ground floor. It includes important examples of work from between the 17C and 19C from Orissa, Jain, work of the Pahari School, temple ornamentation from south India, work from Rajastan and Mughal miniatures. There is also a small but high quality collection of Burmese Buddhist art and wood carving, Japanese prints, including work by Hiroshige, and a large display of African wood carvings from Mali, Benin and elsewhere.

The other aspect of the collection that should not be missed is the **Deltcheff Bequest** upstairs, with works by Rouault, Matisse, Renoir, Delacroix and Derain, and many less well-known French 19C and early 20C artists. Most of the upper floors are taken up by a very large exhibition of contemporary Bulgarian art. In the basement there is a good reconstruction of an **early Roman tomb** and church from the 4C found when the building was constructed. It must have been part of an ancient Serdican necropolis.

The building is very Mitteleuropean in atmosphere, and embodies in its architecture the strong links between Bulgaria and the Habsburg world at the time of its construction in the 19C.

The University and the Orlov Bridge area

To the east of the park, about five minutes' walk across it, you come to the imposing and monumental neo-baroque façade of the **University of St Clement of Ohrid**. In the pedestrian area below the roundabout in the road in front of it are some good second-hand book stalls.

History of the University

The University, the first in Bulgaria, was developed in the years after the Liberation, and began to produce an educated elite for the new nation in the last decade of the 19C after the first faculties opened in 1888. Female students were admitted after 1901. It has a grandiose neo-baroque façade that was constructed in 1934, and completed in 1952, but the interior is worth visiting. It can be reached from the narrow alleyway from the street that leads into a central courtyard. There is a large colonnaded vestibule with impressive chandeliers and stained glass windows showing St Clement of Ohrid and other church fathers. There is a very good 19C ikon of St Clement by the central entrance doors. There is a large mosaic floor, and marble steps leading to the upper floors.

Behind the main building is **Shipka Street**, one of the nicest 19C streets in the city centre, with the university drama department and other university buildings occupying the centre of it, opposite a small park. To the right is the **Russian Cultural Centre**, a large glass-fronted modernist building. It is worth visiting for the good shops selling Russian craft goods and to see the **Vostok Spaceship**, which took the famous dog Leika into space in 1963. Nearby are some very fine **19C houses**, now mostly occupied by businesses and embassies.

Walking past the University about 800m down Tsar Osvoboditel Street, the **Turkish Embassy** is on the left, in an impressive 19C mansion, although its appearance is rather spoiled by the very high and formidable security fence around it. After another 250m, turn left up towards Shipka Street for the **Greek Embassy** and **Greek Ambassador's Residence**. This latter is one of the most beautiful 19C buildings of its kind in Sofia, heavily influenced by contemporary French architectural fashions. Both are presently undergoing an extensive restoration to the plan of the recent Greek ambassador to Bulgaria, HE Anastase Sideris, and the blue and white paint is very sympathetic. The doorway of the Residence is particularly impressive, with very fine metalwork and wood carving. A new garden is being laid out. In the interior central hall there is a marble bust from Italy of Lord Byron, dating from about 1840 that was purchased in London in 1995.

Next to the Residence is the headquarters of **Bulgarian Television**, while down a small street by the side of this office block is the **British Council** at 7 Tulovo Street, ☎ 44 33 94/47 33 46.

Opposite the Residence and television offices, there is a jumble of old buildings which used to be a brewery that was built on the site of the original Greek Orthodox Patriachal church in Sofia.

Across the main road is **Orlov Bridge**, named after the eagle sculptures (*orli* in Bulgarian). The huge **Soviet Army War Memorial** towers over the middle of the park. The main road continues to the outskirts of Sofia in the direction of the airport and Plovdiv (132km).

To the British Embassy and the Church of Sveti Sedmochislentsi

If you cross the park by the memorial and turn right, you are back in Blvd Levski. Immediately opposite is the **Iranian Embassy**, an attractive early 20C building. Cross the road here and either walk or take a taxi (about 10 minutes) or bus along Vasil Levski Street.

About five minutes' walk along here to the left, at No. 65, is the **British Embassy**, a depressing and ugly five-storey office building with red and white brickwork. It is said to be a very poor place in which to work.

About five minutes' walk from the British Embassy up Graf Ignatiev Street is the **Church of Sveti Sedmochislentsi** (Church of the Seven Saints), named after the seven famous saints who converted the Slavs to Christianity. This is a very large building indeed, set in a little park to the side of the middle of Graf Ignatiev Street. It was converted into a church after the Liberation, having been the **Black Mosque of Sofia** for hundreds of years under the Ottoman Empire. It was originally built in 1528.

The church is very impressive in its way, but it is difficult not to feel that it may have looked much better as the Black Mosque than it does now, with numerous small marble columns and arches added to the original structure in often haphazard and inappropriate ways, after it became a church in 1901–03. There are similar problems with the interior, where the main nave adopts the mosque prayer room space, but it is very dark and gloomy and it is impossible to see the wall paintings. There are some garish modern fresco paintings on the main entrance arch from the narthex.

Once, it must have been a very fine building indeed and is worth visiting to give an idea of the scale and urban prosperity of early Ottoman Sofia, but apart from the fine original patterned brickwork there is little to admire in its architectural development. It is possible to get a good view of the beauties of the original Islamic structure by walking to the far west end of the surrounding little park, where the interlocking domes are very impressive. The minaret has disappeared. Next to the British Embassy is the very impressive **Residence of the British Ambassador**. This is one of the largest mansions remaining in Sofia, an early 20C house in the grand style.

History of the Ambassador's Residence

Until 1912 the British Legation in Sofia occupied a building a few minutes' walk away from the present premises that is now a corner shop in Graf Ignatiev Street. Prior to 1912 the present Embassy site was a vegetable plot. Construction of a new building started in 1911 and was completed after the Second Balkan War. The first ambassador to occupy it was Sir Henry Bax-Ironside KCMG. The building cost £26,000 to construct including the stables nearby, in 6 September Street. This part of the property was destroyed by Allied bombing in 1944. The current Embassy premises was originally a block of flats built in the interwar period. It was first used as the British Military Mission after the war, then it became the Embassy.

In the gardens, which resemble in atmosphere those of an Oxford or Cambridge college, there is a swimming pool and tennis court. The house was restored between 1993 and 1995.

A little further up Graf Ignatiev Street, you cross **Rakovski Street**, which takes you back to the Russian Church, then the Sheraton. If you walk it takes about half an hour. It is well worth doing so, as Rakovski Street is one of the best shopping streets in the city, with off-licences which specialise in regional wines, and garages, antique shops, gun clubs, banks and government offices.

Rakovski Street is named after Georgi Sava Rakovski (1821–81), one of the early heroes of the 19C nationalist movement, and someone who embodied the close links between Greece and Bulgaria in the anti-Ottoman struggle. He was born in Kotel, on the Plain of Thrace and was educated at Athens University. He was a leader of the Bulgarian Society in Athens. In imitation of the Greeks in Thessaly and Crete, the Society sought to foment risings in Thrace. He was a leader of the later Bulgarian Legion, and fought against the Ottomans for many years.

On the left after about 10 minutes' walk by the old Suzuki garage, you come to an open pedestrianised area outside part of the university. In term time the area is full of new and second-hand book stalls. Most books are in Bulgarian but it is worth looking out for atlases, artbooks and dictionaries in Western European languages, which can be very good value indeed. About 100m beyond the university building is the **National Theatre**, an imposing, well-proportioned building in the Mitteleuropean style. On the right a little further up Rakovski Street is the **Restaurant Budapest**, somewhere to patronise if you enjoy nostalgia for old communist Bulgaria, with rather mediocre, very heavy food but highly atmospheric, gloomy and conspiratorial surroundings.

Some 100m further up the street, to the right in Slavyanska Street, is the **Slavyanska Besseda Hotel**, a redoubtable old Sofia institution with a long and chequered history. It was opened in the 1920s under the name of the Hotel Sofia, then took on its present name in 1940. In the Second World War it was a brothel for German officers from the Military Club (see p 100). After the war it was *de facto* taken over by the Secret Police, the NHD, and was notorious for the degree of surveillance of any visiting foreigners who happened to stay there. Nowadays it is one of the few budget-price hotels in central Sofia, and is recommended, being generally clean and reliable with reasonable security. Most of the staff are friendly and helpful and very loyal to those they remember as regular visitors. Some of your fellow guests can best be described as colourful. On the opposite side of the street is the **Ministry of Finance**, housed in a deeply gloomy and Germanic edifice.

On the corner with Ivan Vasov Street, 250m away, is the **Ivan Vasov Museum**. This is an interesting collection of material about the great 19C Bulgarian novelist Ivan Vasov (1852–1921), author of *The Yoke* (well worth reading to capture the atmosphere in Bulgaria at the time of the Liberation from the Turks). It is housed in an attractive but rather gloomy 19C mansion house. The offices of *Reuters* news agency (Ms Talia Griffiths, ☎ 41 21641, fax 64 80419) are nearby.

Opposite, a little further up the street, is a cinema, and some top of the market clothes and antique shops. At the end of the street is the park on Blvd Tsar Osvoboidtel and the Military Club (see above). To the right there are some fine buildings, such as the **Residence of the Austrian Ambassador**, a grand white painted town house. Opposite is the old Museum of the Bulgarian Communist party. It was ransacked in 1990 and then became a main haunt of homosexuals in central Sofia but is now being restored for commercial use. The fine buildings in front of it were once part of the Royal Palace stables.

Beyond on the street corner is an office of **Balkan Airways**, then a small theatre and the **Grand Hotel**. Like many Sofia hotels, this is expensive for what is really offered, but is a good central place for the business traveller to stay, with helpful staff. There is a good hotel shop selling top quality souvenirs, particularly ikons. Recommended.

In front of the hotel, across from the Sobranje building, is the bronze **equestrian**

statue of Tsar Alexander II of Russia. This is a very impressive monument indeed and is generally considered to be the best equestrian statue in the country.

History of the monument

The foundation stone for the monument was laid in 1901 and it was completed in 1907. The pedestal is granite from Mount Vitosha, and the bronze monument shows the 'Liberator Czar', as he is known by Bulgarians, holding in his hand the declaration of war against Turkey. The pedestal is worth a close look, as it shows some seminal scenes in modern Balkan history, particularly the signature of the treaty of San Stefano in 1878 on the west side.

Next to the hotel is the Mladezhki (Youth) Theatre, with a pretty 19C façade with a balcony.

Return to the junction with Rakovski Street and the Military Club—five minutes' walk.

Continuing up Rakovski Street, with the Flea Market on the right, you walk up a slope. On the left is a small public open space that adjoins the park at the rear of the Military Club, then 200m ahead on the right is the **Opera House**. It was opened in 1909. The opera in Sofia is well worth visiting, although the establishment is short of money, and many Bulgarian musicians now work in the West, but the standard of the singers and productions is high. Immediately in front of it, above the entrance to the Opera café in the basement, is the colossal **bronze statue of Alexander Stamboliiski**. This commemorates the assassination of the internationally famous Bulgarian political leader on this spot in 1923. He was one of the first 'Green' politicians in the world, as leader of the Agrarian Party and saw the future of the Balkans as one of mutually supportive peasant societies. The statue is very powerful and impressive, about twice life size, some 5m high.

Outer Sofia

Generally speaking there is not a great deal to interest the foreign visitor to Sofia outside the historic centre and the inner ring road, but there are a number of places which it may be necessary to use or visit, some of which are listed below.

The Central Railway Station area

Sofia is an important rail terminus and used to be a key station on the Orient Express route from Western Europe to Constantinople and beyond. The train services between the main cities in Bulgaria are reliable and reasonably efficient and are well worth using, particularly in the winter months. See p 30. The **Centralna Gara** (Central Railway Station) is an appalling monstrosity of late communist architecture which was opened in 1973. It is one of the largest examples of modernist reinforced concrete construction in Bulgaria and is vast, dark, depressing and profoundly authoritarian in atmosphere. **Security is poor. Avoid this area at night. Avoid the pedestrian underpasses running from the station at all times**.

Opposite the station is the main park for **long distance coaches** (see p 30) and a **tram terminus**. Behind it is the **Novotel Sofia** (☎ 31261, fax 320011, telex 22051), a modern 16-storey tower block with over 600 rooms. This is not cheap but the rooms are pleasant and warm in winter, and there is a good view from the upper floors. The air conditioning is intrusive. A single room is about $US70 a night. Ask for the 'tourist rate' and pay in dollars only, in an office by the casino. Downstairs there is a variety of shops, car hire offices and a casino. The hotel is a popular meeting place for the Greek business community in Sofia, and a daily coach service runs from the side of the hotel to Thessaloniki, currently at 14.00. There is a well run small hotel **casino**, under British management, with roulette, stud poker and blackjack, for modest stakes. Recommended—though the restaurant is not very good; it is better to eat elsewhere.

The general district near here has many ethnic Greek residents and Greek-run businesses, as it was given for the housing of Greek refugees from the Greek Civil War. Some of the sons and daughters of these people are now prominent in Sofia economic life.

> After the Greek civil war ended in 1949, many thousands of soldiers of the Democratic Army and their families and political supporters left northern Greece and went into exile. About 8000 people settled in Bulgaria between 1949 and 1952, nearly all in Sofia, a few in Plovdiv and Varna. In Sofia, Greek-language schools and cultural institutions were established. The majority of these people returned to Greece after the amnesty for Civil War participants announced after the election of the PASOK government in Greece in 1982.

The Intercontinental Hotel and vicinity

The 5-star **Intercontinental Hotel** was known as the Hotel Vitosha until 1995, when it became part of the international Intercontinental group. Previously Japanese investors were involved in its ownership; the current position is rather unclear. It is a modern tower block up the hill from central Sofia in Boulevard James Bouchier, set back from the main road, with a large car park in front of it. It is a fairly expensive luxury establishment but has excellent facilities for the business traveller, including a modern communications centre. It is popular with visiting Russians and Americans. The staff are efficient and helpful, and it is a good place for residents and non-residents to hire a car. The Panorama restaurant and night club on the top floor have outstanding views of Sofia and Mount Vitosha. A single room is about $US200 a night. **Recommended for business travellers**.

In the vicinity of the hotel there is the headquarters of the 'God Loves Bulgaria' evangelical organisation, in offices a little way down the hill, plus a number of good flower shops and a very good open market in vegetables and fruit over the road. To the south there is a public park which has some good small restaurants. **NB**. Avoid unaccompanied walks in the park and woodlands.

The Hotel Rodina and vicinity

The **Hotel Rodina** (☎ 151631, fax 543225, telex 22200, 24038) is a modern hotel on the outskirts of the city, on the road running south towards Boyana and the southwest of the country. It is cheaper than some similar establishments, with a single room at about $US65 a night, and quite efficient, but some foreign visitors find the atmosphere unsympathetic, with a strong representation of the newer and less respectable type of businessmen and their equally doubtful female companions. The Rodina is particularly popular with visiting Ukrainian *Mafiya* who stand out in the public rooms by the huge size of their personal security staff.

The Rodina downstairs bar is a lively, welcoming and convivial place, with excellent *rakia*. Many of the bar staff can speak foreign languages as they are ex-members of the old security apparat and are well informed and entertaining, particularly about the foibles of the diplomatic corps in Sofia.

The Rodina is very convenient for the long distance bus station in Damien Gruev Street, which runs services to Albania, Turkey, Serbia and FYROM, among other places (see 21). This is about five minutes' walk away; turn left at the Rodina front entrance, then left at the roundabout. The small **Hotel Shipka** next door is a clean, cheaper but slightly noisy alternative.

The Ambassador Hotel and vicinity

The Ambassador Hotel (☎ 962 5602, fax 962 5590) is situated on the outskirts of town, 5km from the city centre, on the way to Mount Vitosha, on Simeonovsko Boulevard. It is expensive, with rooms at about $US180 a night, and is smallish with 72 rooms and a gym, sauna and conference facilities. The restaurant is not cheap, but it is good, specialising in fish. The general area is becoming a fashionable residential location, with new apartment blocks being built on grazing land. The Chinese embassy and a number of other diplomatic missions are about ½ km away, on the Simeonovsko Boulevard.

The Military Museum and the National Palace of Culture

The Military Museum is in General Skobelev Street, about 10 minutes' walk from the British Embassy. It is a rather mediocre and poorly-maintained collection, most of it made up of old communist period equipment kept on open air display. It is not really of much general interest and those with specialised knowledge of militaria are likely to be irritated by the poor condition and inaccessibility of many of the exhibits. In a display of heavy weapons, there are 87mm cannon from the First World War, magnetic mines, various artillery pieces, a Second World War German 'Nebelwurfer' and much similar material.

There is a very fine early 20C building opposite, which is painted ochre, and used for educational purposes.

The large circular modernist building of the **National Palace of Culture (NDK)** near the inner ring road at the end of Fritiof Nansen Street, is a main landmark on the Vitosha side of the city. It is currently used as a conference and business centre, and for the offices of organisations such as the European Union in Sofia. It was originally built as a monument for Ludmilla Zhivkova, archaeologist daughter of the communist leader, who died of a brain tumor in 1979.

On the large pedestrian Plaza in front of it there is a large concrete and metal sculpture, '1300 Years of Bulgaria'. You can walk across the Plaza to the end of Patriarch Evtimii Street, one of the main shopping streets, and the return to the city centre, along Angel Kanchev Street. The cinema on the right-hand side at the south end of this street often shows English-language films.

Sofia Zoo

The zoo was founded in 1888, and is the oldest zoo on the Balkan Peninsula. It is at 1 Sreduna Street (☎ 68 20 43) in the Hladilhika district, on the outskirts of the city, and can be reached by the No. 67 and No. 127 bus. It covers 23 acres, with about 1100 creatures of 244 species. On the whole it is a pleasant old zoo, although some of the facilities for the larger animals need modernisation.

Environs of Sofia

All the places mentioned in this chapter are within 15km of the city centre and, with the exception of the Royal Palace at Vrania, can be reached by public transport, such as the No. 66 bus, which runs from Sofia city centre to Mount Vitosha. If you are going by car, follow the signs for Boyana, off the main road to Pernik, turn left up the hill on the city outskirts, or via the outer ring road, turn right before the Plovdiv road.

The environs of Sofia are much more attractive and interesting than some modern parts of the city itself, and offer a variety of recreational opportunities such as hiking, skiing and visiting historic buildings. There are a few hotels on the outskirts. **Mount Vitosha** dominates the southern edge of the city and suburban villages on its slopes such as **Dragalevtsi** and **Boyana** are favoured residental locations for the diplomatic community and the business elite, as they were for the communist leaders in the past. **Boyana Church** is one of the most important Byzantine monuments in Bulgaria, a UNESCO World Heritage site with outstanding fresco paintings. There are also other important monasteries, commercial enterprises, the **Residence of the President** and academic institutions in the vicinity. The villages are some one of the best places to eat in Bulgaria, with both traditional restaurants with folklore displays and cosmopolitan establishments.

Vrania is the old royal residence, set in very beautiful grounds, and although it is not always easy to gain access to the old Palace buildings, it is an atmospheric and interesting monument to the world of the Bulgarian monarchy in the late 19C.

Mount Vitosha

Mount Vitosha, with its central peak of *Cherni Vrah* (2290m), dominates the Sofia region and is one of the higher ranges of mountains in Bulgaria. It is about 11 miles square, mostly granite rock, and has a damp climate. In antiquity it was known as *Mount Scomius*. The name Vitosha is said to be of Thracian origin, and to mean '*twin peaks*'. It is an outstanding landmark on the central plain, and has always played an important part in the life of the city.

History of Mount Vitosha

In ancient times Thracian tribes settled on the mountain, usually near the numerous springs and water sources. In later antiquity mining began, mostly for copper and gold, which continued until Byzantine times. A fortress near the modern village of Boyana was built in this period by the *voivode* Botko. In the Middle Ages over 40 monasteries and churches existed on Vitosha. Mining resumed in Ottoman times but ceased in the 19C when much of the mountain became seriously deforested, and there was no timber for the mineshafts. It was replanted under the guidance of King Ferdinand in the 1880s and 1890s.

In 1895 Vitosha saw the birth of the **Bulgarian hiking movement** when Aleko Konstantinov led a mass walk from Sofia up to the top of Vitosha that summer. This movement had been predicted by the 19C French travel writer Ami Boué, who wrote, 'I foresee in my soul that when railways are built in Turkey, the members of the Alpine Club and many others will begin creeping up Mount Vitosha'.

The lower slopes are forested with beech while the upper pine forests are dominated by Norway spruce. The upper plateau on top of the mountains is largely covered with peat bogs. The Vitosha range is an important **wildlife reserve**, with hazel grouse and birds of prey in evidence, a very large range of woodland birds, and mammals such as wild cats, red deer and a few brown bears. **Wolves** are said to have returned to Vitosha after a long absence although many local residents are sceptical.

There are many pleasant walks on all parts of the lower slopes of the mountain. Those wishing to walk to the top, which on fine days has **outstanding views** of the Sofia plain, should make for the **Aleko Hut**, named after the founder of the hiking movement. It is directly above the village of Simeonovo. This is best reached by taking the No. 66 bus from the city as far as Hotel Moreni. On the way up, the bus crosses one of the **stone rivers** of Vitosha, a run of large boulders, all of similar size, down the mountainside. It was originally believed that they were glacial moraines, but it now appears that they are naturally occurring phenomena formed by erosion of the Vitosha strata. In antiquity and the Middle Ages some of them were worked for alluvial gold.

■ **Accommodation**. The **Aleko Hut** can be reached on foot from the Hotel Moreni by a well-signed path, or by the ski chair lift. It is possible to stay at the **Hotel Moreni** (☎ 671059), and also the **Hotel Kopitoto** (☎ 575051). The larger Shtastlivetska Hotel is not currently recommended. Apart from the Aleko Hut, there are also various other *hizhi* (hikers' huts), dotted about all over the mountain.

■ **Walking**. Serious hikers should read *A Walker's Companion* by Julian Perry which gives directions for a long Vitosha hike, among other Bulgarian walks.

■ **Skiing**. Mount Vitosha has various skiing facilities, though nowadays used more by Bulgarians than foreigners—it has mostly been dropped from skiing package holidays. Though basic, the facilities do work, and there are a number of runs of varying levels of difficulty. The hotels mentioned above can be used for accommodation in the winter, but they are all in a somewhat problematic state as a result of the privatisation process, at the time of writing, and it is a good idea to get a Bulgarian friend to check up on the actual situation with them before booking.

Boyana

Follow the signs for Boyana from the outer ringway, to the south of the city. Boyana is the most favoured suburb of Sofia, overlooking the city from the north-facing lower slopes of Mount Vitosha—a leafy, wooded refuge from the pressures of life in the capital city. It was a scattering of village houses in the pre-industrial era but grew in prominence with the royal patronage of the area in the late 19C, and the rise of the **diplomatic corps** in the capital. The diplomatic corps has always had a significant and distinct social role in Sofia, by comparison with many Balkan cities: large houses were built in the 1930s to accommodate them. These homes became those of communist party leaders after 1945 after which access to some parts of Boyana was difficult. Many houses have been returned to domestic use. Boyana is known to Sofians as 'The Island', indicating the remoteness of these elites from the struggles of everyday life.

Boyana is the home of the last communist leader of Bulgaria, **Todor Zhivkov**. To see his home where he is currently under house arrest, as he has been for the last few years, take the second turn on the right into Boyana on the right as you reach the village, above the turn for President Avenue. About 1km on the right is a large house surrounded by trees, with a small guard post at the garden entrance.

NB. There are no restrictions about approaching the Zhivkov house, but photography should not be attempted. This applies elsewhere on Vitosha, where most houses are inhabited by spies, foreign arms dealers, various *Mafiya* figures, diplomats and other privileged members of the new *nomenklaturas*, all of whom value their privacy highly. Savage dogs which help protect their homes are a hazard for walkers. It is not a good idea to wander around after dark.

Todor Zhivkov

Todor Zhivkov (1911–) was the last communist leader of Bulgaria. He was born in Pravets, a village not far from Botevgrad, trained as a print worker and joined the communist party in 1932. He was a leading organiser of the defence of Georgi Dimitrov which led to his rise in the party. His power base was always the Sofia region. He married Mara Maleeva, a fellow comrade, in 1938. He was said to be involved in Partisan activities in the Sofia region during the Second World War. He was elected secretary of the party central committee in 1950, and prime minister in 1962. He remained leader until the end of communism in 1989. He was a close friend of the disgraced British media tycoon Robert Maxwell, who produced a sycophantic biographical volume in English in his honour in 1982, the mistitled *Todor Zhivkov—Statesman and Builder of New Bulgaria*. It is now a rare book and much sought after by collectors.

The **President of Bulgaria**, currently Mr Peter Stoyanov, has his **official residence** a little way down the hill from Boyana village (not open to the public). It is a modern building, in what can best be described as the high Stalinist style, with a vast, cavernous interior, enormous Expressionist wall mosaics of scenes from Bulgarian history and huge oak doors and gargantuan chandeliers. The **largest table in Bulgaria** is in the rear reception room. It seemed designed to give a sense of status and importance to the leaders of a small country that was under Russian domination. The building is set in somewhat austere gardens and pine woods, behind a high fence. The external guards, in Bulgarian national dress with pheasant feather hats, are impressive.

About 400m to the south is a **conference centre and residence** that is used by the government for official purposes. It is also a modernist concrete affair, although comfortable and with good views up the hillside towards Mount Vitosha. The architecture is more sophisticated here, with clever use of a series of interlocking slopes on the hill, and extensive use of marble in the interior, and attractive landscaped courtyard gardens. It is often foggy here in autumn and winter, so the diplomatic houses in President Put and other Boyana streets above the presidential complex are lost in a sad grey mist.

Boyana Church

This is a foundation with **frescoes** of the highest quality that have an important place in the development of European art. It is easy to find, turn left from the main road out of Sofia as you enter Boyana, and proceed about 1km and turn right up a steep hill. You come to a small open area, with a famous spring, restaurants, and the church and museum on the left. Near the entrance to the church is an interesting war memorial, with photogravures of IMRO heroes of the Balkan wars.

History of Boyana Church

Boyana Church of St Nicholas was built in 1250 by Sevastokrator Kaloyan, a local feudal lord. It stands just below a medieval fortress which has virtually disappeared. Archaeological research in 1972 indicated a construction date in the 9C. The fortress is mentioned in Byzantine chronicles in 1015. The first frescoes were painted about 1260, and indicate the work of a great master, whose name is unknown. They have a deep humanity and dignity, and although following the formal traditions of Byzantine art, show a new and profound interest in the individual human being.

The church was first properly explored by the early 19C Russian antiquary Grigorovic, and the paintings were analysed by the Bosnian archaeologist Stefan Verkovic in 1876. Their work led to the exhaustive study published by the Czech historian and art critic Constantin Irecek who left detailed descriptions of the frescoes in his *Travels through Bulgaria*.

There were three main stages of building construction, in the 10C, the beginning of the 11C and in the 13C. The original church was a small, almost square cruciform building with a semi-circular apse with one window. This survives as the eastern end of the present building. The façade decoration is dominated by the wolf's tooth motif that was common in the First Bulgarian Kingdom. In the 13C a major extension of the church was built at the west end, with two storeys. The lower storey is a vaulted rectangular room. This extension is known as the **Kaloyan Church**, after the patron, who was a grandson of King Stefan the Holy of Serbia. The original dome seems to have been destroyed in an earthquake in about 1630. The upper storey is reached by a small door in the north wall, up wooden steps. The frescoes show over 240 figures and are a great living gallery of images of medieval Bulgarian life with remarkable naturalistic details about social conditions of the time. The church was made a UNESCO World Heritage monument in 1979. Restoration is in progress at the time of writing. **Open** 10.00–17.00 Sat and Sun. On weekdays it is usually closed, but you can ring 6855 304 to try to join an official party.

The **Boyana museum** is worth visiting if it is open, with good, well-lit displays showing the history of the church and locality, and some items removed from the church such as the 19C iconostasis. There is a good small restaurant on the ground floor. If the church is not open, which is often the case, it is possible to appreciate something of the quality of the frescoes from reproductions in the museum.

It is in a pleasant light airy building, on the right, 250m below the church. There is a gallery for modern art exhibitions on the left, and a Business Club, on the right, of the entrance hall. In the main hall, on the upper floor on the left, is material about medieval Boyana, including a display from the *Historium Compendium* by George Cedreni, a carved iconostasis, with mythical animals, and a copy of Andre Grabor's *L'Eglise de Boiana*, written in 1924, and the first scientific survey of the building. It is meant to be **open** 09.00–12.00 and 12.30–17.00, shut Monday.

Just outside the north wall of the church, under a plain granite slab, is the **Grave of Queen Eleonora**. This was vandalised in communist times, but was restored in 1994–95, and is a frequent place of pilgrimage.

There is also a modern church in the village, a rather run-down, late 19C building, austere, with grey oblong walls and a small white bell tower. It is surrounded by fir trees. There are excellent cold water springs nearby.

The good quality reproductions of the wall painting show what the catalogue describes accurately as their 'cool emotionality', and the sense of understanding pain and suffering underlying the artists perceptions.

To reach Dragelevtsi, take the road from Boyana back towards Sofia and follow signs.

Dragalevtsi

Dragalevtsi is the more accessible and useful of the two villages for the foreign visitor and has a more relaxed atmosphere and fewer security problems than Boyana. Above the village on the way to Aleko are very fine beech woods.

There are numerous **restaurants** dotted around the village, and also small **hotels** and people offering bed and breakfast for the tourist. It is a good place to stay if you do not wish, or need, to be in central Sofia, with a pleasant general environment and very good walking and skiing nearby. Transport is important, though; the buses are not always very reliable and the journey to the centre of the city can take over half an hour. Taxis can be few and far between.

The village is the site of **Dragalevtsi Monastery**, the oldest monastery in Bulgaria, now occupied by nuns. It was often used as a place of refuge by the 19C revolutionary Vasil Levski. Set deep in old deciduous woodland, it is a remarkable, evocative old building that should be included on any visit to Sofia. There are very pleasant walks in the vicinity. In winter there is often deep snow on the road here, and chains on tyres are needed.

History of Dragalevtsi

The area around the modern village has been inhabited since antiquity and benefited from urban growth in the Byzantine era. The monastery was built in the time of Tsar Alexander, between 1331 and 1371. It is thought that most of the original buildings were burnt down during the Turkish conquest, and only the church remains. In the late 19C, the village grew somewhat as a fashionable place for a summer house, and under communism benefited from the opening of the National Film Studio on the outskirts.

The **monastery** is a wonderful, dreamy, atmospheric building. Although it is within 30 minutes' journey from the centre of Sofia, it manages to capture the central elements of Bulgarian monasticism, and conveys to the visitor the spiritual power and historical resonances of these buildings and their denizens. On the left, as you approach , is a modern accommodation building for the nuns, perfectly framed by trees and hidden deep in the mountain valley. The church is a low single-storey building, undergoing restoration, with the original very small Byzantine building enclosed by scaffolding. It is possible to see the interior, on request. It is a tiny barrel-vaulted chamber, with very serious subsidence and deep cracks in the walls, which are in process of repair.

About a kilometre outside the central village is the **Millers Inn**. This is an old mill converted into a restaurant which was a set-piece tourist attraction in the communist era. It remains an interesting place for an evening meal, with very traditional Bulgarian food and **folk dancing**, of high quality. It is a good place for bread made with yoghourt, the special 'flaming stew' and somewhere to reflect on the essential Central Asian origins of the Bulgarian people. Prices are very reasonable.

The Royal Palace at Vrania

Vrania is a small settlement about 5km east from the centre of Sofia on the road towards Sopot and Kazanlak. The Royal Palace is situated in dense woodland lying back from the road on the left. Access is difficult, and help from Bulgarian friends is generally needed to persuade the state officials and police to admit foreigners to the grounds. It is well worth trying, as the buildings are deeply redolent of the early days of national independence in the late 19C and early 20C in Bulgaria, when the country was directly governed by the monarchy. The surrounding woods and park are very attractive landscaped areas with some traditional wooden farm buildings.

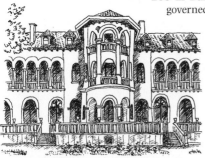

Request permission from the police to enter at the main gate, after driving about half a kilometere into the grounds from the main Sofia–Plovdiv road. There are no signs; the royal palace is set in the first deep forest to the left of the main road after you have left the city. There is then a straight drive of the same length

Royal Palace of King Ferdinand

towards the palace. Near the palace, on the right, there is a very attractive **traditional wooden farm building**, an example of King Ferdinand's fondness for the picturesque in landscaping.

The Royal Palace is an imposing, rather heavy grey building, with a massive central front entrance up a double staircase, and a high, partly turreted roof. It has the style and ambience of some minor German princeling's house of the late 19C. The interior is not open to the public but appears to be in a rather poor condition. There is extensive water penetration in some parts of the building. The atmosphere is melancholy, expressive of the chequered history of the Bulgarian royal family. For a time after the communist takeover the royal buildings were used as a residence for the party leader Georgi Dimitrov (see p 98) and then as an hotel for important foreign visitors and a conference centre, but the Palace was not used much after 1975. On the south end there is a charming traditional **National Revival house**, built of wood, which is in process of restoration.

The **royal grounds** are very attractive, with some parts left as wild woodland gardens containing a large number of native plants, a *Jardin Anglais*, and a pretty landscaped area around a small **lake**. In the German manner, there are a number of very fine specimen trees. There is a picturesque wooden hut by the lake, expressive of the romanticisation of the traditions of Bulgarian peasant life that the late 19C monarchy encouraged. About 300m from the lake, in an open field, there is a very small concrete structure, about 1m x 3m, with a makeshift corrugated iron roof. This is above the **Grave of King Boris III**. It is a moving, sad, little edifice, set in long grass and wild flowers.

Boris III

Boris III (1894–1943) was King of Bulgaria during times of great difficulty for the nation, and many aspects of his career and policies remain highly controversial, even in royalist circles. A central issue has always been the nature of his relationship with Nazi Germany and the Axis powers. His supporters have claimed that his policies of accommodation with Germany kept Bulgaria out of the worst of the Second World War, while his detractors believe he was a traitor, collaborator and enemy of democracy. This view has always been strongly held by the Bulgarian communists, but Boris was also execrated on the political Right by supporters of the Internal Macedonian Revolutionary Organisation which blamed the royalist state apparatus for many of the deaths of IMRO activists during the bloody conflicts in the organisation in the 1930s. For an expert and dispassionate account of this period see *A Short History of Modern Bulgaria* by Richard Crampton. Also worth reading is *Boris III of Bulgaria, Toiler, Citizen, King* by Pashanko Dimitroff, for a pro-royalist position. For the repression of IMRO in the early 1930s see *Terror in the Balkans* by Albert Londres.

King Boris's grandson, Simeon, made a well-received return visit to Bulgaria in the summer of 1996. He currently lives abroad, but takes an active and committed interest in the progress of the country. There is widespread political debate in Bulgaria about whether he should return as a constitutional monarch.

The Dragoman Pass, Vidin and the Northwest

- **By car**: From Sofia, to the Serbian border at Kalotina, 55km. From Sofia to Vidin, via Belogradchik, and the Petrohan Pass, about 180km, depending on exact route taken. Via Vratsa, and the Iskar Gorge, about 50km longer. All routes are basically on good wide asphalt roads, but can be very difficult in winter.

- **By train**: Sofia–Vidin, about 4 hours, from Sofia main railway station. Trains also go direct to Lom.

- **By coach**. Coaches leave from the park by the Novotel.

The northwest of Bulgaria is one of the least visited parts of the country, even by Bulgarians, and is very unjustly neglected. The historic Danube town of **Vidin** has very well preserved 19C buildings, left from the time when it was an important stop on the downriver route from **Vienna** to **Ruse**, and a remarkable **medieval Bulgarian** and **Ottoman fortress**. There is a large number of Roman, medieval Bulgarian and Turkish military edifices in the northwest, such as the fort at **Lom**, and the outstanding and dramatic Ottoman fortress at **Belogradchik**. The northwest played an important part in the revolution of 1923, and in general has a strong **socialist tradition**. Many families have relatives over the border in **Serbia**.

It is possible to reach any of these places from Sofia in a day's drive, and this chapter is planned and written on that basis, although it is better to stay in Vidin and elsewhere in the region. In the winter, it is advisable to do so, as snowfall can be heavy in the northwest and plenty of time should be allowed for journeys. Train travel and the use of local taxis is preferable in the winter.

In the past, the northwest was very much a Balkan through route, between Yugoslavia and Bulgaria, but although the frontier is open at the **Dragoman Pass** and there are no difficulties in using it, you must have the correct documents, and in practice there is often little traffic. The end of most UN sanctions against Serbia has not yet brought about a restoration of previous trade and travel patterns. If you wish to cross the border to Serbia you must obtain a visa from the Yugoslav Embassy in your country of residence before leaving (see p 19). Visas are not obtainable at the border.

- **Recommended road routes**. There are three main routes north from Sofia to the northwest. **NB**. If using the Petrohan Pass in winter, take advice on the state of the road and weather before leaving, as it rises to over 1500m and conditions can be anything from difficult to absolutely impossible after snowfall.

Sofia to the Dragoman Pass and Serbia

This journey (55km) takes about an hour, on a very good road, that is generally passable in all but the very worst winter conditions, and snowploughs are operative then.

■ **By train**. The international express between Sofia and Belgrade stops at Kalotina station, on the Bulgarian side of the border, and it is possible to get on and off there. Although a very beautiful journey, particularly through the Dragoman Pass in Bulgaria and in the Morava valley in south Serbia, it can be very cold indeed in winter—take warm clothes and food, drink and cigarettes. It is worth paying the modest extra charge for a first class ticket.

■ **By coach**. The international coach between Sofia and Belgrade also stops at the border.

■ **Taxis and car hire**. Although it is possible to hire a car in Vidin, and other towns have some taxis for local journeys, bear in mind that this is one of the poorest parts of the country and it is much easier to find a reliable vehicle in Sofia before departure. Petrol stations are fairly few and far between in some places; keep tanks reasonably full or carry an emergency supply. When travelling outside towns, supplies and a full tool and spares kit are advisable. It is a good idea to travel with a companion in what is often lonely and depopulated country.

Leave Sofia by the northwest main road, making for the Central Railway Station but turning left onto the inner ring road before you reach it and following signs for **Beograd**. The road leaves the city through industrial suburbs and crosses the Sofia Plain. On the outskirts of the city is the desperately poor **Roma** suburb of Filipovitsi. In 1963 the British traveller Lesley Branch attended a wedding here. She saw

> 'a long, wide unpaved street lined with little shacks, fenced with broken down palings, over which rather seedy vines trailed...the entire population seemed to live outside, cooking on braziers, or lolling on rags, or on broken iron bedsteads, set under the stumpy acacia trees.
>
> 'They were dancing a *horo* outside no. 27, spinning round, shrieking, their bare blackened feet kicking up clouds of dust. They all crowded round, very friendly, almost menacing in their advances.'

On the left, after 6km, there is a turn for **Bankja**, a small hydrotherapy and thermal centre.

After 30km, **Slivnica** (Slav for 'river junction'), where the countryside begins to change to pleasant rolling upland grazing land, with occasional flocks of sheep among the brambles and scrub.

History of Slivnica

A small Roman settlement, *Alkalija*, was established here, then a minor Ottoman administrative centre. In 1886 an important battle between Bulgarian troops and the forces of King Milan of Serbia was fought at Slivnica. The Serbs were attempting to prevent the union of the two

Bulgarian states that was later embodied in the Treaty of Bucharest. The area was developed for small-scale coal mining and quarrying under communism.

The climate is dry, with snow often providing most of the precipitation, and agriculture suffers accordingly. Most of the rural northeast is very depopulated, and some villages are inhabited only by elderly people. It remains to be seen what their future will be in the long term.

After 42km, the road climbs across bare low hills, with the town of **Dragoman** appearing on the left, an exposed upland settlement. 2km further on, the road enters the **Dragoman Pass**, with its fine scenery. The road goes on through a wild narrow wooded gorge of the Nisava river to Kalotina and the border with **Serbia**, 8km. The Dragoman Pass takes its name from the Turkish word for a travel guide/interpreter, who used to be retained here on arrival in Ottoman Bulgaria. There are many amusing accounts of English travellers relationships with their dragomen in 19C travel literature.

In 1959 Anton Zischka noticed that only eight cars a day passed through Dragoman, and that 'it is not more than an hour's journey from Sofia, but the road has a frightening effect, passing along, as it does, beside dark and almost perpendicular mountainsides. The telegraph wires hum and you can now and then hear the cry of a bird. But nothing else interupts the loneliness of this frontier region, which was for so long the scene of fighting that nobody has ever dared to settle in it.' The area was the focus of Eric Williams' novel of espionage and conspiracy in 1950s Bulgaria, *Dragoman Pass*.

In Ottoman times the area was notorious for banditry and wolves, and in the 19C was a centre of Haiduk attacks on the Turkish occupiers. During the Croatian and Bosnian wars, 1991–95, it was a focus of sanctions-busting activities, smuggled petrol in particular.

The border with Serbia is reached at **Kalotina**, where there is an old Byzantine church. Beyond Kalotina is **Berendi**, with another church with very good frescoes.

Many ethnic Bulgarians live over the border, particularly in and around the town of Pirot, in south Serbia, and as far up the Morava valley as Nis. In 1996 they were recognised as a national minority within the new Federal Republic of Yugoslavia. There is some outstanding scenery on the Serbian side of the Vidlic mountains, the Morava Gorge in particular.

Nis (ancient *Naissus*) is an important Serbian city with efficient transport links to Belgrade and FYROM, and some wonderful Roman and Ottoman monuments. It was the birthplace of the Emperor Constantine the Great. Nis used to be a strong centre of support for President Slobodan Milosevic of Serbia, until November 1996, when his town boss in Nis, Milo Illic, was overthrown.

Sofia to Vidin via the Iskar Gorge

This is the better all-weather route to Vidin although the winter weather can cause serious difficulties in the **Iskar Gorge** section. The road has a particular resonance for British visitors to Bulgaria, as it passes near the village of **Batulija** and **Thompson Railway Station**, named after Major Frank Thompson, a hero of the Special Operations Executive in World War II, who died here while fighting with the Bulgarian partisans.

The scenery of the **Iskar Gorge** is very impressive. The Iskar river is the only Danube tributary which flows north through the central mountains, and a very deep gorge has been made in the limestone as a result, hundreds of metres deep in places. On the way you pass through **Vratsa**, an historic town and industrial centre with medieval buildings and a good museum.

■ **Public transport**. The Iskar Gorge carries the main **rail line** north from Sofia towards the Danube and the north, and it is possible to reach many of the places mentioned in this itinerary by rail. **Coach services** to the northwest towns do run, but are rather intermittent to many places, and the train is often a better bet, particularly in winter.

Leave Sofia by the main road north, via the suburb of Novi Iskar, on the outer ring road. You drive across the fairly flat land of the Sofia Plain for a short time, and then go into more wooded and hilly country with the Mala hills on the left. The road runs close to the railway line up a rather gloomy wooded valley. After 24km, Batulija.

Batulija

Batulija is a rather glum and nondescript little place, very hot in summer and lost in grey mists in autumn and winter, with a small railway station named after the British resistance hero, Major Frank Thompson. The **station** is worth visiting, below a large old-fashioned coal depot, as there is a moving little bronze monument to Thompson on the booking office wall; he is portrayed smoking his pipe. The railway winds northwards up the steep valley.

History
Major Frank Thompson (1920–44) was the brother of **E.P. Thompson**, the prominent historian of the British labour movement. He was a brilliant Classics student at Winchester College and at Oxford University where he was a very close friend of the philosopher and novelist **Iris Murdoch**. He joined the communist party as a result of activity in support of the Spanish Republican cause in the Spanish Civil War. Thompson volunteered for military service early in the Second World War, and took part in Allied activities in Italy before joining the **Special Operations Executive** and becoming a British Liaison Officer attached to the Bulgarian Partisans in April 1944. He was taken prisoner on 24 May of that year, after his *ceta*, his partisan group, was betrayed by a Bulgarian peasant informer, and Thompson was shot with some of his Bulgarian comrades three days later, the German occupiers taking the view that as someone attached to irregular forces, Thompson should be regarded as a spy and therefore not entitled to treatment according to the Geneva Conventions.

A useful volume about Frank Thompson and the final events in his life was published in Sofia in 1979, *Grateful Bulgaria* by Slavcho Trunski, also *There is a Spirit in Europe* (Gollancz, London, 1947). A general picture of SOE in Bulgaria is given by Stowers Johnson, in *Agents Extraordinary*. A commemoration ceremony on the 50th anniversary of Thompson's death was held in June 1994, organised by the British Embassy in Sofia.

The **monument** to the Thompson *ceta* is 2km off the main road—follow the road to the east, climbing slightly. It consists of a concrete edifice, a platform with two curved walls, about 6m high. There is an upper section, surrounded by rose bushes, and an underground chamber, with the names of all the Partisans killed by the Germans on the wall. The monument is in a neglected condition and subject to some vandalism. In view of the fact that this is the only British World War II monument of its kind in Bulgaria, urgent restoration work for an important war memorial would be highly desirable.

The Iskar Gorge

About 10km north of Batulija, the road enters the gorge of the river Iskar, and it narrows and winds through the gorge, clinging to the side of the rocky slope with endless hairpin bends. The route was an important thoroughfare in ancient and medieval Bulgaria and has seen many important military actions throughout history. The gorge was much admired by 19C travellers with a liking for the picturesque, Isambert noting in 1881 that it compared with '*les plus belles horreurs de la Suisse et de la Savoie*'. There are many pleasant walks along the gorge although local accommodation is difficult to find. The road through the gorge runs for about 30km, then drops down to **Mezdra** (93km). 15km south of Mezdra is **Cherepish Monastery**, a charming tiny foundation. There was once a much larger monastery on the site, which was destroyed during the Ottoman conquest. The black and white buildings with great slate tiled roofs hide below the cliffs of the gorge. Most of the surrounding buildings were constructed in the late 19C when the monastery was prosperous. Travellers by rail wishing to see the monastery should get off the train at Zverino station.

Mezdra is a minor provincial centre on the road north, with a very poor hotel, not recommended unless you really have to have somewhere to stay if exploring this part of the Iskar Gorge. It was a village before the railway was built in the 19C. Vratsa is only 17km north, and is a much more civilised and interesting place with decent amenities.

32km south of Mezdra, on the road which meets the main Varna–Sofia motorway at Plavets, is **Botevgrad**. This used to be quite an important Ottoman market town, and had some industrial importance in communist times, but has fallen on hard times. It is not worth visiting except as a stopping point on the road south to the motorway.

Follow the main road 17km to Vratsa.

Vratsa

Vratsa is a regional centre and an interesting historic town worth a short visit. It nestles in a hollow on the very southernmost edge of the Danube Plain below the Vracanska mountains. Many of the pastoralists who live near the town are of Vlach descent. It has an important **museum**.

History of Vratsa

The area was important in ancient Thrace, coming under the Triballi kingdom. Royal burial tombs were found in 1965. Under the Romans there was probably a very small settlement on the site. In medieval times a village called *Zgorigrad* occupied the present site of the town. It was totally destroyed in the Turkish invasions, and a new village was built at the beginning of the 15C. The Turks built a fortress at a place called *Kaleto* nearby. Originally it was an almost entirely Turkish settlement, but Bulgarians moved there in the 16C and 17C. In 1829 the town was a base for the Russian general Kisseleff in the battles against the Turks. *Vratsa* played an important part in this and other patriotic movements, and the patriot and guerilla leader Hristo Botev was killed nearby, in May 1876, fighting with his *ceta* southeast of the town on Mount Okolcica. In the late 19C it was a well-known centre for wool production and manufacturing, with goods exported as far away as Athens and Marseilles.

Drive to the town centre through the usual industrial outer suburbs. All the places of interest are in or near the main square, at the far side of which is a fortress, known locally as the **Sahatnata-koula**, the Clock Tower.

This is a very evocative, brutal-looking tower, set near the steep limestone cliff at the edge of the central square. The visible structure probably dates from the early 16C, when the town was growing fast as a regional centre after the Ottoman invasions. It is 17m high and 9m square. There is a monument to Hristo Botev. On the far side of the square, below limestone rocks, is another small **tower**, of unknown date.

A short walk away on the far side of the square is **Vratsa Museum**. This is a pleasant modern building that suffers the usual current neglect of provincial museums, which it does not deserve as it gives a good picture of the history of the region. The main interest is material from the **Thracian tombs** of Vratsa, which was discovered in 1965 near the town centre. This was one of the most important discoveries illustrating the history of ancient Thrace. Excavations continued until 1969, and revealed the burial of a prince, a princess who was almost certainly ritually murdered, slaves and various artefacts. These include a chariot, two horse skeletons and remarkable jewellery. The chariot on display is the oldest so far discovered in Bulgaria, with the skeletons of ritually slaughtered horses. The tomb provided conclusive proof of **Herodotus's** descriptions of the ritual sacrifice of a favourite wife among the Thracian rulers. The burial dates from the 4C BC, and also contained some Greek artefacts.

Some of this material is on display in Vratsa, although not the bridal wreath and some other outstanding items which are currently in Sofia. The displays give an evocative picture of the ancient Thracian world, and it is a great pity that museums of this quality in provincial Bulgaria are so little visited.

Vratsa is a good centre for **walking excursions**, and there are many caves in the vicinity. The most spectacular is the **Ledenika cave**, 15km to the east, up a narrow road from Vratsa.

The main road continues 40km northwest towards Montana. About 8km along the way, you will notice the road suddenly becomes very wide indeed across a flat plain. These road widenings, which are not uncommon throughout Bulgaria, were designed to allow Warsaw Pact aircraft to land throughout the country in the event of a NATO invasion.

Montana

Montana (Communist period name, *Mihajlovgrad*; Royalist period name *Ferdinand*) is a very dull, run-down and grey, middle-sized concrete town with few cafés or decent shops. It has, however, been very important in two historical epochs, the Roman period, when it was the site of the **Temple of Apollo and Diana**, the most important cult centre in this part of Bulgaria, and as a centre of communist support and rebellion in the post-1918 period. The **1923 Rising** started here.

There is little from either period to see now, except the foundations of part of the temple in the old fortress area near the river, and numerous monuments connected with the Rising. The **Museum of the Rising** is currently closed, and some of the communist period monuments to it have been vandalised.

History of Montana

The town has been inhabited since Thracian times, when a cult grew up around the spring issuing from the base of the fortress hill. The site was developed after the Roman invasion as a roadside centre along the road linking *Marcianopolis* with the *Naissus* highway. By 162 it had achieved the status of a *Municipium*. Fortifications were constructed in the middle of the 3C and remained functional for the next 300 years. The temple was excavated in 1915, and numerous remains of votive offerings to Diana and Apollo found. It was probably destroyed by the Slav invaders in the 5C.

In medieval and Ottoman times a small regional market town grew on the site, called *Kutlovitsa*, and there was some early industrial development. In 1891 it was renamed *Ferdinand*, after the reigning monarch. The workers in the region were mostly strong supporters of the Agrarian Party, and rose under the leadership of Hristo Mihailov against the right-wing Tsankov government which had overthrown the Agrarian government. The rising was put down with great brutality, with tens of thousand of people in the northwest being killed, and the population levels of many villages in the region have never reached their pre-1923 population levels since. Mihailov went on to become a communist leader and was killed by the Germans in the battle for Sofia at the end of the Second World War.

The town was elevated in importance by the communists, who made it the capital of an *oblast*, an administrative region, and a centre of the food manufacturing industry. In the post-1989 period it has declined, and unemployment is high.

Chiprovci

30km west of Montana is Chiprovci, a picturesque mountain village best known for rugmaking, with a very severe winter climate. It is reached by a left turn from the main road going north to Vidin, about 6km out of the town, then along reasonable minor roads. It is an interesting excursion in its own right, best attempted in spring or summer when the **wild flowers** in the mountain meadows are outstanding.

Apart from the scenery, and rugs, Chiprovci is best known for its **Monastery of St John of Rila**, which is about 6km north of the village itself, in a secluded mountain setting, and is unusual in Bulgaria for originally being a Catholic foundation. It is a poetic, pastoral place that is close to the hearts of Bulgarians as the home of the 1688 rising against the Turks, the leaders of which are buried here. A small river runs around the monastery, which possesses a famous Bible presented by a Russian tsar which is said to work miracles for the sick; a sign of the close links with Russian monasteries that have always been maintained here after Orthodox monks moved onto the site at the end of the 17C. The monastic buildings date from the early 18C, rather dull rectangular constructions, but the 16C **church** and ossuary in the interior courtyard are very fine. The church is a single nave oblong building with a low roof and a simple whitewashed interior.

45km north of Montana, the direct road north meets the **Danube** at Lom.

Lom

Lom is nowadays a rather dismal and very run-down Danube town, and is not worth a special visit, but it was important in Roman times when its fort was a significant element in the post-Trajan defences of the Empire. It grew in industrial importance in the 20C as a main Danube railhead for Sofia, although that role has declined in importance with the reduction of Danube trade, and, in the last few years, United Nations sanctions against Serbia. Coal and iron ore for the Sofia steelworks are important commodities. It has a good open air street market in the summer. The mild climate is good for melon growing and early vegetables.

There is a hotel, the Hotel Danube by the river, which can be used *in extremis*. The town museum is said to display some interesting Bronze Age material but is currently closed.

History of Lom

The Romans built a fort at Lom and called the little garrison town that grew up round it *Almus*. Little is known in detail about the settlement, except that like Montana, it was known for the cult of Diana the Huntress. In medieval times there was a small fishing community here, and the Turks made a small administrative centre. In the 19C the town grew as an industrial port on the river.

There is little to see in the town, except a small and very badly neglected site with remains of foundations of Roman urban buildings. Another reason to give the town a wide berth is that it is the nearest town of any size to the nuclear power station at **Kozloduj**, 39km to the west along the Danube. This plant has been plagued by technical and operational problems for many years, and is currently the subject of a major EU-funded safety scheme. It cannot be shut down as it provides a large proportion (about 35 per cent) of Bulgaria's electricity. **Avoid**.

If you have taken this detour, follow the road to Vidin along the bank of the Danube (47km).

Sofia to Vidin via the Petrohan Pass and Berkovitsa

The **Petrohan Pass** route is the most scenic route north, and it is the way to the historic but sad and lonely town of **Berkovitsa** and the magnificent **Ottoman fortress of Belogradchik**. You climb over the *Hemus* range of Classical times, through remote and deserted beech forests to Berkovitsa. The road is generally fair to good asphalt but care is needed on the numerous hairpin bends. Note winter weather warnings above.

If taking the Petrohan route from Sofia direct, Berkovitsa is 73km from the capital.

Berkovitsa

Berkovitsa, is an interesting small historic town near the magnificent peak of **Mount Kom** (2016m) and the border with Serbia. It was much more important in the 19C than it is now and has some very good buildings from that period. The town captures the difficult and poverty-stricken present of post-communist Bulgaria more than any other, with the lonely beauty of its surroundings—although it is often very cold in winter—and sense of loss of what many older Bulgarians still see as an ordered and worthwhile society with positive human values. There is some very fine walking country in the vicinity.

■ The **Hotel Mramor** in the centre of town can provide basic accommodation. There are virtually no restaurants and it is best to try to eat there, or to take your own food. It is possible to buy fish and stuffed peppers from local people, who are very welcoming to visitors. The local strawberry wine is famous.

There is a very pleasant drive up Mount Kom from a track to the east of the town, with wonderful views to the east from the lonely beech forests.

History of Berkovitsa

Although traces of minor Thracian and Roman settlement have been found in the vicinity, Berkovitsa was only a small rural community in Byzantine times. It became a Turkish administrative centre of some importance, so that by the mid-19C it had a population of about 15,000 people, about half of them Turks. In this growth trading relationships with the rich *vilayets* of south Serbia and Macedonia were important, and modern borders and ideological conflicts have not helped the economy of this part of Bulgaria. Under communism Berkovitsa was used for training Democratic Army recruits in the Greek Civil War, and later, star athletes and weightlifters.

The town is centred around a long oblong pedestrianised area, at the far end of which is a **clock tower**, an attractive Ottoman building built in 1762. There is a very fine **view** of Mount Kom to the west, a magnificent brooding presence on the border with **Serbia**. It has been compared, justifiably, to the presence of the Matterhorn above Zermatt.

Most of the interesting churches and houses in Berkovitsa lie beyond the clock tower. An exception is the **Church of St Nicholas** which has very fine wood carvings in local style, birds of prey in particular, on the iconostasis, and a small bell tower. It is to the south of the main square, in an open grassy area, with a long, rather strange glass-windowed cloister along the north wall.

In the Turkish quarter there are many fine traditional houses, usually large low buildings with high garden walls and red tiled roofs. The writer Ivan Vasov lived for two years in this part of the town, recovering from tuberculosis. His near-miraculous return to health gave the town its reputation as a health centre. The **Church of Sveta Bogoroditsa** is an outstanding sunken building, unfortunately often closed, with a Zograph ikon, and a very pretty surrounding garden.

Drive on to Montana (24km), then travel northwest on the Vidin road (52km), then take signed left turn to Belogradchik (another 10km along a minor road). The main road crosses empty, open farming country, with some deciduous woodland. It follows the route of the old Roman road to *Ratiaria* (see below).

Belogradchik

Belogradchik is nowadays a rather nondescript little settlement in a lonely and depopulated part of the country near the border with Serbia, but it is well worth a special journey to visit the great **Ottoman fortress** which is undoubtedly one of the best-preserved and most remarkable examples of Turkish military architecture in the Balkans. It is built on a spectacular natural site, incorporating extraordinary **natural rock formations** on top of a hill. To the northwest there are stupendous **views** of the landscape of the **Sveti Nikolska Mountains** and the **wilds of southeast Serbia**. It is best appreciated on an autumn afternoon, where the combination of the autumn colours in the woods, the fortress, and the vast and elemental landscape to the north and east, create a landscape of breathtaking scale and magnificence. It was described by a French writer in 1933 as a '*région de falaises découpees, de rocs érodés, de rochers striés aux formes bizarres de monstres antediluviens*', after being originally first properly described in Western literature by Blanqui in 1841.

■ The spartan but clean 2-star **Hotel Belogradchishkite Skali** is in the centre of the town, in the main street. It is cold in winter; take a sleeping bag.

Follow the road into the modern village and drive to the top of the village, up hairpin bends through houses set in pine woods on the steep hillsides. Park in the central square near a small church, and the National Bank building. It is possible to walk directly from here onto the rock formations, and up to the Citadel, past a monument to Todor Titorenov (1881–1923) and to enjoy the stupendous views, on a scale in the Balkans that can perhaps best be compared to vistas in northern Albania and Montenegro. It is a place that can diminish human concerns, in a landcape stretching to infinity.

On the right there is a **mosque**, a small squat building with a minaret faced with cement. There is an oblong prayer hall and double windows covered with wooden latticework. The interior is in very poor condition. There are fragments of what appear to be Byzantine masonry in the garden. It was the mosque for the Turkish garrison of the *kale*.

The **citadel** is entered through a very attractive small Turkish gatehouse.

History of the citadel

The name of the fortress comes from a Slav root, the same as that of Belgrade, '*white town*'. The origins of the fort lie in the Roman period, and some remains have been found from the First Bulgarian Kingdom. In Roman times the importance of the fortress diminished as settled urban life was established in the Danube provinces, and most of the visible remains date from the Ottoman period, when the fort was developed as a military strongpoint dominating the routes between Serbia and northwest Bulgaria. This structure was completed in 1837, and consists of an outer bailey wall and associated earthworks, and the development of a central strong-point using the remarkable natural rock formations. The fortress and surrounding region were important for the bandit *cetas* in the fight against the Turks, and in 1850 a large number of Bulgarians were executed here.

Follow the minor road back to the main road, then 39km to Vidin. After 10km, it is possible to make a detour to the right at Dimovo to meet the Danube at the small town of **Archar**, the site of ancient *Ratiaria*.

History of Archar

Ratiaria was an ancient town, originally founded by the Celts in the 3C BC. In Roman times it was an important centre and harbour for the Danube fleet. It was the terminus of the road that led to *Naissus*, modern Nis, in Serbia, and was the capital of the province of Upper Moesia. In 29BC it was described as 'strongly fortified', when Crassus campaigned in the region. In Imperial times it became a centre of munitions manufacture. *Ratiaria* was destroyed by Attila the Hun in 447, rebuilt by Justinian and totally destroyed by the Avars in 576.

The Roman settlement was centred on the modern hamlet of **Turska Mahala**, where some remains are visible on a small hill, including the foundations of an aqueduct, a road going in the direction of Vidin, and a partly excavated necropolis.

Follow the riverside road to Vidin (18km).

Vidin

■ **Hotel**. Much the best place to stay is the **Hotel Bononia**, near the river, east of the main square, old fashioned but well run and very friendly, with a reasonable restaurant serving standard Bulgarian dinners.

■ **Restaurants**. There are plenty of pizza and burger bars, and some good cafés, in and around the main square. Most restaurants only seem to open in the early evenings; picnic lunches may be necessary.

■ **River ferries**. For up-to-date information, ask at the Danube river services office, ☎ 30767. The frontier checkpoint number is ☎ 26242.

Vidin is a pleasant medium-sized town near the border with **Serbia**, with outstanding views over the river Danube and important medieval and Turkish monuments. Although the outskirts are ugly and run-down, it has a well-restored historic centre near the river. The population is ethnically mixed, with a preponderance of Bulgarians but also many people who have Serbian links, and a good number of Roma, Turks and Vlachs. Its position on the Danube has given the town strategic importance throughout the ages, and the **Baba Vida castle** is an outstanding example of medieval Bulgarian and Ottoman military architecture. The economy of the town has been badly affected by the disintegration of Yugoslavia and UN sanctions against Serbia, and remains depressed. It is possible to cross the river to Romania here, to Calafat 4km to the north of

Vidin, by ferry. There was a plan to build a new bridge here over the Danube, but it appears to have been recently abandoned by both governments.

History of Vidin
In Roman times, the town was known as *Bononia*, a name that is probably cognate with Boulogne and Bologna, and indicates Celtic settlement before the Roman invasion. *Bononia* was closely linked in the time of Trajan with the fortress at *Ratiaria*, 10km downstream. It was originally a fairly small legionary encampment, but it increased in importance in the 3C after the evacuation of Dacia when the Danube forts became the northern frontier of the Empire.

In Byzantine, medieval Bulgarian and Turkish times it remained an important military strongpoint (it was capital of a separate Bulgarian Tsardom in the late 14C). For a time in the late 18C and 19C it benefited from the increase in river trade and passenger traffic between Bulgaria and the Habsburg lands. But the industrial revolution passed Vidin by, like all the Danube towns, and it only grew as a result of industrial development under communism, and the depopulation of much of the surrounding countryside. Progress was also severely hampered by the propensity of the town to serious flooding before the Danube dykes were built. In a particularly disastrous flood in March 1942, whole districts of Vidin were swept away. It is one of the very few places where the Bulgarian bank of the river is lower than the Romanian.

The main sights of the town can be seen in a couple of hours' walk. If staying at the Hotel Bononia, turn left out of the main entrance and walk to the riverbank. There is a good view of the Danube above a boat station.

On the left, in a small park, is the remains of the **mosque of Osman Pazvantoglu**, dating from the 18C, with a small hexagonal building in the gardens nearby. It is in poor structural condition, and requires urgent renovation. Opposite is the large 19C Church of Sveti Nicholai, a standard building of its time, but to the north side is the very fine long, low **Church of Sveti Panteleimon**, a very well-preserved Byzantine building, with tiny windows that conjures up the disorderly past of the region. Nearby is the **Stambul Gate**, an impressive large fortified Turkish gatehouse dating from the 17C, part of the old town wall.

Past it along the riverbank walk are some charming late 19C buildings, including a small **theatre**, which evoke perfectly the long-vanished world of the Danube steamers, when travellers, including the cream of Mitteleuropean society, would disembark onto the land for nightly entertainment and elegant dissipation. About five minutes' walk further to the northwest is the impressive **Fortress of Baba Vida**.

History of the fortress
The fortress dates from Roman times, when it was a central element in Trajan's Danube fortification system. It was taken over by the Byzantines and in the Middle Ages was the centre of a small Bulgarian independent state. It was finally captured by the Ottoman Turks in 1398 by Sultan Bazajet's army, who added various elements, including the fortified river walls. It is built around four great corner towers, and was largely impreg-

nable, except during the longest sieges, as with the Austrian army in 1689. In later Ottoman times it was the seat of a virtually autonomous *pashlik*.

The fort is entered by a wooden bridge slung across a deep moat, about 18m deep. Inside there is a complex of inner fortifications and a church. It has a picturesque, sinister atmosphere and is well worth visiting, although it is often not open during normal weekday opening times, and it can be necessary to call at the town hall and request entrance. Vidin museum used to contain some interesting artefacts but is currently closed as a result of a property restitution dispute.

The central square of the town is the usual echoing and inhuman concrete parade ground but there are some well restored **19C buildings** in the pedestrianised shopping area, around Targovska Street, mostly two storeys and painted in bright colours, and some quite good basic shops for a remote provincial town. Local music and dancing traditions are very strong and very much alive, with some Serbian and Romanian influence. The Hotel Bononia band at wedding parties is outstanding.

24km southwest of Vidin on the road to Vraska Cuka and the Serbian border are the remains of **Castra Martis**, a late 3C fort, in the little crossroads town of Kula. A small square fort with round towers has been partly excavated. In medieval times the road through the village to the Vraska Cuka Pass into Serbia was an important trade route.

Return to Sofia by either designated route. An interesting excursion on the return journey can be made near Sofia at Kremikovci.

Kremikovci

Kremikovci is a hill village 25km north east of Sofia in a rundown industrial area, off the main road to Buhovo. On top of a small hill is **Kremikovci Monastery**, with a very fine church behind a fortress wall. It was originally founded in the Second Bulgarian Kingdom. The current building and its beautiful frescoes date from 1493, after restoration by the Radivoi *boyar* family. The famous Kremikovci Gospels were written here in 1497. There is an ugly modern church nearby, but the site is full rural beauties and a sense of a very long Christian tradition. It is particularly attractive in winter snow.

Svishtov and the Central Danube Valley

From Sofia, take the motorway northeast—following signs to Pleven and Ruse—to Pleven (174km), then north to Svishtov (237km). The last section is a fairly good wide asphalt road.

The **Central Danube valley** is rich in Classical and medieval sites, and attractive traditional villages and small towns in the river valley. **Pleven** is a medium-sized provincial centre with some important factories. It was the site of the great battle of Pleven, then known as *Plevna*, in 1877, when the Russian army helped defeat the Turks. **Svishtov** is a rather dull, mostly modern town that faces the large Danube island of **Belene**, but it makes a convenient base to explore the surrounding region, including the important sites of ancient *Nicopolis* and *Oescus*. Belene used to be a forced labour camp, but is now an important nature reserve and wildlife site. Like all Danube towns, the economy was very negatively affected by the end of communism, the imposition of United Nations sanctions on Serbia and other problems of the transition period.

Sofia to Pleven

■ **By rail**. Pleven is on the main line to Varna from Sofia and there are plenty of trains.

Leave Sofia by the main east road—most signs are for Ruse. After passing through residential areas, and crossing the outer ring road, you come to the main east motorway. This is good quality dual carriageway for the first part of the journey, built in a major road project in the 1970s. The road is a considerable engineering achievement, with some long sections through the central mountains in tunnels. Fast driving should be avoided, as there are unpredictable hazards such as deep potholes on some parts of the road. The tunnels about 25km east of Sofia are dangerous, drive slowly with lights on.

Pleven

Pleven, 157km from Sofia, lies on the open grasslands south of the Danube valley itself. It has an important place in the Bulgarian nationalist imagination, and was generally favoured with investment by the communists after the Second World War. A number of museums were opened in this period, some of which no longer survive. It is now a rather run-down, mediocre town, although with much for anyone with interests in Russian or Bulgarian history. There is a pleasant pedestrianised precinct in the centre of town, with some cheap restaurants, cafés and shops.

History of Pleven

In antiquity Pleven was known as *Storgosia*, which was a Roman renaming of an existing Thracian settlement. It grew to be a minor market town by the road from ancient *Oescus*, then into a small city in Imperial times. It was destroyed by the Huns in the 5C, refortified by Justinian, then taken over by the Slavs and renamed *Kamenec*, after the limestone cliffs nearby. The name Pleven first appears in 1270, after the area had been captured by the Magyars for a time.

Pleven prospered under the Turks, with the 17C Turkish traveller Evlija Celebi recording that there were 2000 houses in the city. In later Ottoman times it was one of the largest market towns in the Balkans, but it was in a poor defensive position, and in the Liberation war of 1877 the large Turkish army in Pleven found itself unable to resist the Russian siege tactics of General Totleben.

Under communism it became a centre of the food and munitions industries.

32km south of Pleven is the town of Lovec.

Lovec

Lovec is an attractive medium-sized town on the banks of the river Osam that is worth a short visit if you are interested in Bulgarian 19C history, as it was a centre of activity for Vasil Levski (see p 102), and it is near **Troyan monastery**, one of the finest ecclesiastical buildings in Bulgaria. Neither takes very long to visit and a detour on a journey to the Danube valley is quite feasible. The river has cut a winding route through a limestone gorge, and Lovec is somewhat similar in situation to Veliko Tarnovo, on a tiny scale.

■ The **Hotel Lovec** (☎ 23905) is adequate.

History of Lovec

There was an ancient Thracian settlement on the site of the present town, where the Romans later built a town called *Melta*. A fort on the Strates hill was built to control the north–south route through the central mountains to *Nicopolis ad Istrum*, and to help safeguard the east–west road to *Odessus* (Varna). In Turkish times it was a centre of leather manufacturing. Under communism a bicycle factory was opened but that has now closed and unemployment is very high. Under communism, Lovec was also the site of a notorious forced labour camp

The modern town is predictably dull and run-down but the Old Town is very attractive, although many of the houses are actually modern replicas of Ottoman constructions. The Levski Museum used to be in one of these houses, but has been moved to a large concrete block on the Strates hill. There are a few minor remains of the Roman town of *Melta* visible here, on top of the hill. A section of the original wall has been reconstructed.

The Old Town is reached by a bridge across the river. To the south of the modern bridge is a very fine reconstruction of the **medieval covered bridge**. It was built in 1874, with shops for leather merchants, then destroyed by a fire in 1925. The present structure dates from the late 1920s.

The **Levski Museum** has one of the largest collections of material about the Liberation struggle in one place in the country, and is of considerable interest to specialists, and worth a brief visit for non-specialists. It is currently closed, due to lack of funds to pay staff.

At the top of the hill there is a good view of the river valley, with the ruins of a medieval **fortress**, and a statue of the revolutionary hero. In the lower street of the old quarter there is an attractive, but crumbling Ottoman **mosque**, painted yellow.

Troyan

Troyan is 18km south of Lovec, in the centre of the Troyanska Planina range. The first 10km of road are quite reasonable, but the last 8km are on a mediocre minor road with a steep climb. The town is small and nondescript.

To reach the **monastery**, turn left before you reach the main part of the town up a minor road towards Oresak (7km), the monastery is 5km further up the hill to the southeast.

It is a very large building, the second largest in the country after Rila, and has always played a leading part in the life of the church and the nation, particularly in the mid 19C when Vasil Levski lived in it for a time. It is beautifully situated in deep pine woods by the small Cerni Osum river. The monastery is a good place for those unfamiliar with 19C National Revival art to begin to appreciate its qualities, as the beautiful surroundings are stimulating to the imagination, but it lacks the overt 'Bulgarianisation', and some sense of the mythologisation of the national identity and history that some visitors experience at Veliko Tarnovo.

Most of what the visitor sees nowadays dates from the 19C although the monastery was founded in the early years of the 17C. According to legend, a small wooden church was built near the river by a hermit, and the foundation grew as followers joined this holy man. It consists of long, low, two- and three-storeyed wooden buildings forming an external courtyard, with the **Church of the Holy Virgin** standing in the middle, and a four-storey white bell tower a little way away. The outer courtyard buildings are very pleasant, but similar to many that can be seen elsewhere, but the church is outstanding, with a beautifully painted external cloister that was built in 1835.

Work continued on different parts of the buildings until the begining of the 20C. The church has some wonderful **paintings** by Zachary Zograph, who was invited to decorate the church in 1847, and it is perhaps the most sympathetic display of his work available in Bulgaria today. The wood carving and painting of the ikons on the iconostasis is equally fine.

South of the town the road continues to the **Troyan Pass**, across the central range. It is the highest road in Bulgaria and the **views** are magnificent. **Snow** can be a major problem on this route in the winter, take advice before attempting it then. There are warning signs indicating whether the road is passable at either end of the pass.

Pleven to Svishtov

■ **By car**. This is a good asphalt road across open rolling farmland, but it is not dual carriageway and can involve encounters with farm animals, slow-moving farm carts and vehicles, and dangerous overtaking. It is a good place to buy fruit and vegetables from peasants at roadside stalls in the winter.

■ **By rail**. Svishtov can be reached by train from Sofia but it is a very slow journey involving changing trains. It is better to take an express train to Varna, alight at Pleven en route, and take a coach from there.

Svishtov

Svishtov is the best place to stay as a centre in the region.

■ **Accommodation**. The **Hotel Dunav** is the main hotel in Svishtov. It is a dreary and frowsty, but is an acceptable place to stay for a short time.

History of Svishtov

The low cliffs overlooking the river Danube on the Bulgarian side of the river have been inhabited since the earliest times. Settlement in the Roman period was concentrated at *Novae*, near the modern village of Stuklen, 4km east of modern Svishtov. Traces of earlier Thracian occupation have also been found on the site. From 46AD to 69AD *Novae* was garrisoned by the Legio VIII Augusta. It was then taken over by the Legio I Italica, and was made into the site of an important river crossing. It remained so for centuries, and the urban settlements nearby grew up as a result. Thanks to the bridge, the town also prospered in Ottoman times. In 1877 the Russian army crossed the Danube at Svishtov on the march that led to the Battle of Pleven. In the communist era the town developed close trade links with Yugoslavia, dealing in commodities such as scrap metal and coal.

The remains of Svishtov fortress are on a small hill in the town above the river (difficult to find; ask for local assistance). Across the road from the hotel is a small open space, beyond which are good views of the river Danube. To the left, about 500m, there is the **Church of the Transfiguration**, an attractive 19C building with a wooden interior. Opposite is the Vasil Levski School, the first to open in the town. It is well known locally for the quality of its choral singing.

To the right, about five minutes' walk into the remains of the old Ottoman town, is a fine Turkish **konjak** that has been converted into a restaurant. The food and wine are quite good, in very attractive surroundings. Recommended. Behind it there is an Old Quarter, with a few nice old merchants' houses with trailing vines and a sense of the lost world of Danube prosperity. There is a good open street market in the town.

Belene Island

Belene Island is a large, uninhabited, almost rectangular island in the centre of the Danube, mostly covered in stands of fir trees and marshy areas. It is an important wildlife reservation, and one of the best places to watch wading birds in Bugaria. It is about 12km north west of Svishtov. Belene has an important place in the Bulgarian popular imagination as the site of the notorious **Belene Forced Labour Camp**, established by the communists in 1948, and finally closed in 1989.

Belene was chosen to be a political prison because of its remoteness and the ease of preventing escapes by inmates. At the end of the Second World War it was little more than a swamp, notorious for malarial mosquitoes. In the early years inmates spent much of their time cutting timber. There was a very high death rate from disease and maltreatment by camp guards. The camp was closed in 1989. In recent years a highly controversial plan to build a new nuclear power station here has been debated in Bulgaria.

The Central Danube Valley

Nicopolis

The most interesting excursion from Svishtov is to ancient *Nicopolis*, about 51km away to the northwest, on the banks of the Danube. This is a very evocative site high on a cliff above the river, although the view is ruined by the appallingly ugly and polluting chemical plant at Turnu Magurele on the opposite Romanian bank. **This plant discharges highly coloured effluent into the river. Avoid contact with the water.**

The site is near the modern village of Nikopol, on the Danube. Follow the main road out of Svistov past the railway and veer right across very pleasant rolling countryside and through traditional Danube villages. Good wine, brandy, honey and fruit are sold by the roadside. The general atmosphere is perhaps a little reminiscent of France in the 1930s with many peasants still using traditional techniques and implements. Keep to the main secondary road west, but it is easy to get lost, with many intersecting minor roads. If you do not read Cyrillic it is a good idea to get somebody in Svishtov to write the word Nikopol in Cyrillic on a piece of paper for you before leaving. The villages probably reflect closely the ancient settlement patterns, where settlements grew up along the small feeder roads linking the river towns and fortresses with the main Serdica–Odessus (Sofia–Varna) legionary route. **Asenovo** is a pleasant little place to stop for refreshments if returning from the site towards Pleven.

Modern **Nikopol** is a pleasant little riverside town, with some good Ottoman and National Revival houses and one or two attractive cafés. It is very poor and Western visitors should behave without ostentation. It used to be well known for fishing, but has suffered from the decline of stocks caused by diminished Danube water flows and serious pollution. Although most Bulgarian governments have attempted to persuade the Romanians to modernise their riparian industrial plants in this vicinity, in practice little appears to have been achieved.

History of Nikopol

Nicopolis means 'city of victory' in Greek. It was refounded as a city by Emperor Heraclitus I in 629, but a Roman fort existed on the site before that, and traces of pre-Roman occupation have been found in recent excavations. With its fine defensive site above the Danube, it was a natural place for a medieval stronghold, and it played an important role as such in the region for centuries.

The fortress was captured by the Ottomans after a long siege in 1393, and it was an important part of the Danube fortification system until 1810, when it was destroyed by the Russians. In Turkish times there was a large Nicopolis Jewish community.

The road up to the fortress is near a block of flats in the middle of the village, and winds up a little way to the base of the massive **earthworks**, about 12m high.

You can walk into the centre of the fortress from here, which is a great basin within the earthworks, with picturesque grazing animals within the fort. There are remains of foundations of very thick external walls, and of one or two massive towers. There were once 26 of them in the outer fortification system.

Environs of Ancient Nicopolis

The Danube valley in this region has a good climate, with much milder winters than many places in Bulgaria, and plenty of very fertile land. As a result it is possible to visit **villages** in the Nicopolis vicinity which are deeply traditional, with a rich rural culture, but without the grinding poverty and serious depopulation which is so often found in rural Bulgaria. Nonetheless, the visitor should not expect luxury, even small shops are few and far between, but it is one of the few parts of the Danube littoral where it is possible to enjoy at least some aspects of the world of the river before it was ruined by industrialisation (best described as it was in the late 1930s in Patrick Leigh Fermour's book *Between the Woods and the Water*). There are many very good local food specialities, duck and goose, in particular. Water supply is a problem in some villages; it is a good idea to drink bottled water although do not worry if you cannot. Avoid paddling or swimming in the river Danube itself.

The Bulgarian rural environment, with the survival and relative prosperity of traditional family-based agriculture, compares favourably to the enviroment on the Romanian bank, with its vast fields, destroyed villages and Stalinoid 'agro-industrial complexes'.

Ancient Oescus

It is about 32km west, depending on the route taken, from Nikopol to the village of **Gigen**, which is near ancient *Oescus*. This is a little-known but sprawling, spectacular Roman site that is well worth visiting. The road crosses open farming country inland, then turns down towards the river. Gigen is about 3km from the river.

History of Oescus

Oescus was a very important, cultured Roman town and military stronghold that was central to the defence of the Danube frontier. It was founded in the 1C AD, on the site of settlement of the Thracian clan, the Triballi. It was the base of the Legio V Macedonia, and was attacked by the Dacians on many occasions. It flourished in pagan times, when many temples were built, and it had a theatre and many urban amenities. It appears to have been largely destroyed by the Visigoths at the end of the 4C.

In 328 the longest bridge constructed in antiquity was built by Constantine the Great, across the Danube north of the city. It seems to have been burnt down by 367, when the Emperor Valens had to cross the river on a bridge of boats. According to local tradition, the bridge was built of copper but there is no evidence for this. Romanian archaeologists have found very large timber foundations on the north side of the river opposite the Romanian village of Orlea.

The site is in open fields south of the modern village, and considering its importance is not as well kept as it should be. Foundations of massive external fortification walls can be seen, and low walls and foundations of many urban buidings. The most impressive part consists of the forum and remains of demolished pagan temples, with a very large area covered by pieces of broken ancient masonry, carved stones and other debris from ancient times. The buildings were probably destroyed by a combination of Visigoth attacks, Christian demolitions, and earthquakes.

Excavations at the site began in 1905, although the existence of the place had been known since the 18C when the Italian aristocratic antiquary Count Marsigli identified it. Some notable works of art have been excavated, particularly marble statues, and mosaic floors of buildings.

Ruins of a large complex of buildings outside the existing fortress walls can also be seen, and the foundations of some of the series of huge defensive towers that protected the city. Roman burials have also been found in many places outside the walls.

It must be a great cause for concern that such an important and attractive site as this, with tourist potential, is in the neglected state that it is. It is also impossible to see any of the works of art that have been found here.

Return to Pleven by direct minor road via Trastenik (about 35km).

Ruse and the Eastern Danube Valley

- **By car**. From Sofia, 322km, via Pleven (174km); from Varna, 205km.

- **By rail**. Train services from Sofia are good.

Ruse

Ruse (pop. 321,000), Ottoman *Ruschuk*, is the largest town in northeast Bulgaria on the Danube, and a very interesting historic city with some fine 19C period buildings. It is a good centre for the region, with a developed commercial culture and close links with Romania, as it is the site of the only bridge crossing of the Danube between Romania and Bulgaria. In the past the city, and the region generally, had a very ethnically mixed population and to a large extent this continues today, with substantial numbers of Turks, Armenians and Roma in evidence. There are also growing numbers of Russians who use the city as a base for their business operations in Bulgaria and other traders and *Mafiya* from the Caucasus, Moldova and Bessarabia. There are also a few Jews who have survived from the extensive community that used to exist here. The Jewish community was described in *Tongue Set Free*, the autobiography of the Nobel Prize-winning novelist **Elias Canetti** (1905–92), one of the most famous residents of Ruse. Local white wine is of high quality. The city played an important part in the struggle for democracy under communism, linked to the environmentalist campaign against the appalling pollution from the Giurgiu chlorine plant on the opposite bank of the Danube in Romania.

- **By air**. The airport is 6km to the southwest.

- **By rail**. Regular fast trains to Sofia and Varna from the Central Station, ☎ 222213. Recommended.

- **By coach**. There are two Ruse terminals, one on the east of the town, ☎ 443836, and one on the south side, ☎ 222974.

- **River ferry services**. There are a number of Danube river ferry services connecting Ruse with Silistra and Vidin, and also offering pleasure trips. Enquire locally for details as regular schedules have not always survived the end of communism; the reception desk of the **Riga Hotel** is a good place for accurate information.

- **Hotels and restaurants**. Given the low price of most Ruse hotels, it is hardly worth trying to find private rooms. The **Dunav Hotel** (☎ 082 226518, fax 224679) in Svoboda Square is a friendly if rather decrepit old place, with large, fairly clean rooms and a very attractive view over the main square. A single room is about $US16 a night. The restaurant has quite good food, excellent wine, and in summer has a delightful open air inner courtyard with a small orchestra. **Recommended**. The **Hotel Balkan** is a very pretty building, and cheaper, at about $US10 a night, but the sanitary conditions are

Ottoman. The best hotel in Ruse is the **Riga Hotel**, a modern concrete block in Pridunavski Street, but it is expensive, at about $US42, for what is offered, and the staff are not particularly helpful. The view over the Danube is very good, though, if you do stay there, ask for an upper floor room. There are some business and conference facilities. (Tourist office ☎ 33629.)

■ **Hospital and medical services**. The hospital is on the outskirts of the town, ☎ 230437. The dental clinic is on ☎ 221427. There are chemists in Nikolaevska Street and Aleksandrovska Street.

■ **Free trade zone**. Ruse has a free trade zone, near the river and border crossing, which has warehousing, manufacturing and freight-forwarding facilities. For information contact Ruse International Free Trade Zone, 5 Knyazheska Street, POB 107, Ruse 7000, ☎ 272247, fax 270084, telex 62285.

History of Ruse

Primitive small fishing and hunting communities developed along the Danube in neolithic times. A town first grew up under the Roman occupation, based around the fortress and harbour of *Sexaginta Prista*, Sixty Ships. During the period of the Slav invasions, the population left, and founded a new town called *Cherven*, 24km inland from the river (see p 143). It became a small but prosperous town in Byzantine times, based on metalworking. It was burnt down completely by the Ottoman Turks, who restored the harbour of the old Roman town, and the new town was called *Ruschuk*. It was known by Bulgarians as Ruse.

In the 17C the place was almost entirely Turkish, with 15,000 Turks and only about 1000 Bulgarians. It increased rapidly in size and importance in the high Ottoman period, with over 6000 houses, fine public baths, and numerous mosques and markets. This prosperity was closely linked to the development of suspension bridges across the Danube, and the importance of the town in the Ottoman Danube fortification system. *Ruschuk* played an important part in the Russian–Turkish wars, falling to Russia in both 1774 and 1812. In the mid 19C, under the rule of the enlightened Pasha Midhad, it became an important and progressive capital of a *vilayet*, with the construction of the Ruschuk–Varna railway line between 1864 and 1866, and the building of schools, the foundation of newspapers, and housing and public health reforms.

After the Liberation, Ruse was the largest town in the Principality of Bulgaria, with 26,163 inhabitants in 1880, compared to only 20,000 in Sofia. There was a rapid increase in trade along the Danube with the Habsburg lands, and this began to influence the architecture and social ambience of the place. The town did not particularly benefit from the industrialisation of Bulgaria in the late 19C and early 20C, being far from supplies of coal and iron, and has never regained the importance lost in those years. Shipbuilding, on a small scale, and ship repair were the only significant industries. In 1919 a short-lived Commune was established by the Ruse trades unions. In the inter war period the town stagnated, and there was little new building.

After the Second World War there was a revival, with the 1954 opening of the new Danube bridge a major landmark. In the last five years there have been many interesting developments in the town under the new economic system, but the municipality remains very short of money and many public buildings and museums are closed or affected by property restitution disputes.

Life in Ruse revolves around two areas of the city—the main square, Svoboda Square, and the Danube. The bridge crossing to Romania is a short distance outside the town to the east. If you are travelling into the city, be careful with signs. The Bulgarian customs and border control post is at the bridge access road. **NB**. Security in this area is not all it might be. If planning to cross into Romania, drive straight to the border control post and avoid business with moneychangers and other 'dealers' who hang about nearby.

Exploring the town is best started from **Svoboda Square**, which used to be called Lenin Square. It is dominated by the very fine **Monument to the Liberation of Bulgaria**. This was erected in 1908 in memory of Ruse citizens who died in the struggle. It shows a figure of Freedom on top of a granite and bronze column, about 18m high. The bas reliefs, which were made in Italy, show the battles of Shipka Pass (1877) and Buzludza (1868). The small gardens in the square are very well kept and have a much more imaginative and sophisticated planting design than many Bulgarian public gardens.

The general atmosphere is very relaxed and pleasant, with a great *corso* in the spring, summer and autumn evenings. There is, though, a distinct sense of a city with many elements of the old socialist society remaining, and although there are plenty of small private businesses in evidence, there are also relatively few cars and a generally egalitarian atmosphere. There is also a strong echo of the late 19C, in many of the Mitteleuropean public buildings, when for a time Ruse was an important European travel hub from the Danube, before the Orient Express ran through to Constantinople. Like other Danube towns such as Vidin, this brought a temporary boom, when many of the distinguished urban buildings were constructed, and rapid decline with the coming of the railway. Ruse also suffered from the rise of Varna at the same time, and the coming of larger ships which made the Danube increasingly unimportant for Bulgarian trade.

Opposite the monument is the **Town Hall**, which was built in the Stalinist style in the 1950s as the House of the Ruse Soviets. Following the edge of the square, there are one or two fine 19C buildings, then the **National Theatre**. This is a very impressive Italian-designed building with a neo-baroque façade that was opened in 1891, but is in process of restoration and is currently boarded up.

Other interesting parts of the town centre adjoin this square. There is a very fine 19C street to the north of the square, towards the river. Most of the large merchants' houses have been converted into shops. At the end of it is the **Hotel Balkan** (see above), with a very attractive façade. French influence on the architecture of this part of the city is evident, a product of the process where, as the literary critic Walter Benjamin wrote, 'Paris became the capital of the 19C'. As a rising star in this part of the Balkans, Ruse sought to emulate French architectural models. In the same way, Velinkov Street nearby is also very attractive.

The **river area** is much less animated than the town centre and has a rather downbeat atmosphere. The focus is the **Riga Hotel** (see above) which is worth a

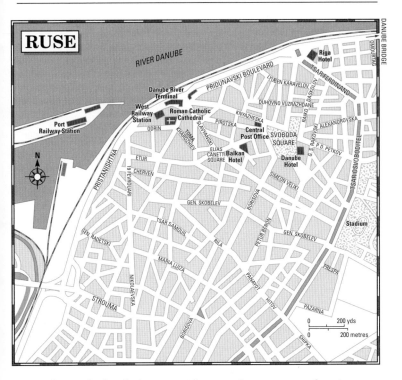

visit to have a drink, whether you wish to stay there or not, as there is a very pleasant terrace looking over the Danube. The Romanian town of Dzurdzu can be clearly seen to the right, to the centre and left there is a very fine **view** of the deciduous woods on the opposite bank.

About 300m downriver of the hotel there are some very fine houses, two of which used to be museums to heroes of the Bulgarian national liberation struggle, but they are both affected by property restitution and are closed. There is a nice café 400m away, with good *rakia* and fine river views. A little further along, up a small side street to the left, is the **Catholic church**. This is a rather grim dark grey building in the Gothic style that has been partly restored in the last three years and is now open for services. They are held at 10.00 every Sunday. Ruse is unusual among Bulgarian cities outside Sofia in having a Roman Catholic community, a sign of long-standing trade links with the old Habsburg lands to the north, the 19C boom and the influx of a mixed population in late Ottoman times. The ambience of the charming houses with their large rambling gardens and minor decrepitude is characteristic of the best of old Ruse.

The **Danube Bridge** was opened in 1954, and is a key East European transport link. It became a centre of appalling congestion during the ex-Yugoslav war, when lorries were re-routed through Romania and Bulgaria to avoid the war zone, and queues of vehicles miles long waiting to cross were normal. It is built across what are really the last two main rocky outcrops on either side of the river, before it enters its final lowland course, and the delta area. Over 2000 tonnes of steel were used in the construction work, which took five years.

The first plans for the bridge had been developed in 1881 and international negotiations took place in 1895, 1898, 1909, 1914 and 1918. Final agreement between Bulgaria and Romania was reached in 1942.

The Eastern Danube Valley

Leaving Ruse by the main road east towards Silistra, turning inland, after 59km you come to Tutrakan. This is a pleasant, interesting little town on a small hill above the river. It has a long history as a centre of Danube river fishing. It reached a prosperous state in the late 19C and early 20C, but has suffered economically recently as a result of the decline of the Danube fish stocks. It was originally fortified by the Romans and called *Transmarisca*.

After another 65km, Silistra.

Silistra

Silistra (pop. 29,500) is the most easterly town on the Danube in Bulgaria and is closely linked in its trade with the Dobrudzha plain inland. Under communism it used to be a favoured place, with a strong Russian flavour, but in the last five years it has fallen on rather hard times with a decline in trade in agricultural products from the interior, broken connections with the ex-Comecon countries and problems relating to United Nations sanctions against Serbia. Although a modern, fairly tidy town, it is a rather depressing place. There are nonetheless some fine public buildings from the 19C, and a very impressive Ottoman fortress.

Unfortunately, the 4C **Roman tomb** in the town is no longer open to visitors. It dates from the time of Emperor Theodosius and is said to have very fine wall paintings.

If you visit Silistra, do not miss the **view** of the Danube, which has a great bend beyond the town on the Romanian border, and is over 2km wide. The local apricot brandy is very good.

■ **Ferries and border crossing**. There is a ferry across the Danube, crossing to the road in Romania leading to the town of Calarasi (19km). The border post with Romania (24 hours) is to the east of the town.

History of Silistra

The Roman occupiers found an existing Thracian settlement on the site, which was fortified as part of the system of Danube river defences. The new fortress was called *Durostorum* during the time of Trajan (97–117), and a town grew up around the fortress. In medieval Bulgarian times it flourished as a small market town, and was visited by the Arab traveller Idrisi in 1154 who recorded that he saw busy streets and many shops. During the First Bulgarian Empire it was the seat of the patriarch. In Ottoman times it was refortified as part of the defences against the Russians. Under communism factories for producing tinned food, furniture and textiles were established.

17km west of Silistra on the Ruse road is **Lake Srebana**, an important nature reserve with very rich birdlife, pelicans in particular.

Razgrad

Razgrad (pop. 21,127) is a modest town 67km southeast of Ruse situated on the Beli Lom river on an open plain. It is not worth making a special journey to visit it, but if travelling in the region it is worth stopping briefly to see the ruins of Roman **Abritus**, parts of the walls of which are visible as you come into the town from the south, and also the very fine Mosque of Ibrahim Pasha in the town centre.

History of Razgrad

Abritus was known to be an important legionary stronghold guarding this part of the road between *Sexaginta Prista*, modern Ruse, and the south. The exact location of the fortress was unknown until 1953, when it was discovered accidentally. It was probably built on the site of an earlier Thracian settlement. The excavations made so far indicate that a large and wealthy town had developed here by late Roman times, most of which is probably still buried beneath the modern town. The Emperor Decius died at *Abritus* in 251 while fighting the Goths.

The fortress and town were completely destroyed during the Slav invasions and little happened on the site until Ottoman times when it became an important market and trade centre, with a substantial Albanian minority in the population. In communist times it was developed as the main centre of antibiotic production in Bulgaria.

On a nice day Cherven is an interesting excursion from Ruse. Take the main road towards Razgrad, and turn right off it towards Straklevo (12km).

Cherven

Cherven came into being as a hilltop refuge for the inhabitants of ancient Ruse, fleeing from barbarian invasions in the 5C and 6C. It is 16km directly south of the city. There is not a great deal to see, in terms of visible remains, but it is a pleasant atmospheric spot with good hill walking in the vicinity.

It was very much a clerical and monastic city, built on a high place above the modern village, with a dramatic view, from a small flat area with sheer cliffs on three sides. There are surviving low walls from the foundations of several churches, boyar houses, and other smaller buildings. After the Turkish invasion the medieval Bulgarian clerical establishment remained at Cherven for some time, until the site was finally abandoned, with the rise of Ruse in the 17C. The birdlife in the local woods is very rich. There is nowhere to stay or to get a meal nearby.

Varna, the Northern Black Sea Coast and the Shumen Region

- **By car**. From Sofia, 469km, take the Ruse road, via Pleven (174km); good road on the whole but often busy.

- **By rail**. From Sofia, about six hours by express train, nine hours otherwise.

- **By air**. From Sofia. There are frequent internal flights from Sofia airport.

Varna

Varna (pop. 295,038), ancient *Odessus*, is the third largest city in Bulgaria, and the most important port in the country. It is a relatively sophisticated, cosmopolitan town, with good tourist facilities nearby and has some important secular and ecclesiastical monuments from all historical periods. The **Roman thermae** are the largest and best-preserved Roman baths on the Black Sea coast. This is a most outstanding monument and worth a special trip.

The town has a reputation for friendly people and is well used to foreign visitors. Some business people find it a more pleasant and efficient place to use as a base for commercial operations in Bulgaria than Sofia or Burgas. It is the home of major Bulgarian industries, such as the chemical plant at Devnja, on the western end of the Varna lagoon.

Varna is also a good base to use for exploring the **Shumen region** of the interior, which has pleasant wooded and open countryside and antiquities of great importance, such as the ancient Thracian rock carving, the **Madara Horseman**, and ancient **Pliska**, the capital of the First Bulgarian Kingdom.

For a beach holiday, some of the resorts to the north of Varna have been upgraded, and offer pleasant, good value beach facilities in a quiet wooded environment. The drive north from Varna up to the border with Romania makes an interesting day out, crossing the vast open spaces of the **Dobrudzha plain**, on the edge of the Eurasian steppe.

Most of Bulgaria's minorities have a presence in Varna, with a strongly developing Greek-speaking community in the city itself, and ethnic Turks, Roma and Gagauz nearby. There are also numerous Russian, Georgian, Ukranian and other Black Sea businessmen and *Mafiya* lowlife types in the city on a temporary or permanent basis. Russian is understood and spoken by many people in the city, and some knowledge of Greek is widespread.

- **Airport**. The airport is about 12km northwest of the city centre. As well as frequent internal flight services from Sofia, and holiday charters, there are some international destinations with direct links to Varna; these include Dubai, Kiev, Tehran, Beirut and Moscow. (**Balkan Airlines**, ☎ 052 222604, fax 223496). Varna is in general a well-run, uncongested, medium-sized airport, with good café, restaurant and car hire facilities. It is sometimes subject to fog problems in the autumn and winter. There are regular buses from the airport to the city centre, and to the Sunny Beach resort bus station, from the car park at the front of the terminal building. Allow 30 minutes to the city centre by taxi.

■ **Taxis**. There are generally plenty of taxis plying for hire, with large ranks near the cathedral. It is often quicker to walk in the old town, rather than take taxis.

■ **Car hire**. Most major operators are to be found at the airport, including Avis (☎ 52 440793), Hertz (☎ 52 650210), Europcar (☎ 52 435054). Vehicles should be checked before acceptance, tyres particularly.

■ **Ferries**. Varna is a major port for Black Sea ferries and general shipping and it is possible, with some ingenuity, to reach almost anywhere on the Black Sea littoral from Varna. There are various shipping agencies and ticket offices near the harbour which can provide information. There are particularly good links with Odessa, in the Ukraine, with passenger ships and roll-on and roll-off ferries (**Bul Union** ☎ from UK 00 359 2 259 262).

■ **Hotels**. Varna is a busy commercial town and although there are adequate hotels in all price ranges, most people will find it much pleasanter to stay in one of the northern suburbs or towns near the sea, such as **Sveti Konstantin** (see p 152). These hotels are only 10–15 minutes from central Varna by taxi or bus, and are generally not expensive. The Grand Hotel Varna (☎ 52 861491) is the most popular business hotel in Sveti Konstantin, and is popular with the international conference market, although there is competition in this class from newer buildings.

■ **Post office and international telephone**. From the Central Post Office, on the west side of the park at the rear of the cathedral.

■ **Security**. The Bulgarian police have made a particular effort to enforce the law more efficiently in the fashionable resorts north of Varna, and in the city itself. In the resorts there has been a considerable improvement compared to the mid 1990s.

NB. Some caution is nevertheless needed in Varna at night, and common-sense precautions should be taken. If you do not have a Bulgarian friend with you, **avoid** casinos and night clubs. **Avoid** any dealings with bodyguard companies, or people offering 'security services' or commercial insurance. Most hotels have safe deposit facilities for valuables. Use them.

History of Varna

Primitive people have inhabited the area since the neolithic period, their cultures based on the fish of the Varna lagoon. They built villages by driving piles into the lagoon mud. About 1200 BC a Thracian tribe called the *Krobisae* established a settlement. Ancient Greek settlers from Miletus in Asia Minor founded a colony called *Odessus* in 585 BC. In the 4C BC *Odessus* came under the rule of the Macedonian kings, and from 431 to 280 formed part of the state of Macedonia. Later it was a leader of the Euxine League, along with *Tomi, Callatis, Mesembria* and *Apollonia*.

Odessus fell to the Romans in 15AD, and became one of the most prosperous and powerful cities anywhere in the Black Sea under their rule. It was refortified by Augustus, and then by Justinian, and a theatre, acropolis and baths were built. In the 5C the Huns and Goths attacked the city, and the Emperor Theodosius II signed a peace treaty at *Odessus* with Attila the Hun in 443. Procopius mentions the scale of the fortifications in this period. Over a hundred years later the Avars laid it waste, in 586. Fifty years earlier Justinian had made it the military and administrative centre (*quaestura exercitus*) of a vast area including Cyprus, the Cyclades, Caria and Moesia Secunda. The Church seemes to have accumulated substantial wealth by this period.

The city, now called **Varna**, a Slav name, was taken by the Bulgarians in 681, but recaptured by the Byzantines in 970. In 1173 the Arab geographer El Idrisi admired the economic prosperity of the port. In 1201, Varna returned to the Bulgarian Kingdom. After another period of prosperity, the town was brought into rapid and severe decline by wars between the boyars in the 14C, and it was captured by Sultan Murad I for the Ottoman Turks in 1393. In 1399 it was ravaged by the Tartars.

Varna was an important defensive fortress for the Ottomans for centuries. A Greek-speaking population remained in the city throughout the Turkish period. Varna was besieged by large armies of Poles in 1443, and Russians in 1773. Trade prospered, with cattle exports particularly important. In 1828 invading Russian forces won control of Varna for a time, and in 1854 the Crimean War allies—Britain, France and Turkey—established a headquarters in the town. A Bulgarian language school opened in 1860. The Ruse–Varna line, the first railway in Bulgaria, was opened in 1866. The Ottoman garrison withdrew under the Treaty of Berlin (1878), and the new fortifications built by Sultan Mahmud II after 1830 were dismantled.

The port was rebuilt by British engineers after 1878, and was finally completed in 1906. Commerce was badly affected by the Treaty of Bucharest in 1913, which gave most of the Dobrudzha to Romania, and by the decline in Black Sea trade between the world wars. Under communism, there was a heavy industrialisation programme, with the construction of the first shipbuilding facilities in Bulgaria. For a time after World War II, Varna was called *Stalin*, after the Soviet leader.

In 1947, Tito and Dimitrov signed the Varna Agreement which envisaged a customs union of Yugoslavia and Bulgaria as a step towards a **Balkan Federation**.

To see Varna properly a day or so is needed, but it is possible to see the main sights, apart from the Museum of History and Art, on a three or four hour walk. If approaching from the airport, drive into the centre of the town along Varnenchik Street. This is a broad shopping thoroughfare, with many private shops and small businesses, an indication of the deeper roots of the commerical culture here, compared to many other parts of the country.

Begin the walk near the **Cathedral of the Assumption**, on Mitropolit Simeon Square. This is a large, imposing building dating from 1886, designed by the architect Pomerantsev and heavily influenced by the Russian church architec-

VARNA

ture of the time. Like many Bulgarian cathedrals from this period, it is as much a war memorial and patriotic monument as a church. Although it undoubtedly holds a strong place in the affections of many Varna residents, the heavy architecture and gloomy atmosphere do not always appeal to foreign visitors. There is a small circular entrance porch, and a single large nave with some good wood carving. The frescoes were painted between 1948 and 1950. There are craft stalls in the small gardens surrounding it.

The **Varna Museum of History and Art** is about five minutes' walk north of the cathedral, along old Dimitar Blagoev Street. It is well worth visiting. Housed in the fine 19C building that was the first girls' school in Varna, opened in 1898, its collection illuminates the long and interesting history of Varna, and includes ancient Greek and Thracian material, ancient and medieval jewellery and some outstanding Roman sculpture. **Open** 10.00–17.00; closed Mon.

The **ground floor** shows the large palaeolithic and neolithic collections, with emphasis on the material from the early tribal settlements in the Varna lagoon.

On the **upper floors** there is very beautiful Thracian and Hellenistic **gold jewellery** from locally excavated tombs of the 6C BC, gravestones, some good ancient **Greek vases** and other ceramics mostly from the 4C, and a large quantity of Roman and later material, including a **statue of Heracles** from the Thermae complex, and the font from Galata church. The Byzantine and medieval gallery rooms are mainly of specialist interest, apart from an interesting display of medieval Varna **glazed pottery**, which was an important local industry.

On the south side of Mitropolit Simeon Square is the **clock tower**, a finely proportioned National Revival building that was built by the Varna trade associations in 1884, although the nature and position of the building owes a good deal to Ottoman urban traditions. By the base of the tower is a good **craft market** in summer, with stalls selling embroidery, jewellery and other gift items.

Walk south-eastwards into the pedestrianised area, and follow this towards the port. Most of **old Varna** is to be found in this area. On the right, after 500m, is the **Opera House**, a very cheerful red-painted building in the late 19C style, perhaps modelled on the smaller sort of provincial opera house in Italy. There are many bars and cafés down here, though some of the very attractive traditional Bulgarian pubs are being ruined by the worst kind of copying of American bar styles. Opposite the Opera House is the **Town Hall**. Below the Opera House on the same side is the **National Bank** building.

After about five minutes' walk, turn left into Chioka Street. On the left is the **Church of Saint Nicholas the Miracleworker**, an attractive 19C building that was consecrated in 1866. It is worth a visit to see the very fine interior wood carvings, particularly the iconostasis.

Return to the main pedestrian street, Preslav Street, and carry on down towards the port.

Varna and Count Dracula

The port of Varna has a minor place in English literary history, and in many films, as the embarkation point for **Dracula**, the famous vampire hero of Bram Stoker's novel who travelled buried in soil in his coffin from Transylvania to England via Varna port. The novelist writes:

> The sequel to the strange arrival of the derelict in the storm last night is almost stranger than the thing itself. It turns out that the schooner is a Russian from Varna and is called the Demeter. She is almost entirely in ballast of silver sand, with only a small amount of cargo—a number of great wooden boxes filled with mould.

Bram Stoker (1847–1912) was a theatre manager of Irish extraction before he became a novelist. His masterpiece, *Dracula*, was published in 1897, and shows some study of social and economic conditions in the Ottoman Balkans. The choice of Varna as the port of embarkation indicates its regional importance at that time.

Varna's **port** is the centre of a very large industrial area, with extensive dry dock, naval and ship repair facilities. Most of it is on the south side of the town centre, and is easily found by car if you drive towards the cranes that tower above it. The main railway station is also in the port.

Across Boulevard Primorski the main coast road to the port about 400m by 700m north of the main harbour entrance are the ruins of the **Imperial Roman baths**. The baths were built in the late Roman period, and fed by an aqueduct. Remains of this, and of a small Roman necropolis, have been found nearby.

This is a disappointing and very badly neglected monument, almost totally overgrown with brambles and other vegetation. It is not worth spending much time trying to see it. There is an entrance gate on the east side but it appears to have been locked for a long time. You can get a reasonable general impression of the site from the coast road.

There are pleasant gardens by the sea on the far side of the port, with good views and the town **aquarium**. There is a **municipal beach**, but is perhaps rather close to the town and harbour for safe swimming.

Also on the seafront is the **Naval Museum**, at the corner of Graf Ignetiev Street. This is a rather gloomy and badly lit collection, with no foreign language captions, and is really only worth visiting if you have specialised interests in naval, Black Sea, or Bulgarian history.

About 2km along the coast road from the Imperial baths is the **Military Museum**, an open air collection on a clifftop site of old aeroplanes and other, mostly Soviet-period, military equipment such as artillery pieces. It is in theory open on weekday mornings, although in practice it often appears to be closed at the moment. It is possible to see most of the main exibits through the fence, of which the elderly MIG fighters are the most interesting to non-specialists.

The Roman thermae and vicinity

This area, containing the most important monuments in the city, is found at the bottom of Khan Krum Street, off to the left of the lower pedestrianised area.

On a small square site, enclosed by railings, is the **Armenian Church of St Sarkis**, where Khan Krum and Sveti Klement Street meet, a very dignified and attractive whitewashed church that was opened to cater for the city's large and influential Armenian community in 1842. The masonry surrounding the church door is particularly finely carved. The interior is simple, painted pale blue, with a white wooden barrel-vaulted ceiling, designed in the manner of many Turkish Armenian churches. There is a very good **fresco**

Armenian Church of St Sarkis

on the east wall showing the Virgin meeting St Sarkis.

It is not often open, but it is usually possible to find somebody to unlock it in the adjacent **House of the Armenian Bishop**, a very fine ochre-coloured four-storey building.

The **Church of Sveti Bogoroditsa** is about three minutes' walk southwest down Khan Krum Street, and is well worth visiting, as a very fine example of Varna ecclesiastical architecture. Entry is by a small gate in the railings. The church is sunken about 6m into the ground, as Ottoman legislation required, and in general shows a strong Russian atmosphere and influence. On the roof at the west end is a very fine small bell tower. This is constructed on the foundations of a demolished minaret that was built in Ottoman times when the building was a mosque. Half-way down the north wall is an attractive entrance porch, with inscriptions around the door.

The Roman thermae

The massive, fascinating Roman thermae are a couple of minutes' walk from Sveta Bogoroditsa, and can easily be seen from the road outside the church.

■ Open 09.00–17.00. Entrance is through a gate in the perimeter iron railings on the north side.

The thermae are a remarkable, atmospheric monument that evokes clearly the size, power and importance of ancient *Odessus*. They can be seen in 15–20 minutes, though a longer and more leisurely walk around the site is recommended. It is very pleasant to linger among the picturesque ruins in spring and summer and enjoy the atmosphere and wild flowers. On the left as you approach the entrance corner is a very large pithoi and a statue of Karel Skorpil (1859–1946), the great and long-lived Bulgarian archaeologist of Czech extraction who was mainly responsible for excavating the site. There is a small monastery to the north of the site.

History of the thermae

The *thermae* were built on the foundations of earlier buildings, probably in the middle of the 2C AD. Water was provided from the new aqueduct that was completed in 157. The site occupies about 7000 square metres, within an overall fortified area of the ancient city that in Roman times covered about 43 hectares. It was surrounded by temples, cult centres and a market area. The *thermae* probably continued in use until the 4C when they were superseded by the minor seafront complex, a sign of the decline of the city. The buildings were damaged in the Gothic invasions. The great **Varna earthquake** of 544 may also have assisted in their destruction, when a tidal wave from the Black Sea is said to have flooded most of the city.

Entering the site past the ticket kiosk, you bear left and immediately walk over a wooden bridge. Below it are parts of the heating system, with large underfloor vaults visible, and there are a number of later Roman tombstones.

The **thermae walls** survive from a height of 2–18m and are up to 3m thick, with stone alternating with bands of brick. The largest surviving block of masonry that you see when you enter the central bath complex was part of the monumental entrance to the *vestibulum*, within which there was a very large hall that was used for athletic exercises. To the side were the normal hot, warm, and cold rooms, all of which were interlinked with the central halls and heated by the same hypercausts. Large numbers of marble fragments found indicate that the floors and walls were made of white marble.

The Black Sea coast from Varna to the Romanian border

The Dobrudzha region

North of Varna is the Dobrudzha region, an extensive cereal-growing plain that is the furthest direct extension of the **Eurasian steppe** into the Balkans—it is a very flat, featureless area with seemingly infinite horizons, which can be very cold and bleak in winter. It has always been of economic and political importance as a result of the tireless productivity of its soil. In the 19th and early 20C it was a bone of contention with neighbouring Romania who at one time controlled all of it. The population is very mixed, with members of nearly all of Bulgaria's ethnic and religious minorities present.

Ovid and the Black Sea

In antiquity this region was the place of exile of the great Roman poet Ovid (*Publius Ovidius Naso*, 43 BC–AD 17). He is believed to have spent most of his banishment from the Rome of Augustus in 8AD at ancient *Tomi*, modern Constanta, just over the frontier in Romania, but much of his writing about his exile describes conditions of life that were general then throughout the Black Sea region and the Dobrudzha inland. More than any other figure in Western literature, Ovid has been responsible for the images of the Black Sea coast as a wild, bleak, barbarous and uncivilised part of the world, fit only for exile and lonely isolation. In the *Tristia*, he prays for his ship as it passes *Anchialos*, modern Pomorie, near Burgas:

> may she steer her way along the Thymnian bays; and hence impelled past the city of Apollo, may she pass on her course the walls of Anchialos. Thence may she pass the harbours of Mesembria and Odessus and the towers, Bacchus, that are called after thy name.

Other condemnations of conditions in this region at the time are found in his *Epistulae ex Ponto*. Ovid conveys very well the perpetual threat of attack from barbarous Scythian and other local tribes endured by the Roman occupiers. Modern Classical scholarship has cast doubt on the validity of some of Ovid's grumbling, with one or two critics even arguing that the poet was never long in the region at all.

It takes a day to drive from Varna up to Romania and back, allowing for some stops, but more time is needed to appreciate the region fully. Although it includes the first parts of the coast to be developed for mass tourism north of Balchik, it is a generally little known and neglected part of the country, which is a pity as the **Dobrudzha steppe landscape** inland has an evocative and unique quality, and the coast itself has some interesting small places and undeveloped areas with very fine seascapes. Although it is possible to find places to swim en route, many of the coastal approach roads to the beaches are very poor, and it is best to use Tuzlata or one of the other beach resorts nearer Varna if you need a quick dip.

In antiquity the region was much less important than the coast south of

Varna, and there were no urban settlements that could be compared to highly cultured and prosperous Greek cities such as *Apollonia* (modern Sozopol) and *Mesembria* (modern Nesebur). The region was later regarded, largely through the influence of the Roman poet Ovid (see box), as a bleak, windswept and thoroughly uninviting wilderness. In Ottoman times it was important for cereal export production, and some small ports grew up along the coastline. After 1878, the Dobrudzha was bitterly contested between Romania and Bulgaria.

Leave Varna by the port road and then drive north through the modern suburbs towards Sveti Konstantin. There are a variety of hotels of all price ranges en route, and the road goes along a pleasant, wooded coastal strip with some attractive large houses many of which were built by the Varna business community as summer houses between the wars. It is a good quality asphalt dual carriageway for most of the way. The village of Viricia, on the outskirts of Varna, is inhabited by Vinitsa **Gagauz** people, Turkish speaking Orthodox Christians.

After 6km, you come to Trakata, with a right turn to **Euxinovgrad Palace**. This is a large and sprawling building that might well be called a 'stately pile' if it was in Britain. It was built in 1882 in the reign of Alexander I of Battenburg as the summer palace of the Bulgarian kings. It was used as a workers' sanitorium in the communist period then taken over by the communist leaders and became a summer playground for the Politburo and their friends. The vineyards nearby produce some of the best brandy in Bulgaria.

Sveti Konstantin
Sveti Konstantin was the first purpose-built tourist complex to be built along the Black Sea coast.

History of Sveti Konstantin
The resort was originally known as *Druzhba*, meaning Friendship, but has now regained its original name, after a monastery dedicated to St Constantine which was built here in the early 18C. The monastery was destroyed in 1828, and rebuilt before the Second World War, then demolished again after it. The building of the tourist complex was finished in 1956, after construction of the first hotels started in 1948.

The centre of the resort is reached by a right turn from the dual carriageway about 4km north of Varna. Tours from the West started in the mid 1950s. Thanks to its age, and modest size, it has matured into a very decent little resort, with well-run hotels that are not built on the elephantine scale later favoured. Sveti Konstantin has a relaxed atmosphere and a cosmopolitan mixture of visitors. (Recommended.) It is very well-planted with what are now mature deciduous trees, and has attractive gardens and lawns. There are three sandy beaches which are well kept. Although the sea here is clean it has quite a high level of natural vegetable matter in it, and sometimes jellyfish of a quite fearsome size make appearances.

With the decline of the international package holiday industry, it is easy to find somewhere to stay without booking, even in July and August. The **Grand Hotel Varna** (see p 145) is, on paper, the best hotel but it is quite expensive with a rather mediocre restaurant and is trying to break into the international conference market. Facilities for businessmen are good. The hotel swimming pool is very impressive. Unless you are on expense account it is better to stay at one of the smaller and cheaper places nearer the Varna road turn. The **Hotel Rosita** is pleasant and relaxing with reasonable food and friendly staff. There are some good craft stalls and shops nearby.

Carry ID documents at all times, as the police operate frequent security checks on people entering and leaving the resort.

Zlatni Pjasatsi (Golden Sands)

Zlatni Pjasatsi was the first mass market holiday resort to be developed in Bulgaria. It is about 10 minutes' drive north of Sveti Konstantin. Construction began in the late 1950s, and it was soon taking thousands of tourists a year for standard beach holidays. Initially most of these came from the Warsaw Pact countries, but after a time Western visitors followed. Despite these unpromising origins, it should not be written off, as in the last three years a good deal of time and effort have gone into upgrading and reorganising the resort, and many hotels and restaurants have improved under privatisation. The wooded surroundings are pleasant and well looked after.

The main attraction is the wide sandy **beach**, 3.5km long, and a variety of budget hotels and restaurants. There are 64 hotels in the resort, mostly two- and three-star category, 10 villas, 30 restaurants, and numerous shops, cafés, bars and folklore pubs. Although international demand for the standard 'Sea, Sun and Sex' holiday seems to be in serious decline, Golden Sands will probably be able to continue to compete with the Costa del Sol on price and the improving quality of the facilities. Most of the hotels seem to offer the same sort of food and standard of accommodation. If booking a package holiday in the UK, it is a good idea to stay in one of the smaller places.

Aladzha Monastery

5km west of Golden Sands is the Aladzha Monastery, one of the Bulgarian rock monasteries that flourished under the *hesychast* rule of solitary asceticism in the Middle Ages. The cliff with the caves is set in Hanchuka forest, which is a pleasant place to walk. The caves themselves are rather tatty but show the complex social world of some rock monastery settlements. Remains of churches and hermits' houses have been found nearby.

Return to the main road, drive north to Albena via **Kranevo**, a small beach resort. A few remains of a small 5C Byzantine fortress have been found in the village. Turn right 2km off the main road to Albena.

Albena

Albena is a standard, medium-sized modern resort with a wide and exposed, kilometre-long beach which is good for small children as the sea is shallow for up to 100m from the beach. The main place to stay is the **Dobroudja Hotel**, a well-managed but supremely ugly concrete block which has a large conference centre. There are good sports facilities, nine swimming pools, tennis courts, and various discos and night clubs. There are 27 other hotels in the resort, all two- or three-star, all modern and much of a muchness. Although a bit short on night life, it is a quite well-organised and pleasant place, and spotlessly tidy.

(Recommended.) There is a hydrotherapy treatment centre at the hotel which has a good reputation. The winter climate is sheltered and some hotels are open all the year round.

Obrochishte and Dobric

Inland from Albena, on the road to Balchik, is the village of **Obrochishte**. This is a mixed Bulgarian and ethnic Turkish village, with an interesting historic **Dervish tekke**, with a hexagonal *turbe* dating from the 16C. In the 18C there were said to be 26 monks living here.

The tekke is situated in countryside just outside the village and is difficult to find; ask for directions in the village. Although an important monument, one of the largest Dervish monasteries in this part of the Balkans, it has been closed for many years, the roof is in poor condition and urgent restoration is needed. This state of affairs is an indicator of the general neglect of Ottoman monuments in Bulgaria, that was supposed to improve with the end of communism.

A road leads inland towards the town of **Dobric** (33km). In the communist period Dobric, on the road to Silistra and the Danube, was known as *Tolbuhin*, after the Russian military leader. In Ottoman times it was called *Bazardzik*. The name Dobric originated in a re-naming ceremony after the Liberation, following the name of the boyar Dobrotica, ruler of the Dobrudzha in the 14C. Nowadays it is a rather dull and poor market town and not worth a special visit.

After 1940 there was substantial **ethnic cleansing** and population movement in this part of Bulgaria. In World War II about 40,000 ethnic Turks were sent to Turkey from the Dobrudzha by the Bulgarian government, and after 1946 the Russians expelled more and also many ethnic Greek, Romanian and Turkish inhabitants of Varna and the coast nearby.

Russian 'colonies' were then planted, on both sides of the Bulgarian–Romanian border involving about 30,000 people, some of whom were employed in large-scale agricultural schemes. **Stalin** also planned a grandiose scheme to construct a Danube–Black Sea canal in the region, to enable the Soviet fleet to reach the Danube without large ships being stopped by the Delta. Little was achieved and it was abandoned soon after his death. The general area remained closed to foreigners until 1956.

Return to the main coast road and drive north towards Balchik 15km.

Balchik

Balchik is a more interesting historic town than anywhere else nearby, huddling below sandstone cliffs, and with some good old Ottoman and National Revival small houses. It does not have much of a beach—the breakwaters constructed for the small commercial harbour only serving to collect vast amounts of seaweed—but it is well worth a short visit. When it was part of Romania **Queen Marie** built her summer palace here, parts of which can still be seen. There are one or two small hotels and private rooms may be available.

History of Balchik

Balchik was established as a very small Milesian colony by Greek settlers in the 5C BC. It was then called *Krounoi*, or *Dionysopolis*. Current scholarly debate about the ancient history of Balchik is focused largely on whether *Krounoi* and *Dionysopolis* were one or two cities. There is little information about its early history except that it seems to have been established to control shipping around the Kaliakra peninsula, and that it was known for wine exports, hence its alternative name, after Dionysus, god of wine. Some of this trade may have been with the area the Romans later called *Scythia Minor*, to the north.

The harbour silted up about AD 500, and urban life seems to have collapsed as a result. Balchik is a Turkish word meaning 'mud', and geographical conditions seemed to have changed little when in Ottoman times it grew up as a very small port, probably little more than a landing stage surrounded by a seasonal market linked to the export of agricultural products from the interior. Many of the inhabitants are ethnic **Tartars**, very warlike people who were used by the sultans as frontier guards. In the interwar period under Romanian rule there was little development and the interior remained a backward part of the country.

There are some interesting cafés and small restaurants near the harbour, and good fish can be found, with a little luck. In the town there is a **mosque**, a pleasant little 19C building, and a good **street market** with fruit and vegetables from the surrounding countryside. Beans are a local speciality. There is a good view of the strange little dome-shaped hills around the town from the road leaving the seafront to the north.

The **Palace of Queen Marie of Romania** is about a mile west of the town, on a hillside, surrounded by impressive gardens, with numerous follies and weird grottos and terraces.

Tuzlata

Tuzlata (communist period name—*Silberstrand*), 5km east of Balchik, is a rather run-down, nondescript resort on an exposed part of the coast, with little to recommend it apart from a reasonable beach and the extensive balneotherapy centre. This rather gloomy establishment was opened in the 1950s, based on the saline mud from the lagoon. It is supposed to be good for gynaecological and rheumatic conditions.

North of Balchik, the landscape changes substantially, to the vast flat open fields of the **Dobrudzha**, with sunflower and barley fields stretching into the distance and to immense horizons as far as the eye can see. 18km north of Balchik, you arrive at Kavarna. Kavarna is not a very exciting place in itself, but it is a good centre for the exploration of the very fine coastal scenery of the Kaliakra peninsula.

Kavarna

Kavarna is a minor Black Sea coast port which developed as a centre of trade in Dobrudzha grain. Attempts to set up an oil industry here in the early communist period were not successful. Some of the underlying strata were linked to Romanian oil-bearing strata, but quantities of oil and gas discovered were not commercially viable.

History of Kavarna

Kavarna stands on the site of the ancient Greek colony of *Bisoni*, a short-

lived city that did not much prosper; the settlement collapsed after an earthquake in 312. In the 14C Kavarna was the capital of an independent
statelet set up by the boyar Balik who rejected the authority of the
Bulgarian kings and allied himself with the Byzantines. In Ottoman times
Karabuna, meaning 'black cape' in Turkish, was established, a more
successful town that traded mostly with Venice, Genoa and Dubrovnik.
Most of the inhabitants then were either ethnic Greek or Greek speaking.

Kaliakra peninsula

History of the area
In antiquity the peninsula was known as *Cape Kaliakra*, and was an important focus for Greek shipping activities in the region. A fort was built in the
5C BC, and remained in use for centuries until the Ottoman conquest. It was
the headquarters of Vitalian who led a popular revolt against the Byzantine
emperor Anastasius early in the 6C. A major sea battle was fought here in
1791 between the Russian and Turkish fleets.

Kaliakra, probably ancient *Cape Tirisis* mentioned by the ancient Greek geographer Strabo, is a pleasant open headland with good sea views; some remains of
the old fortifications can be see on the point beyond the village of Balgarevo.
Kamen Brjag is a nice traditional village to the north, although it is a long walk
from the village to the sea and the roads on the headland are poor and virtually
non-existent in some places. The cliff is a notable landmark on this part of the
Black Sea coast and is buffeted by violent storms in winter. Colonies of seal live
in the caves in the rocks although numbers have been affected by the environmental crisis affecting the Black Sea. It is also an important site for rare seabirds,
such as the hooded cormorant, the pink starling, and the rock blackbird.
    Continue north 11km towards Shabla.

Shabla to the Romanian border
Shabla is a rather miserable little town, with communist-period buildings dominating what was an Ottoman market centre. There is a very poor hotel where it
is possible, *in extremis*, to stay. A dirt track leads to the sea at Nos Sabla (5km).
Proceed northwards through the town towards Ezerec (6km). The road runs
fairly near the coast, and the village of **Krapec**. Here there are some remains of
attempts to develop an oil industry, with 'nodding donkey' installations dotting
the tops of the cliffs near the sea.

> In the 1950s and 1960s, it was a perennial hope of the Sofia government
> that a substantial petroleum industry might be established here, as the oil-
> bearing measures are similar to those of neighbouring Romania, where a
> commercially successful industry has been established for many years.
> Neither oil nor gas has ever been found in commercial quantities in
> Bulgaria, in Krapec or elsewhere, and the little Krapec field was abandoned
> over 20 years ago. In recent years there have been various attempts to find
> offshore gas along the Black Sea littoral, and exploration is still in progress
> in some places.

North of Ezerec, the road crosses vast open fields of sunflowers and grain, and goes through the small village of **Vaklino** (7km), where there seem to be more geese than inhabitants. To the east the large coastal **lagoon** of Vaklino can be seen, across farmland. It is surrounded by deep reed beds which are very good for birdwatching. The lagoon itself is said to be mildly radioactive, and modern settlement has never developed nearby, although remains of ancient fishing settlements have been found in the vicinity.

Proceeding northwards towards the border, the very tall cranes of the Mangalia shipyard, in Romania, can be seen on the horizon. Pass through the village of **Durankulak** towards the border post 6km to the north, passing a military post and radar installations. Durankulak is a good place to buy very cheap semi-contraband goods, such as Romanian cigarettes. To the west there is a dramatic open landscape, with vast distant forests in Romania.

The **border** is open 24 hours a day, for people and vehicles. It is a rather bleak, open spot, with few arrangements for travellers who do not have their own transport, and anyone planning to use it as a pedestrian should have someone to meet them on the Romanian side. The Romanian port of **Constanta**, ancient *Tomis*, is 43km to the north, which is linked to Bucharest by dual carriageway and by rail.

The Black Sea coast south of Varna

■ **By car**. Generally it is a good main road to Burgas (132km), via Obzor, although it is often congested.

■ **By rail**. The train is slow and not recommended.

■ **By coach**. There are plenty of coach services, although services are less frequent in winter.

Leave Varna by the main road going south past the port and dry docks. To the left is the turn for **Galata** (3km), on the southern point of Varna Bay. There was an important **church** here, which was built in the early 5C on top of the ruins of a Thracian temple dedicated to the Madara Horseman (see p 164ff). The building was burnt down, probably by pirates, in the 6C. It has been fully excavated, revealing many votive reliefs of the Horseman which were incorporated into the Christian foundations. A large baptismal font found here is in Varna Museum of History and Art. Return to the main road by the same route.

The road passes through some deciduous woods with many small vineyards until you reach Bjala (1km). To the east of this road there are a number of very small resorts such as **Kamcija**, where it is possible to find somewhere to stay, but generally they are not very interesting places and this is a part of the coast that can be neglected. In antiquity the small Kamchiya river was known as the *Panysos*. There was a small Byzantine fortress called **Ereta** at the river mouth where it meets the sea, and the remains of a church that was destroyed in the 7C were excavated in 1939.

The road turns inland and crosses the end of the Stara Planina mountains (ancient *Hemus*) with fine views to the west, and thick deciduous woods. The road is not well maintained here, and frost damage is bad in some places, care is needed.

Bjala

Bjala is a quiet little resort with a wide beach with good sand although it is rather exposed to the prevailing wind. There are some cafés and places to eat.

History of Bjala

Bjala, from the Slav root word meaning 'white', takes its name from the cognate Greek word *Aspro*. It was the site of a small Dorian colony. The Romans established a garrison here after the conquest. A small Greek community survived through the medieval period, but largely disappeared in Ottoman times. Most modern inhabitants are descended from Bulgarians settled here after the First World War who were expelled from neighbouring countries. Post-1989, it has become a fashionable place for Sofia professionals to have a small summer house.

Obzor

South of Bjala you come to Obzor with a very fine long open **beach**, and a camping site. There are some ancient Roman columns in the public park.

History of Obzor

Modern Obzor is built near the site of an ancient Greek colonial settlement called *Naulochus*. It was an important religious centre, founded by Dorians from *Mesembria* (modern Nesebur) with a temple of Zeus by the sea. After the Roman conquest it was called *Templum Jovis*, and prospered as a small port. A medieval fortress was built here in the 14C, which was taken over by the Ottoman conquerors and called *Gozeken*. The surviving Greek-speaking people in the vicinity called the little town that grew up *Heliopolis*, City of the Sun. It took its present Bulgarian name after 1878.

Emona

To the south of Obzor, there is a good view of **Cape Emine**, now a thickly wooded outcrop into the sea, with little cultivation, but in antiquity the site of ancient *Emona*, a small city established by Greek colonists.

History of Emona

The small settlement of *Emona* was primarily a religious centre in ancient times, with a Thracian temple dedicated to the culture hero Rhesus, the son of Strymon, mentioned by Homer in *The Iliad*. The Greeks must have built a temple in the same place, which was taken over by the Romans and dedicated to Jupiter. In Roman times, according to Pliny, the place was known as *Aristaeum*. In medieval times a monastery was built, dedicated to St Nicholas, the patron saint of mariners.

It is worth a detour to see the Cape properly, with lovely unspoilt beaches although they shelve steeply with strong undercurrents and great care is needed by even the strongest swimmers in all weather conditions.

Take the small road to the left of the main road towards the hamlet of **Erakli**, ancient *Heraclea*. This leads to the sea through attractive small fields and woodlands where herds of wild boar are pastured, along a dirt track to the left of the road junction before Erakli village. The area was used in communist times for holiday homes for senior party officials and so has remained unspoilt. There is a small concrete and wooden landing stage, and a nice little beach. It is a beautiful and peaceful place.

Regrettably the same cannot be said of the coast south of Cape Emine, where after returning to the main road by the same route and travelling south through woods and fields for a few kilometres, the tower blocks and ribbon development associated with the vast mega-resort of **Slancev Brjag** (Sunny Beach) are visible. It opened in 1959, and is the largest resort in Bulgaria, with over 25,000 beds, and is one of the largest purpose-built seaside resorts in the entire world. About 400,000 people a year take their holidays here, a substantial proportion of which seem to come from the old GDR region of Germany. It is an overweight concrete dinosaur—a monument to the communist planners.

The real achievements in upgrading the mass market beach resorts north of Varna, such as Sveti Konstantin, have not been matched at Sunny Beach, or even perhaps attempted, although security has improved since the mid 1990s. It remains a vast soulless complex with all the faults of impersonal communist town planning involving ugly modernist buildings that have not all been well looked after.

Some effort has been made to mitigate the vast and impersonal scale of the place with the **Elenite holiday village**, 8km away to the northeast—take the Sveti Vlas turn off the main road, with smaller and more traditional accommodation. This is a much better place to stay than central Sunny Beach with quite pleasant little apartment blocks, a good beach 800m long, and a three star hotel, the Emona. It specialises in water sports, water skiing in particular.

There are 113 hotels in the Sunny Beach complex, and five campsites, and seeemingly endless bars and discotheques, tennis courts, a yacht club, open air theatre and riding club. It is possible to hire boats and motorboats to explore the nearby coast.

■ **Security**. Although the authorities have attempted to improve security in the resort, they have been hampered by its vast size and the fact that many of the modernist buildings could have been designed as a thieves' and muggers' paradise. Care is needed, and safe deposit facilities for valuables are essential. Tourists should check to see that they are available at any hotel where a booking is planned.

The beach itself is clean with good sand but vast and open, producing chills if there is a north wind, and rapid sunburn in high summer. There are a few noteworthy 'British' landmarks, such as the **Red Lion**, an exact replica of a mock-Tudor English pub, although there is no real ale and few of the staff speak any English, and numerous establishments designed to cater for the tastes of less sophisticated Teutons. It is somewhere to avoid unless you are looking for a beer swilling, disco bopping, bottom pinching, budget holiday.

One of the few positive features of the place is a good locally produced brandy, *Slancev Brjag*, which is distributed all over Bulgaria and is well worth buying.

Follow the main road south from Sunny Beach for 7km to reach the historic town of Nesebur.

Nesebur

Nesebur (96km from Varna) is one of the oldest Greek colonial settlements on the Black Sea coast, now a picturesque tourist centre, built largely on a small rocky peninsula, south of Cape Emine, below the Stara Planina mountains. It contains some of the finest treasures of **Byzantine church architecture** in Bulgaria, some of which require restoration work. Most of the area of the town is either out of bounds for cars, or so crowded that you are better off without one. The main sights can be seen in a day, but two days allows a more leisurely and rewarding visit. It can be a little crowded in summer and has suffered some exploitation for commercial purposes and the serious student of the buildings may find spring or autumn a better time to visit.

Accommodation in high season is not always easy to obtain at a sensible price, and should be pre-booked if possible, although if in difficulties it is always possible to stay somewhere in nearby Sunny Beach. Some of the fish restaurants in the town, and the local wine are both very good. Souvenir shops vary from appalling tat emporia to interesting craft centres. As a result of its proximity to Sunny Beach, it is a classic tourist trap, and prices need watching, especially the currency rates offered by local exchange bureau.

Some inhabitants understand and speak some Greek, but on the whole Nesebur has been slower to rediscover its Hellenic heritage in the post-communist period than Varna and Sozopol.

Street fountain

History of Nesebur

Nesebur was originally a Thracian settlement—dating from the second millennium BC—called *Menebria*, named after the tribe of the chieftain Miniji. The original town was much larger than modern Nesebur, before changes in sea level during antiquity and the continual erosion of the eastern shore of the peninsula by heavy storms. This continues to this day. Material such as earthenware pots and dwelling foundations from the Bronze Age have been found. In 510 BC Greek colonists from Chalcedon, Megara and Byzantium established the town of *Mesembria*. It was a Dorian colony, unlike adjacent *Apollonia* and *Odessus*. In the 5C the inhabitants started minting their own coins, and wide-ranging economic relationships with the interior were established, mainly based on copper mining. For a time the Greeks came under the protection of the Thracian king Seuth III (see *Seuthopolis*, p 198). **Herodotus** mentions the town when the Persian King Darius marched against the Scythians in 513 BC.

By the end of the 5C, *Mesembria* was a rival of *Apollonia*, and war broke out between the two cities in 400. Active commercial relations with Athens also developed in this period, and the city gained control of the important salt production at *Anhialo* (modern Pomorie). The results of the war with *Apollonia* were inconclusive, and by the middle of the next century both cities were allies against the rising power of the Macedonian kings. Trade continued to grow at this time, and the houses of a large number of wealthy merchants date from this period. Temples to Zeus, Asclepius and Apollo were constructed over this time, followed by shrines to the Egyptian gods Isis and Seraphis. Unlike *Apollonia*, the city did not attempt to fight the Roman invaders in the 1C, and under Lucullus Roman occupation began after the year 72 BC when the town surrendered to avoid destruction.

It was then known as *Mesembria*, and fell within the Roman province of Moesia until AD 86 when it was in Lower Moesia and from the mid 2C the new province of Thrace. The port did not prosper under the Romans, and trade declined, although a statue of the Emperor Claudius was erected in the 1C. It minted coin from the time of Emperor Hadrian to that of Philip the Arabian who banned all the Black Sea mints in 244. Mesembria was unaffected by the Goths' invasion in the 3C, after which the name disappears from history until the early Byzantine era when the role of Constantinople as capital of the Eastern Empire brought revival. It was then part of the Imperial Province of Memimont, when a strong external fortification was built, four basilicas constructed and coin was once again minted. In 587 the hinterland was sacked by the Avars, but the town escaped.

In 681 the Byzantine Emperor Constantine sought refuge in Mesembria after the defeat of his army by the Bulgarian Khan Asparuh. At this time the town was one of the best fortified towns in the Balkans, and it remained a Byzantine stronghold until 812.

Prosperity continued under the onslaughts of the early Bulgarian kings, when the Slav name **Nesebur** was adopted. The fortress was important for the Byzantines in their naval operations against the First Bugarian kingdom based on Pliska and Preslav. In 812 the city fell to Khan Krum, without destruction, but remained an important economic link with the Byzantine Empire. It was a vital entrepôt between Byzantium and the other Black Sea regions.

The city remained of mixed Byzantine and Bulgarian and Slav population, and alternated between Byzantine and Bulgarian control until 1336 when it was ceded by Amadeus of Savoy to his cousin, the Byzantine Emperor, John V Paleologus. In this period the town expanded onto the mainland and the population grew considerably. Chroniclers refer to the town as 'populous Mesembria', and it was involved in the complex political intrigues between Byzantium, Bulgaria and Venice. In 1441 the last Byzantine Emperor, Constantine, fled to Mesembria to escape the Ottoman Turks. In February 1453 Nesebur fell to the Ottoman Turks. It soon achieved a favoured position under the Sultan, and for 200 years kept a modest prosperity and independence. It was refortified in the 17C to try to protect it against Cossack pirates. Throughout this period the Church survived, and new buildings were constructed. The Turkish traveller Evlija Celebi noted in the mid 17C the quality of the local vineyards and fish, but noted that the fortress was in ruins and piracy was causing serious problems for the town.

In the 18C and 19C a long process of decline began, which acclerated after the liberation of Bulgaria from the Ottomans and the beginning of the development of Burgas as a modern port. Throughout this period the ethnic Greek community maintained itself, and Greek was the normal language of trade and religion for most inhabitants. The German traveller, Wentzel von

Outer walls of Nesebur

Bronyar, visited the town in 1786 and noted the active religious life of the 13 Orthodox churches. Nesebur was seized by the Russians for a short time in 1828–29, during the Russo-Ottoman war. It was liberated from the Turks in 1878. It remained a small fishing village, as the sheltered Burgas harbour nearby could take much larger ships. In the 20C the economy has revived with tourism, and there has been an extension of the town onto the mainland. Important underwater archaeological explorations are planned near the much-eroded north shore of the peninsula which are likely to lead to a great increase in knowledge of the ancient town.

Park in the car park under the walls on the north side of the peninsula. Walk back towards the main entrance gate on the west side of the peninsula. In front of you are remains of the medieval Byzantine **fortifications** and sea defences, imposing walls about 6m high, in stone and red brick. Passing through the walls, on the right is the town **Archaeological Museum**. Open 09.00–13.30, 14.00–18.00.

This is an interesting, well-laid out collection, although the museum building itself is obtrusively modernist. On the **upper floor** there are ancient Greek vases, coins, terracottas and other ceramics, votive objects, a very fine Byzantine **Ikon of the Virgin**, and some very good examples of medieval folk art, the carved wooden figures in particular. Other outstanding exibits include a bronze hydria, 'The Abduction of Oreitheia by Boreas', coins from ancient Mesembria, and Slavonic and medieval-Bulgarian ceramics. **Downstairs** there is an ikon museum, with some very fine works of art, the medieval examples in particular. The metal ikon of the Virgin and Child is a breathtaking masterpiece.

Leaving the museum, and turning right, the road forks. It does not matter very much which way you take, in either case you pass a large number of very fine 18C and 19C wooden houses. Taking the right (south) side, you are soon in a small open square with the **Church of the Pantkrator** on your left. This is an impressive 13C building from the outside, but it is difficult to see the interior properly as it has been transformed rather badly into an art gallery, an example of the insensitive commercial pressures to which parts of Nesebur are being subjected.

Near the sea is the **Ethnographic Museum**, in a pretty small wooden house. The exhibits are the usual mixture of folk costumes and peasant artefacts, but the house is a fine example of an old Nesebur house, dating from the Turkish period and worth seeing. The best church in Nesebur is the **Church of St Stefan**, down a slope to the right of the main central lane going towards the sea. It has outstanding frescoes, in a low medieval building, with a large amount of Byzantine masonry scatterred around in the courtyard. Below it, by the seashore, is the ruined **Church of St John**, an evocative early Byzantine building with very good patterned brickwork. Local musicians, often Russians, sometimes give impromptu performances inside. There are several other very fine small churches in the town, but at the moment many are closed. If you have a particular interest in Byzantine churches, it is best to visit on a Sunday, or even better, a major religious festival.

Returning to the main road, continue south towards Pomorie 21km, past a turn to the small resort of Ravda (7km).

Pomorie

Pomorie, ancient *Anchialos*, 21km south of Nesebur, is the last significant settlement before Burgas is reached. It is a popular holiday resort and has one important extractive industry, the local **saltpans** which supply much of Bulgaria's salt; they have been in continuous use since ancient times. Pomorie is also famous for the quality of its **wine** and *rakia*, particularly *Grozdova* which many good judges consider to be the best *rakia* in the entire country. The town itself, although welcoming and with some good fish restaurants, is much less interesting than Nesebur as it suffered in its history from a series of disastrous fires, the most recent of which, in 1906, destroyed virtually every historic building. This was linked to IMRO pogroms against the local Greek community. It is nevertheless a friendly unpretentious place for those on a limited budget. A private room rental is a good holiday option. Buses from the main bus station go to Varna and Burgas. There is a hydrotherapy centre in the town with warm mud baths, which are used to treat arthritis and sciatica.

History of Pomorie

Pomorie was originally an ancient Greek colony called *Anchialos*, founded in the 4C BC by Ionian settlers from *Apollonia* (modern Sozopol). It became involved in the trade and political rivalries between *Apollonia* and *Mesembria*, and remained a small place until Roman times when it prospered after being made an Imperial administrative centre. It was then called *Ulpia Anchialos*, in the time of Trajan. Very large fortifications were constructed in this period, but the town was captured by the Goths in 270. The Roman poet Ovid stayed in Anchialos on the way to his Pontic exile. In 812 the town fell to Khan Krum, and became a centre for agricultural trade and exports. It was awarded a salt monopoly by the Ottoman Turks. It was a centre of Greek business activity in the Black Sea in the 19C, and was the seat of a bishop, but many Greeks were ethnically cleansed from here in the 1906 pogroms, when the town was set on fire.

You enter Pomorie through small industrial suburbs, then into a rather run-down, nondescript town centre dating from the 1950s. The few remaining buildings from the pre-fire period are mostly perched on the top of the cliff at the end of the peninsula—two or three National Revival wooden houses. There is a wide and quite good **beach**, with good surfing waves on the right day, and without such severe shelving of the sand as on many southern Black Sea beaches. In the town it is possible to find good fried fish. There are a few Greek-speakers, but in general the cultural atmosphere is still a little more that of skilled working-class Bulgaria than in the fashionable and increasingly Hellenised areas around Sozopol. This is largely because the town was chosen in communist times to be the resort for a number of trades union holiday centres, and a large chalet settlement on the outskirts of the town remains in use. These chalets adjoin the large Pomorie **saltpans** which must be one of the oldest industries carried on in the same place and by the same methods in Europe, if not the world. Salt was obtained here for the fish-curing industry which began in early antiquity.

5km west of Pomorie, off the main road, a large Thracian–Roman **tomb** was found, probably dating from the 4C.

The Shumen region and the First Bulgarian Kingdom

The Shumen region inland from Varna contains some of the most important monuments from the First Bulgarian Kingdom (681–1018), and if time is available should form part of any itinerary. It is possible to stay in Shumen itself, and elsewhere, but Shumen is a run-down and depressing town and it is much pleasanter to remain based in the Varna area and to hire a car for a day or two, or use public transport and taxis to reach the sites and monuments, all of which can be done on a day trip. It is also possible to reach them from a Ruse base, see p 138. It takes about two hours to drive from Ruse to Shumen (111km), on a good asphalt road, about one and a half hours from Varna (93km). Shumen is on the Varna–Sofia rail line.

Leave Varna by the A2 motorway to the west. About 4km on, to the left, is the petrified forest, **Pobiti Kamani**, a collection of fossilised trees protruding from sandstone that used to be regarded as a great tourist attraction in communist times. They were formed when this area, known as *Dikilitash*, lay under a shallow sea.

After 15km you pass the western end of the Varna lagoons and then **Devnya**, site of a vast chemical and plastics plant which has severely polluted the surrounding countryside. **Avoid this locality**.

History of Devnya

Devnya is near the site of ancient *Marcianopolis*, founded by the Emperor Trajan and named after his sister Marcia. It was built as a military centre, with a fortress defended by 14 towers, and as a Roman counterpart to the powerful but essentially Greek city of *Odessus* (modern Varna). It was prosperous for a time, but was destroyed in the Gothic and other barbarian invasions. Remains of a large amphitheatre, baths and villas have been found, although much remains to be excavated.

After about an hour's journey across pleasant open country with good quality arable and grazing land, you come to Shumen (63km).

Shumen

Shumen is close to three sites of major importance in the early development of the Bulgarian nation: **Preslav**, **Pliska**, and the **Madara Horseman**. The old town of Shumen itself is worth a look around, with a large fortress, a very well-known mosque, and some old houses and small streets which have a good Ottoman atmosphere. Many of the museums dating back to the communist period in these houses are now closed as a result of property restitution.

Shumen, a regional centre of some importance, has suffered heavily from its past associations with the communist regime. It was a favoured centre that received a good deal of attention and investment money. Since the early 1990s, these resources have dried up, and there has been little to replace them, although there are a fair number of private shops and small-scale commercial developments. Many people living here are very poor, and unemployment is very high. Some people are xenophobic—behave circumspectly.

■ **Hotels and restaurants**. Staying in Shumen is not particularly recommended at the moment, on both practical and security grounds, but there are a number of possible hotels. The **Hotel Shumen** and **Hotel Madara** both try to charge ridiculous prices for what is offered. Try instead the **Hotel Orbita**, which is at least cheaper. All have just about tolerable restaurants. A pizza is preferable or even a sandwich.

History of Shumen

The hill above Shumen has been fortified from the earliest times, with Thracian and Roman remains being found. Under the First Bulgarian Kingdom (681–1018) a new castle was built that was later modified and extended by the Turks. The town grew considerably in the 18C and formed part of the northern defence system of the Ottoman Empire, with a very extensive rampart defence system. In the 19C many Hungarian and Polish refugees came to the town, adding to the existing ethnic diversity with its Armenian, Jewish and Turkish quarters. Lajos Kossuth, the Hungarian hero of the 1848 revolution, lived here for a while in 1849, and introduced beer brewing into Bulgaria. It was a centre of education in the National Revival period. In 1950 it was renamed *Kolarovgrad*, after a commmunist leader who was born in Shumen in 1877, but reverted back to Shumen in the 1960s.

The Ottoman **fortress** is well worth visiting. The hill was first fortified by the Thracians, and the Romans extended the existing castle. It was developed in the First Bulgarian Kingdom to protect the road to Pliska. The Ottomans made it a military strongpoint and it became part of the strategic defences of the later Empire against Russia. The Turks built huge ramparts, the lower walls of which can still be seen.

Built on top of a natural rock outcrop, 2km to the west of the town, with very fine views over the surrounding countryside, the outer walls are protected by some impressive hexagonal corner towers in the later Ottoman style of military architecture. There are the foundation walls of numerous small Ottoman buildings in the interior of the fortress. It is very much a 'Turkish' monument, in what remains, and as such was not much promoted for tourist purposes in the communist period when the iconography and monuments of this part of the country were heavily angled towards the promotion of Bulgarian nationalism. An example of this is the horrifically ugly, huge and inappropriate **'1300 Years of Bulgaria'** concrete hilltop monument nearby; a gross eyesore and blot on the landscape.

The **mosque of Sharif Pasha** is very fine, and worth visiting, although requiring restoration. It is a large 18C mosque with a beautiful courtyard and fountain, indicating the high cultural level of the Ottoman town in this period. In the 19C the majority of the population of the town were Muslims.

Pliska

To reach ancient Pliska, turn right off the main Varna–Shumen road at Novi Pazar, a dull industrial town and follow a small road northwards across empty countryside. The restored **fortress walls** are on the left of this road, in the middle of farmland, after about 6km. It is a lonely, evocative sprawling site, with remains of low walls indicating the scale of the civilisation the first Bulgarian khans established after their arrival from central Asia. Although there is nothing particularly dramatic to see, it is well worth visiting, with a strong atmosphere of the very remote past when Bulgaria was born as a nation.

History of Pliska

Pliska was the capital of the First Bulgarian Kingdom (681–1018), but was a central objective of the Byzantine Emperors in their wars with the Bulgarians and was sacked by the Emperor Nicephorus in 810. In 855 it was the residence of followers of Kyril and Methodius when the Cyrillic alphabet was brought to Bulgaria. The Pliska settlement was probably Slav in origin, near the route of the old Roman road that linked *Odessus*, modern Varna, with the Danube near modern Ruse, but was taken over by the tribes that formed the Greater Bulgarian Union.

Most scholars consider the people to have been of Turkic origin, and to have come to Bulgaria as mounted horsemen in a horde which originated in the lands between the Volga and Dneiper rivers, and the Black and the Caspian seas. Their chief deity was *Tangra*, the creator of the world, and his will was interpreted by the **Khan**, the priest king. The Khan ruled through a council of six *Boils*. The First Kingdom was composed of these tribes, and the neighbouring Slav *Severae* tribe. Pliska was heavily fortified and became its capital. It extended from the Black Sea coast as far as the crest of the *Hemus* mountains (modern Stara Planina), and extended north over the Danube to include parts of modern Romania and Bessarabia.

The town declined rapidly after the capital was moved to Preslav by Tsar Boris I in 893.

The impressive **ruins** of ancient Pliska occupy a large area, over 20 square kilometres, and can be visited at any time free of charge. You enter through a rebuilt arch in the main front wall, where the restoration, although well intentioned and professional, gives something of the impression of an old-style studio film set for a medieval B-movie. There is a long straight path to the foundations of the **Royal Palace**, with low walls showing masonry work using large interlocking blocks of very high quality. It makes an enjoyable walk to wander around the rest of the site, with many low walls exposed in the grassland. There are good views across the surrounding countryside.

The Madara Horseman

The Madara Horseman is one of the most famous sights in Bulgaria, near the modern village of Madara, about 11km east of Shumen. It is a remarkable carved image of a horseman with a hound fighting a lion, made about 91m up the sheer cliff face outside the village. Unfortunately, it is completely covered by scaffolding at the moment, and cannot be seen, and it is not clear at the time of writing when this situation will change.

The general area has been inhabited since antiquity, with Greek inscriptions having been found dating to the 3C BC. The exact origin of the carving is not known, and scholars disagree about the date of the work. One school of thought claims that it is an image of the ancient Thracian rider god which was taken over as a symbol by the first Bulgarian rulers, while others believe it was carved in the 8C AD, citing evidence of rock inscriptions nearby.

The monument is reached up a set of steps, below which are a number of small cafés, a museum (currently closed), and a very fine fresh water spring. There is a railway station in the village connecting with Shumen, although trains do not run very often at the moment. There are a number of caves in the vicinity, some very large, and a large number of assorted remains of churches, cave retreats for monks and some Byzantine fortification, on top of the cliffs. Evidence has been found of the continuation of pagan rituals in the area connected with the source of the small Madara river nearby.

Most visitors to Madara at the moment seem to find the area a disappointment; apart from the obscured carving, the atmosphere is lonely and isolated, and there are few modern facilities for visitors.

Veliki Preslav

Modern Preslav is a dull and mediocre little town, 13km southwest of Shumen, economically depressed and depopulated. Veliki Preslav (ancient *Preslav*) is on a hill outside the town. On the way, the **museum** is worth visiting, a left turn (unsigned) about 1km to the south on the main road to the ancient site. If coming from Sofia, you turn left over a modern bridge towards the site.

History of Preslav

Preslav was founded by Khan Omurtag in 821 and became the capital of the First Bulgarian Kingdom in the reign of Tsar Simeon (893–927). It soon became a major urban centre but its majesty only lasted for a century or so before it was captured by the Byzantines in 972 and burnt down. Although urban settlement continued, it never regained its pre-eminence and was dominated by Tarnovo in the high Middle Ages. The little town that remained was taken by the Turks in the Ottoman invasion and largely destroyed except for the houses of a few rural inhabitants. The Ottomans developed Shumen as their administrative centre for the region.

To enter the **museum**, drive about 500m up the side road and into a large car park. **Open** 09.00–12.00, 14.00–17.00, in theory.

The museum is a pretentious, ugly modern building with an odd processional path lined with statues up to the entrance that could only have been

Outer fortification wall

designed to provide a backdrop for photographs of visiting communist leaders. It does not seem to be open, but it is possible to get inside by ringing the bell. The staff are unhelpful, and there is not a great deal of interest to see apart from some attractive early jewellery, weapons, coins and ceramics, on the upper floor. The only outstanding exhibit is a stone carving of a **Proto-Bulgarian horseman** on a lump of limestone rock.

Veliki Preslav is a vast, confusing site that seems to stretch endlessly over farmland and into woods. Some excavations are in progress at the moment. The most impressive part for the non-specialist are the remains of the north walls, which convey very well the power and cultural level of the growing feudal kingdom. In essence, Veliki Preslav consisted of two enormous **concentric fortresses**, covering an area of over 1250 acres. A town was built inside the **outer fortress** walls, with a basilica, smaller churches, markets and ceramic workshops. In the **inner fortress** there was a palace complex, baths, a mint and a barracks. At the far end of the site, best reached by returning to the car and driving another 1km in the Sofia direction, is the partly restored **Golden Church**, a pleasant, roofless First Kingdom building with impressive marble columns. Some of the restoration work in concrete is poor and does not help the atmosphere of the church. It was built near the south wall of the outer fortress.

In general, Preslav illustrates the need for a fundamental reappraisal and rethinking of the medieval heritage of Bulgaria in the new post-communist period. The site is symbolic of the crisis in post-communist ideology, where medieval history was 'appropriated' by the communist leaders for basically nationalist purposes, and mythologised. The site needs to be made 'user-friendly' for foreign visitors, with some foreign-language signs and professionally written guidebooks. At the moment it is not even possible to buy a postcard at what is one of the major medieval sites in the country.

Return to Shumen by the same route, through pleasant open countryside with a high limestone ridge to the left.

Burgas and the Southern Black Sea Coast

- **By car**. From Sofia, 410km. From Plovdiv, 264km. From Varna, 135km, by the southern coast road, via Staro Orjahovo (35km), to Nesebur (100km), to Pomorie (121km), to Burgas port (135km), or about 121km by the inland route, via Diulino and Kableskovo. The coastal route is very scenic, and is a wider road, but is congested in the summer.

- **By public transport**. The **train** journey from Varna is slow and indirect, if using public transport, go by **bus** or **coach**. There is, however, a good, fast **train** service from Sofia.

- **By air**. From the airport, it is about 12km in to Burgas city centre, on a good road, delays are unusual.

Burgas

Burgas (pop. 178,239) is, with Varna, the main industrial and manufacturing centre on the Black Sea coast. It is largely a 20C creation, although built on the site of the ancient Greek colonial settlement of *Pirgos*, meaning 'the tower'. Burgas is nowadays a tough and functional industrial city. Most of the suburban architecture embodies the worst of the communist period and there is little to delay the visitor. The **historic centre** is very interesting, though, and generally underestimated, with one or two outstanding **churches** and one of the best provincial **archaeological museums** in Bulgaria. A very good **international folk festival** is held each August. It is quite feasible for the visitor with transport to stay in nearby coastal towns such as Sozopol (see p 173).

- **Security**. The *Mafiya* is a major force in Burgas life and pedestrian journeys at night outside the city centre are not recommended. **Avoid** all 'security' firms and bodyguard companies. **Avoid** casinos and night clubs. Some inhabitants carry **handguns** or other personal weapons, avoid minor quarrels.

- **Airport**. Although about the same size as Varna airport, and modern and efficient, Burgas has never developed to the same extent. It is used by charter companies and for cargo and internal flights. Moscow is the only real international destination, although there are flights by small airlines to the Ukraine and Belarus on some days. (**Balkan Airlines**, ☎ 056 34062, fax 31901.)

- **Hotels**. The best hotel in Burgas, and an indispensible centre for business and general communications, is the **Hotel Bulgaria** in Alexandrovska Street (☎ 42820, fax 47291, telex 83555). At the time of writing, rooms cost about $US70. In the foyer there are bars, telephone booths, a café, and shops selling jewellery, weapons and cosmetics. It is a good place to buy long distance coach tickets or to hire a car. **Recommended**.

■ **Restaurants**. The **National**, near the port entrance, is not cheap but it is excellent, one of the best restaurants on the Black Sea coast. The **live music** is also outstanding.

■ **Car Hire**. Hertz office is on ☎ 563591.

■ **International Folk Festival**. This is a well established and high quality event. It is usually held at the end of August.

History of Burgas

The bay of Burgas and the delta lands formed by the three rivers discharging into the bay were settled in the earliest times by primitive people who formed small settlements based mostly on fishing. They appear to have made villages built on wood piles in the marshlands resembling ancient Irish crannogs. In the Izgrev district to the northwest of the town, Thracian remains have been discovered. In the period of ancient Greek colonisation of the Black Sea coast, *Pirgos* was a minor settlement, connected economically to the important cities of *Apollonia* (Sozopol), and *Mesembria* (Nesebur). The Romans built a coastal fortress, called *Scafida*. In Byzantine times a small port was developed near Burgas, called *Develtos*. In 812 it was captured by Khan Krum and integrated into the Bulgarian Kingdom for a time, before being recaptured by the Byzantines.

For hundreds of years the Burgas lagoons were used by fishermen who reaped their rich harvest, until in the 17C larger settlements began to be established, with some immigration of Turkish fishermen. The new village was called *Sindzirli Bunar*, in Turkish, but it never grew much in the pre-industrial period owing to the very severe malaria in the area.

The 19C small town grew somewhat on the basis of Black Sea coastal trade in the pre-Liberation period. Modern Burgas developed as a port with the industrialisation of Bulgaria in the latter part of the 19C. The port was constructed by French engineers in 1903. Burgas soon became an important centre for foreign capital investment in Bulgaria, particularly corn and flour mills. In 1920 there was a short-lived Soviet declared in the city, which had become a centre of socialism.

Under communism, it was developed as an industrial town, with major investments in engineering, shipbuilding, woodworking and food production. The culmination of this process was the construction of the oil refinery and oil port in 1960–63, covering an area of over 200ha. Subsequently, associated Neftochim chemical plants were added to the complex. It has been an environmental disaster for the entire surrounding area, with serious sea and air pollution, although in the post-communist period, there have been some improvements.

A walk around the most interesting parts of **historic Burgas** takes about half a day or so. Starting from the **port**, where there are some good cafés and restaurants, you see behind you bulk-loading cargo facilities which at the moment seem to be mainly used for timber exports and coal imports.

Walk through a small park and cross the road, towards the modern tower of the

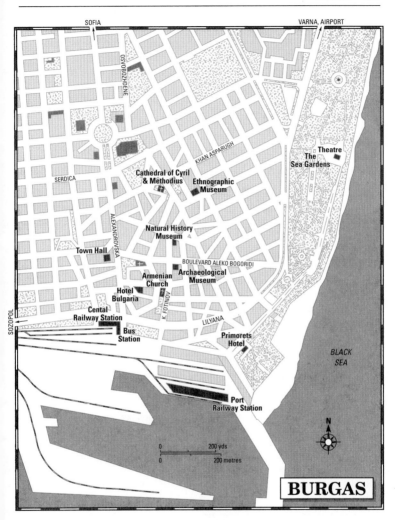

SOFIA

VARNA, AIRPORT

OSVOBOZHDENE

KHAN ASPARUGH

SERDICA

ALEXANDROVSKA

SOZOPOL

The
Sea Gardens

Theatre

Cathedral of Cyril
& Methodius

Ethnographic
Museum

Natural History
Museum

Town Hall

BOULEVARD ALEKO BOGORIDI

Armenian
Church

Archaeological
Museum

Hotel
Bulgaria

K. FOTINOV

Cental
Railway Station

LILYANA

Bus
Station

Primorets
Hotel

BLACK
SEA

Port
Railway Station

N

0   200 yds
0   200 metres

BURGAS

Neftochim headquarters. On the left is the **railway station**, an attractive late
19C building, although needing repair and redecoration. In general architectural style, it has some resemblance to the great Central Station in Belgrade,
which was built at the same time. Over the main road you are near the main
central square, shops and pedestrianised area, with all the interesting buildings
and monuments. Burgas has some surprisingly good shops, and prices, even for
imported goods, are much lower than in Sofia or Varna.

On the right is the modern **Hotel Bulgaria**, see above. Opposite it is the City
Hall. Right behind the hotel is the **Armenian Church**, a delighful little building
that was consecrated in 1858, after a construction period lasting five years. The
exterior is very fine and elegant, of white granite with very beautiful deep blue

The Armenian Church of Sveti Hach

stained glass windows, and a small external porch and two-storey bell tower. The plain wood-panelled interior, with paintings of the Stations of the Cross, has an austere atmosphere; but the custodian is very helpful. It has a great local tradition of sung liturgical worship.

Behind the Armenian Church in Boulevard Bogoridi is the **Church of Sveti Bogoroditsa**. This is a very ugly and unprepossessing 19C building with a huge grey granite west façade wall, but it has a fine **neo-classical marble interior**, with white columns showing more than a hint of Greek influence, and a very good carved priest's throne and iconostasis.

Across the Alexandrovska Street to the left about 350m is a small pedestrianised street, Aleko Bogoridi, that has some attractive 19C buildings, including the **Archaeological Museum**, 500m down on the right, where the collection is kept in a large 19C merchant's house. This should be seen on any visit to Burgas if possible, as it is compact, well laid out, and contains a quality collection from all periods of ancient Bulgarian history, with some outstanding Thracian and Roman sculpture. This is also the best street to eat out in central Burgas.

The museum has five well-lit modern rooms, with material from the neolithic settlements on the Black Sea coast in the first, including stone and horn tools, Bronze Age ceramics and parts of primitive boats and corn grinding stones. The second room has exhibits of Thracian metalwork and ceramics, and material from the Greek colonial period, including coins, votive reliefs, with very fine carvings of a Boy and his Dog, maenads and satyrs.

The third room covers the end of the Greek colonial period and the beginning of Roman colonisation, with metalwork, ceramics, textiles and a wooden chest. There are very fine **votive reliefs** showing the Thracian Horseman. The fourth room shows the Roman colonisation of the interior, with vases, lamps, column bases, a statue of a lion, iron tools and weapons and agricultural implements. The last room covers late Roman and Byzantine Burgas, with fragments of mosaics, ceramics, sculpture and jewellery.

Crossing Aleko Bogoridi Street, turn left into Permetov Street. About five minutes' walk down here on the right is the **Historical Museum of Burgas**. **Open** Tues–Sun mornings, at least in theory.

The museum has an interesting collection concentrating on the 19C Liberation period, with some very fine **weapons** and **early photographs** of Burgas. There are also some outstanding exhibits on inter-war Burgas life, showing the cultural and political vitality of what was then a quite sophisticated provincial city. It is a pity that many of the exhibits are not well lit, and that there are no foreign-language captions on the display cases, as this could be a very informative museum for foreign visitors interested in Balkan history in this region.

On the opposite side of the street, another 300m down, is the **Natural History Museum. Open** 09.30–17.00, closed Mon.

This is housed in a fine early 20C mansion, with double staircases to the street and an entrance at first-floor level. It is a pleasant, rewarding place that has suffered some neglect in Bulgaria's recent past but deserves a visit. Although it has exhibits of all the flora and fauna of the region, the main interest is the material relating to the **Burgas lagoons**, with their specialised habitat.

The museum is on two floors, the lower covering plants and geology. On the upper floor there are some good stuffed specimens of mammal and birdlife from the lagoon—in particular, a very fine **stuffed wild boar**.

300m north is the **Ethnographic Museum**, in a large wooden National Revival house. **Open** 10.00–17.00, closed Mon

This is a fairly standard collection of regional costumes and a room displaying typical 19C peasant artefacts, but the house is a good example of the genre and is worth a short visit. The upper floor has an interesting display of costumes from the Sidarovo ritual fertility dance, while the room downstairs to the left of the entrance is well furnished in mid 19C Biedermeier style. There is a small wooden rural building in the outer courtyard.

Walk down this street a little further to the end and turn left to the **Cathedral of SS Cyril and Methodius**. This is basically an ugly, over-large and down at heel late 19C church, with urgent work needed on many parts of the fabric of the building, but it is well worth a visit to see the extraordinary **art deco stained glass windows**, with a series of portrayals of young women with demonic features but angelic garb, about 1.5m high, set into the plain window glass. They are, in their way, one of the strangest works of Christian art in Bulgaria, with the spirit of the savage devouring females in the 1890s drawings of Aubrey Beardsley. The images are all the more disturbing for their refined and threatening sensuality, with bitter narrow eyes, pouting lips and tangled black hair, in a church that like most provincial Bulgarian cathedrals, is a mixture of war memorial, community centre and place of worship.

Turn left and walk back down towards the main shopping area, the Town Hall on the right opposite the Hotel Bulgaria, and the port.

Burgas to Sozopol and the Turkish border

Leave Burgas by the main road to the south, towards the lagoon and the vast Neftochim refinery in the distance. Here turn left, following signs for **Sozopol**, and follow the edge of the lagoon back towards the sea. Fish are often on sale here by the side of the road, but it is better to buy elsewhere because of pollution problems with the lagoon. After a few kilometres there is a naval base and camp, then the exposed headland of **Chernomorets**, most of which is naval station, and inaccessible to the public. To the west are the Medni Hills. Continue south towards Sozopol, along a wide asphalt road, then through deciduous woods and vineyards. After about 7km, the headland of Sozopol is visible in the distance.

Sozopol

Sozopol, sometimes still called by its Greek name *Sozopolis* (the safe city), is a remarkable and evocative little town with some of the most attractive and best-preserved buildings on the whole Black Sea coast. The **historic centre** of the town is built on the end of a small peninsula that was once an island. Sozopol is busy in summer and accommodation should be pre-booked if possible, as it is very popular with intellectuals and fashionable Sofians for holidays. There are very good **beaches** nearby, wonderful unspoilt **forests** and under a market economy the private sector has developed sympathetically by comparison with some of the Black Sea coast. It is generally free from the problems of excessive commercialisation that affect Nesebur. It is a good base if visiting Burgas, or exploring the very fine natural coastline down to the border with Turkey. Sozopol inhabitants are quite often good Greek-speakers, and basic Greek is understood by almost everybody. Many people also enjoy speaking Russian. In recent years, the town has become the centre of Bulgarian underwater archaeology.

History of Sozopol

The settlement know as modern Sozopol was one of the most important early Greek colonial settlements on the Black Sea coast. It was founded by colonists from Miletus, and known as *Apollonia Pontika*. It immediately became an important market and port on the main trade route between the growing Greek colonies to the north, and the Bosphorus and the Aegean, with fish curing an important export industry. The islands off the coast provided security from attack by the *Nipsei* and the *Skirmiani*, fierce Thracian tribes who lived in the mountains in the interior. Hillside mines were an important trade link between the two communities. Copper is found near the surface of the land, and was mined from the earliest times.

Original links with Miletus remained strong until the Greek cities of Asia Minor came under Persian domination when loyalty was transferred to Athens. *Apollonia* supplied Attica with fish and agricultural products, in exchange for Greek goods which were sold to the Thracian rulers in the interior. By 520 the city was minting its own coinage, and had expanded beyond the original island site onto the mainland. A harbour was built to protect its merchant fleet, and fortress on the mainland, during this very prosperous period. In 460 a colossal bronze statue of **Apollo** was made for the city by the sculptor Kalamis, and the wealth and prosperity of the city led **Herodotus** to compare it with the most famous cities in Greece.

After the decline of Athens after the 5C, Apollonia also went into decline, and it became increasingly threatened by internal disorder on the Balkan peninsula. It came under the protection of Philip II of Macedon, and was involved in his wars against the Scythians. In the 3C it was threatened by rampaging Celtic tribes, and was looted by the *Bastarni*. It continued as a trading centre until the 1C BC when *Apollonia* became allied with Mithridates VI, in his wars against Rome. In 72 BC it was sacked by the Romans, and the statue of Apollo sent to Rome and set up on the Capitol. In 52 BC it was sacked again, by the *Getae*, and the last Greek settlers fled. After AD 31 it became part of the Roman province of Thrace.

For three centuries nothing is known of the city until records start to show a settlement called *Sozopolis* on the site, probably the seat of a bishop. In the Byzantine period it became a centre of exile for dissident members of the Byzantine ruling class, and the town regained some wealth and dignity. A large monastery, the Monastery of St Cyril, was constructed on the island. On the whole the city avoided involvement in the wars between the Byzantines and the Bulgarians, but it was sacked by the Genoese in 1353, and taken by the Ottoman Turks in 1453. After this, like most Black Sea coast towns, it went into serious decline, so that at the beginning of the 20C, it was a village of about 3000 inhabitants almost wholly dependent on fishing. After the exchange of populations with Greece following the First World War, some refugees from Greek Thrace were housed here.

In communist times there was a drive to industrialise the fishing industry which led to a major **ecological disaster**, exemplified by the construction of a factory to can oil from captured dolphins. Wine and melon growing are also economically important.

■ **Hotels**. Private rooms are fairly widely available, and there are a number of small B&B hotels, but both are taken up fairly fully by Bulgarians in the high season. It is usually possible to get accommodation at the Kavatsite, a camp site-cum-hotel about 2km south of the town, by the sea. Despite its rather unpromising appearance (it was originally a Young Pioneer camp in communist times), it offers good basic accommodation, a café, restaurant, hotel block, and cheaper wooden chalets and tent sites. It is clean and well-kept and the staff are friendly and helpful although foreign languages are not spoken. The beach is excellent, although it is unsupervised and care is needed in rougher weather. The naturist section is at the south end. The tidal undercurrents are dangerous for non-swimmers and small children. Some hotels in the vicinity of the town are owned by trades unions and other organisations and are not open to foreign visitors.

■ **Restaurants**. There are some excellent restaurants in Sozopol, particularly those serving fish, as well as the usual grilled meat and pizza establishments. Very good food and outstanding wine and raki from the proprietor's own vineyard can be found at **Restaurant Costas**, near the old windmill on the south side of the town. It is popular with the Greek and Russian 'business' community. (Strongly recommended.) Campers and self-caterers can buy fish directly from boats in the harbour, or from the central market.

■ **Underwater archaeology**. The Director of the Institute is Dr Christina Angelova, Centre for Underwater Archaeology, Sozopol 8130, ☎ 00 30 359 5514 531. There is an annual conference held each year in Sozopol, usually in September.

It takes about a day to see the main buildings of Sozopol, although it is easy to spend much longer in the town. It is possible to use Sozopol as a base to tour the extreme southeast of the country, or if you are a business visitor to Burgas, you can commute into the city. If driving into Sozopol for a visit, it is easiest to find a way through the outskirts and then park under the old walls by the yacht harbour. The main part of the town is effectively pedestrianised and a car is a nuisance.

To the south on the island of St Kyril, with a small mole and artificial harbour construction, is the **Naval Academy**, opened in 1934 in an impressive large 19C building. On the harbour wall below it there are generally some Bulgarian naval vessels, such as coastal patrol craft. There has been a long-running local campaign to eject the navy from the building, and make a modern yacht marina, but it has not succeeded to date.

Walking up into the town from the harbourside, there are remnants of **Byzantine fortifications**, mixed with more modern town wall construction. At the top of the steps, across a small open space is the **Museum of Underwater Archaeology** (open every day in the summer season). This is currently temporarily housed in the abandoned old church of Kyril and Methodius. There are a number of very interesting exhibits on display, including a wooden **statue**, which is over 6000 years old—the oldest wooden statue ever discovered, and ancient wooden spoons, a section of the sea bed, amphorae and ceramics. The map of submerged settlements is very helpful in understanding the history of coastal settlements in this region. The **church** itself has a finely carved iconostasis.

To the right of the church, about 400m away in a small public park, is the charming small **Church of Sveti Zossim**, a 13C building with a very fine stone carving around the door. The interior is in a poor state and needs renovation. It used to be the church of the Sozopol fishermen.

To the left, 200m over the road in a modern building that also contains the town cinema, is the **Archaeological Museum**. In the entrance hall are some foundation stones and timbers from ancient villages, while upstairs the main exhibits are the unique collection of **ancient anchors** and the **Apollonia kraters**. The former are mainly of specialist interest, and there are examples in both stone and cast iron—they are of great historical importance for the light the inscriptions on them cast on local history and Sozopol trade in ancient times.

The **kraters**, although all 12 are very fine examples of Classical Greek vase painting, are poorly displayed and badly lit and likely to disappoint visitors. All were made in Attica in Greece between 360 and 364 BC and exported to *Apollonia Pontika*. Five show scenes involving wine with the god Dionysus, with scenes of feasting, music and celebration. All of them belong to the so-called red figure style, with the use of white paint to depict female figures.

The finest church in Sozopol is the sunken building of **Sveti Bogoroditsa**, which is in the centre of the old town, but it is currently closed except on Sundays.

Ancient Greek krater

It is worth a good walk through the little town to see the many picturesque and generally well-preserved **domestic houses**. In general they are very small, without gardens or courtyard, given the lack of space on the original peninsula. Many are being restored, especially those with a sea view.

Follow the main road south from Sozopol towards the **Turkish border**, passing through the edge of the **Naroden National Park** (open to visitors without a permit). This was created in the communist period as a recreation and nature study area for young people. There is a very fine long **beach** here, which may remind some visitors of the open beaches of southern Ireland. At the end of it is the wooded headland north of Maslen, site of ancient *Archontiko*.

9km south of Sozopol is the modern holiday village of **Djuni**. This is a pleasant little place for a quiet beach holiday, with well-designed apartment blocks built to a sensible scale, a marina, campsite and pine woods behind the beach. The bay is large and sheltered and the beach is safe for small children under supervision as it slopes only gently for about 75m. It is rather isolated and a car is really needed for any stay longer than a few days. For reservations and information, ☎ 5514 2 04 42, fax 5514 495, telex 83584.

The road runs through thick woods towards **Primorsko** (26km), a nice little village where there used to be a communist Young Pioneers camp and an annual folk festival, then, after a few kilometres, to the attractive little village of **Lozenec**. In general this is a very pleasant, unspoilt part of the coast and a good place to stay for peace and quiet and beautiful countryside and woodland.

After 41km you reach Tsarevo.

Tsarevo

History of Tsarevo

Tsarevo used to be called *Micunin*, in honour of a Soviet-period agriculturalist. In Byzantine times it was known as *Vasiliko*, a name that continued in official use until 1913 when it was a Turkish frontier town on the Bulgarian border. It remained part of Turkey until 1912. In 1913 it was renamed Tsarevo.

Vasiliko was the home town of the Greek family of Danielopoulos, whose largely vanished community and lifestyle in this region was recorded by Yiankos Danielopoulos (1899–1987) and published in his autobiography, *In the Trail of Odysseus*, translated by Nigel Clive and published in English in 1994. It is the most accessible account of the lost world of the Greek communities of traders and fishermen in this area.

Tsarevo nowadays is a quiet and unpretentious little port with a good safe harbour whose size indicates the old importance of the place. There are one or two good fish restaurants, although the local fleet has suffered badly from the problems of overfishing in the Black Sea. There is nowhere much to stay apart from some private rooms. South of the town there is a large and extraordinarily ugly old factory that mars otherwise very good coastal scenery. The road runs south to Varvara, a dull little place, and then to Ahtopol.

Ahtopol

14km south of Tsarevo on the coast road leading towards the Turkish border is the small village of Ahtopol. In Roman times it was called *Peronticus*, and it was destroyed by the Huns. Under the Ottoman Empire, the little community was known as *Agathoupolis*, until 1913, when it was detached from what had been the *Sandjak of Saranda Ekklesias* (Forty Churches), and annexed by Bulgaria. At that time its population comprised 8050 Greeks, 1704 Bulgarians and 1251 Turks, according to the last Ottoman census. Most of the Turks and Greeks left under the exchange of populations and it was taken over by Bulgarians.

Although it is a small and rather nondescript resort, it is well worth considering visiting Ahtopol, as it is the most southerly settlement of any size along the coast and a good base from which to explore the beautiful and remote **Strandjha mountains** near the border with Turkey. The coast has some of the last really top quality and environmentally undisturbed beaches on the Bulgarian Black Sea littoral, mercifully saved from ruination by mass tourist development in the communist period by their proximity to Turkey and the politically very sensitive border. The woodlands in the interior are very beautiful and of great ecological interest. Sinemorec, 5km south of Ahtopol, has the best sandy beach, and the very beautiful **Veleka river estuary**. Sinemorec was founded as a Turkish settlement in the 18C under the name of *Kalandza*. It has many rare waterlilies and a pleasant, slightly exotic atmosphere. If there is time, it is worth hiring a local rowing boat and exploring the upper reaches. Mosquitoes can be a problem here.

History of Ahtopol

Ahtopol has been known by many names in its long history. In ancient times it was called *Aulaion Teichos*, then *Aulikon*, when it was a small Greek colony founded by settlers from *Apollonia*. In Byzantine Bulgaria it was called *Agathopolis*, then in Turkish *Ahtembolu*, and finally, in Bulgarian, Ahtopol. For most of its history it was economically dependent on the export of timber from nearby forests, and charcoal, in Turkish times. Until 1913 the population was almost entirely Greek-speaking Orthodox Christians.

There is an interesting **round trip** inland towards Turkey from the coast road to the old mining town of **Malko Turnovo**, south of Burgas, then returning through the forests of the Strandzha towards the sea. Turn off the main road at **Primorsko**. 9km inland is the little town of **Novo Panicarevo**, a pleasant old place with good Ottoman period and 19C houses with red tile roofs. It has some historical significance as the site of a Utopian socialist settlement, founded in the late 19C on Tolstoyan principles. The road then turns south, over rather bleak uplands with abandoned vineyards.

After 25km you reach the upland village of **Vizica**, then after 4km join the main road near **Gramatikovo**.

NB. Some part of this journey are made through lonely forest roads, where it is is easy to get lost. Take supplies and a good map; a compass is essential. Unaccompanied travel is not recommended.

The road then runs southeast towards the mining town of Malko Turnovo, with outstanding views of forests to the south over the **Turkish border**. Gramatikovo and nearby villages of Bargat and Kondolovo are famous for the fire-walking ceremony, when villagers walk barefoot on hot ashes.

Malko Turnovo is now a very poor and economically ruined place, after the closure of a local copper mine about ten years ago, and it is mainly inhabited by very impoverished **Roma**. It used to be a militant socialist centre, and in 1903 was the centre of a syndicalist movement that spread throughout the region. The main street now resembles a poor industrial settlement in Albania, with derelict machinery, hungry dogs and semi-ragged children. The border crossing with Turkey is 9km to the south of the town. To drive to the Turkish border post, find a small sign on the southern outskirts by an old mine. It is a narrow road that climbs steeply through woods for about 10km, to the border post at Derekoy. The coast south into Turkey was regarded in antiquity as a wholly bleak and hostile place. The Greek geographer **Strabo** describes 'a stony deserted shore, much exposed to the fury of the north winds'.

Plovdiv and region

- **By road**. From Sofia, about 156km, by the main road, although there are other alternative routes. The E8 motorway, via Kostanec (49km) and Pazardzhik (88km), is about half-an-hour faster but less interesting.

- **By rail**. About 2 hours direct from Sofia by express train at most times of the day. By coach. Frequent services from the park by the main Sofia station.

- **By air**. From Sofia airport. The flight takes about 20 minutes.

Plovdiv

Plovdiv (pop.367,895), ancient *Philippopolis*, Ottoman *Filibe*, is the most important city of southern Bulgaria and of great historic interest, with some of the best **Classical remains**, **Byzantine churches**, **mosques** and **Bulgarian National Revival buildings** in the country. Many people consider the **theatre** the finest and most accessible Classical monument in Bulgaria. The town is a good centre for exploring the surrounding country, which has some interesting historic towns, and the mountains of the **central Rhodope range**. The climate is generally more temperate than in many other parts of the country, and it is a feasible centre for a winter holiday. A generation or two ago, it was a very ethnically mixed town, with a large Greek, Roma, Turkish, Armenian and Vlach presence, but nowadays it is more homogenous, although representatives of all these minorities can still be found.

Plovdiv could easily have become the capital of the country, had the 19C **Great Powers** not decided to amend the 1878 San Stefano agreements when Plovdiv was designated as capital. The main sights of the city can be seen in a day from Sofia if an early start is made. Two days are better for a relaxed exploration, particularly in summer, when Plovdiv can become very hot. It is built on hills, and July and August sightseeing can be arduous, especially as some monuments are difficult to find. If you are interested in Islamic buildings, you should bear in mind that most of them are only open on Fridays. There are reasonable local hotels, quite good local restaurants and bars, and accommodation in private rooms is possible. In summer an arts festival is held, with theatre performances in the ancient auditorium. Some museums are not open, or do not exist anymore, as the houses in which they used to be have been repossessed by pre-communist owners.

In the last century Plovdiv was known for its colourful Ottoman ambience. In 1876 Jasper More noted 'narrow streets at night pervaded by Stygian darkness', and 'dingy looking billiard rooms where they smoke the narghile'.

- **By air**. Plovdiv airport was built primarily as a military airport in the Warsaw pact era. It is used by some local small airlines, for internal flights, and for charter flights linked to package holidays, e.g. the skiing holidays at Pamporovo. It is not often affected by fog and sometimes fog-bound Sofia flights are routed here. Transfer time to the skiing resort is about two and a half hours by coach. Information ☎ 226937. **Balkan Airlines**, ☎ 032 431977, fax 438177.

■ **By rail**. Plovdiv is a stopping point for several international trains, apart from Bulgarian internal services. It is easy to reach Istanbul, Belgrade and most German and east European cities. Information, ☎ 222729, reservations, ☎ 222720; International Information, ☎ 02 870777, reservations, ☎ 02 875935. Trains run about every two hours to Sofia.

■ **By bus**. The coach station is at the back of the rail station.

■ **Hotels**. There are a number of hotels in the town such as the 5-star **Novotel**, ☎ 55892, the 3-star **Trimontium** (☎ 23491) is a fine old Stalinist block, with vast public rooms, the **Bulgaria**, ☎ 225564 and the **Maritsa**, ☎ 552735, fax 552727. The Maritsa is recommended for straightforward old fashioned accommodation, a single room is $US28 a night, with TV. The **Novotel** (☎ 652505, fax 551970) is a large air-conditioned block with a fine view over the river, with good facilities for the business traveller. A single room is currently $84 a night.

■ **Restaurants**. Most hotel restaurants are mediocre, except the Trimontium. There are several good places in the Old Town, such as **Persenk**.

■ **Hospital**. The hospital is in Hristo Botev Street. There are **chemists** in Raiko Daskalov Street and Ivan Vasov Street.

■ **Post office and telephone**. The post office is in Ivan Vasov Street.

■ **Diplomatic missions**. **Greek Consulate**, 10 Preslav Street, ☎ 23 22 21; **Russian Federation Consulate**, 20 Ivan Vazov Street, ☎ 23 61 41; **Turkish Consulate**, 10 Filip Makedonski Street, ☎ 236511

■ **Security**. Generally speaking central Plovdiv is one of the safer and more relaxed Bulgarian cities with only normal night-time precautions necessary. There are some very poor areas, though, and they are better avoided, unless you are with a Bulgarian friend in daylight.

■ **Business**. Plovdiv holds a large and well-attended international trade fair. For information, contact International Trade Fair Office, 37 Vuzrazhdane Blvd, ☎ 553191, telex 44432 or 44710. It is usually held at the end of September.

■ **Tourist Office**. The Tourist Office is at 34 Moskva Blvd, ☎ 653848.

History of Plovdiv

There has been human settlement on the site of the city from the earliest times, and neolithic remains have been found in the vicinity. The Plovdiv hills were the site of Thracian *Eumolpias*, the chief centre of the *Odyrsae* tribe. The hills gave the settlement a commanding military position over much of the central plain of the country. Very early evidence of Greek settlement has been found, with ceramics and metalwork from the Mycenaean period. The Thracian tribes were soon subject to a degree of

Hellenisation, which rapidly accelerated after the conquest of the town by Alexander the Great in 341 BC. Later Greek rulers built the extensive fortification system. The town was renamed *Philippopolis*, and grew to become an important regional centre, and a centre of Greek learning, particularly philosophy. Apollo was the patron-god. A large temple of Apollo was built outside the city walls, on what was later called Dzambaz Tepe. The cult of Asklepios was also widespread, both gods being identified with the Thracian Horseman God.

Philippopolis was taken by the Roman invaders of the Balkans in AD 46, and a large number of legionary veterans were settled in the vicinity. An extensive system of aqueducts was built to bring water from the Rhodope mountains to the city. The town was refortified by Marcus Aurelius, and was renamed *Trimontium*, and became a rich and famous city, and a centre of learning. Roman policy was to develop Thrace as a province with a strongly city-based economy which benefitted *Trimontium*. *Philippopolis* began to mint coins under Domitian, and had the title *Metropolis* conferred on it by Septimus Severus. Pythian Games in honour of Apollo were held in 214.

Philippopolis was laid waste by the Goths in 249, and became part of the Eastern Empire in 395, then totally destroyed by the Huns in 447. It was rebuilt and refortified by Justinian in the 6C. After the Slav and Avar invasions, it fell under the influence of the First Bulgarian Kingdom. In the time of Kham Malamir it was given the Slavonic name of *Pupuldin*. The city was contested for many years between the Byzantines and Bulgarians, and after 1018 was fully reincorporated into the Byzantine Empire. It was severely damged by the army of the First Crusade, until 1204, when King Kaloyan recaptured what was then known as Plovdiv into the Second Bulgarian Kingdom. The town grew under the reign of Tsar Ivan Assen II (1218–41).

It was taken by the Ottoman Turks in 1364, under Pasha Lala Salin, and renamed *Filibe*, and became the centre of the territory of the *Beylerbey* of Roumelia. The Turks named the three hills of Plovdiv *Dzambaz Tepe*, *Taksim Tepe* and *Nebet Tepe*. It prospered for a while under Ottoman occupation, becoming a supply centre for rice and tobacco and woollen garments for the Ottoman army, and then stagnated until the 19C when it became a focus for the expansion of Greek economic influence in the region. Craft industries, such as soap making and rug making, were developed. Plovdiv merchants opened offices in Constantinople, Athens, Odessa, Manchester and Calcutta, most of the activity in the latter two towns being controlled by the Plovdiv Armenian community. Bulgarian language education commenced in 1849.

Many churches were built in this period, which later became bitterly contested between Greeks and Bulgarians after the establishment of the Exarchate of Bulgaria, and the breach between the Plovdiv Bulgarians church and the Patriarchate in 1861. Plovdiv was liberated in 1878 and under the Treaty of Berlin became capital of the province of Eastern Roumelia. In 1885 it was fully integrated into Bulgaria. In this century it has become an important industrial centre, with textile, metal, food, carpet and chemical factories. In 1936 Old Plovdiv was declared a 'historic preservation area', and in 1979 the town was awarded a European Gold Medal by UNESCO for its work in protecting its monuments. In the post-communist period Greek business influence has again become an important factor in the Plovdiv economy.

Plovdiv lies on the **river Maritsa**, which is quite wide and fast flowing, and most of the city which is of interest to the visitor lies on the south side of it. In Ottoman times the eastern quarters were Turkish, the west Greek, Bulgarian and Armenian.

The **trade exhibition centre** is opposite the Hotel Martisa, on the north bank of the river, in a low long aircraft hangar-like building. The modern architecture here and in buildings nearby is much more sympathetic than most Bulgarian modernism.

The **old city** occupies much of the same area as the Ottoman, medieval and ancient cities. It is possible to see interesting monuments from epochs of history hundreds of years apart within a few metres of each other.

If travelling by car or coach you enter the city from the west past old factories. The Union of Bulgarian Writers building is on the right near the coach station, in Vasil Aprilov Street. There is a good small **street market** on the right. The apartment blocks on the outskirts of the city centre are generally better than those in Sofia, with better landscaped surroundings. If arriving at the railway station, cross the road directly outside the station and walk north into the city centre. The Plovdiv sports stadia are in the district behind the railway station.

It takes about ten minutes to walk from here to the centre of the city, where there is a large pedestrianised area and modern shopping centre, with some ancient monuments restored and set within it. After about five minutes' walk along Vasil Aprilov Street, with a good small street market on the left, turn right into Gladstone Street. On the right, after about 200m is a public park, cross the road here and bear right towards the Old City. On the right, at the far side of this park, is the **post office**, with the **Hotel Trimontium** nearby. In front of you, in the old Ludmila Dimitrova Street (a name still in general use), is the **Balkan Hotel**, with the **Balgarija Hotel** about 300m further on down the street in Daskalov Street. Both are run down, not particularly recommended. You are now near the foot of Taksim Tepe.

A walk around historic Plovdiv

This walk enables you to see most of the outstanding monuments and museums. If you are staying at the Hotel Maritsa, leave the hotel by the front entrance and turn right 250m, with the Novotel on your right, and cross the river foot bridge. The Maritsa is an attractive river, clean and fast flowing, and with rich birdlife along the wide, flat riverbanks. The bridge has good market stalls on it, particularly clothes. On the other side, walk another block, 100m To the right is the **Archaeological Museum**, in a large late 19C building, but it is currently completely closed, and due to be moved to a new building in the Old Town. This is a pity as it is said to contain some important Hellenistic and Roman sculpture. To the left, in Kubrat Han Street, is the **Imaret Mosque**, built in 1444, and named after the *imaret* (pilgrims' hotel) that once stood nearby. This stands in a garden, surrounded by bushes. It is notable for the unusual twisted patterns of brickwork on the minaret, but is neglected, and needs restoration. Walk to the end of this street, about 300m, and on the right is a low hill, **Nebet Tepe** (hill, in Turkish). Walk south along the broad Dimitrov Street, after about 400m turn right into Gorki Street. Follow this street until you reach

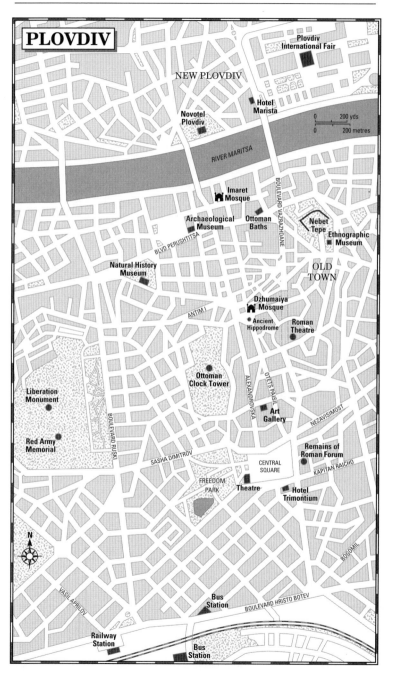

PLOVDIV

NEW PLOVDIV

Plovdiv
International Fair

Hotel
Marista

Novotel
Plovdiv

0   200 yds
0   200 metres

RIVER MARITSA

BOULEVARD VAZRAZHDANE

Imaret
Mosque

Archaeological
Museum

Ottoman
Baths

Nebet
Tepe

Ethnographic
Museum

BLVD PERUSHTITSA

OLD
TOWN

Natural History
Museum

Dzhumaiya
Mosque

ANTIM I

Ancient
Hippodrome

Roman
Theatre

Ottoman
Clock Tower

ALEKSANDROVSKA

OTETS PIASIL

NEZAVISIMOST

Liberation
Monument

Art
Gallery

BOULEVARD RUSKI

Red Army
Memorial

Remains of
Roman Forum

KAPITAN RAICHO

SASHA DIMITROV

CENTRAL
SQUARE

FREEDOM
PARK

Theatre

Hotel
Trimontium

BOGOMIL

N

VASIL APRILOV

Bus
Station

BOULEVARD HRISTO BOTEV

Railway
Station

Bus
Station

The Dzhumaiya Mosque

the very fine **Dzhumaiya Mosque** on the left. This is a very large building, from the time of Sultan Murad II (1359–85) and indicates the prosperity and importance of early Ottoman Plovdiv. There is very fine floral decoration in the interior, and good paintings of holy places. It stands in an open little square, with a raised concrete platform, on the south side below which some lines of seats of the horse-shoe-shaped **Hellenistic stadium** can be seen, in incongruous surroundings. The main shopping street of Plovdiv, the pedestrianised Aleksandrovska Street, runs south from here.

If you walk down it to the end, about 800m, you come to the main central square that was redeveloped in the communist period. On the left is an ugly concrete slab of the post office, behind which there are quite extensive remains of the **Roman forum**, but although it is a pleasant place, it is neglected and there is no information about the layout of the numerous building foundations that you can see. Part of it seems to be used as a car park by post office employees. Over the square is the **Hotel Trimontium**, a classic Stalinist pile, but not without its charm, in a heavy and overbearing way. The Plovdiv Orchestra Hall is next to it, then there is a pretty late 19C Army Club. It used to be the army theatre, but is now used for a variety of entertainments. Beyond it is Freedom Park, well kept and laid out, and a fine view of the little hills of Plovdiv to the west, topped by an enormous statue of a Russian soldier that is the Red Army war memorial.

Walk to the north west corner of the square, past the Eurobank building, and after 250m you come, via a steep side street (turn left by the Filoxenia Restaurant), to the bottom of **Sahat Tepe**, a charming little hill. Walk to the top up steep steps, about 270m high. There is a **wonderful view** east to Nebet Tepe, the houses of the Old Town and the ruined fortress, while to the south you can see the Plain of Thrace and the Rhodope Mountains. Walk past the microwave tower north, 100m, to the **Ottoman clocktower**. This beautiful monument is thought to be the oldest Turkish building left in Plovdiv, dating from the time of the early conquest, was built of hexagonal granite blocks, topped with a charming wooden bell tower, and it still keeps time for the town, a tinny bell clanging out the hours.

Return to the Dzhumaiya Mosque via steps down the north side of the hill, and narrow streets, then return along Gorki Street into the **Old Town** via a sloping old street.

The **Old Town** is one of the finest complexes of late 19C bourgeois domestic buildings in the Balkans. In communist times many of the original owners were dispossessed and their houses made into museums. Some have now returned and it is extremely difficult to establish clearly what it is possible to see. The simplest thing to do is walk up this street into the heart of the area and explore. On the right you pass the **Boyadzhiev Museum** (open 10.00–17.00, expect

Mon) dedicated to the work of one of Bulgaria's postwar artists. Next on the right is the church of Sveta Bogoriditsa, behind high walls, while everywhere there are remarkably beautiful houses, many painted bright colours, that belonged to the Greek and Armenian merchants who dominated the trade of the town. To appreciate one easily, and to see inside, visit the **Ethnographic Museum** (open 09.00–12.00, 14.00–17.00, except Mon), 100m further up the street on the right, with a marvellous formal courtyard garden and fountain, and deep green painted exterior. The local costumes and jewellery collection is outstanding. It dates from 1847.

200m further on you come to the end of the street, and the **Nebet Tepe Citadel**. This is a romantic and evocative ruin, about 250m wide, with huge crumbling external walls 2m thick and with spectacular views to the north, east and west. The interior is full of grassy mounds of rubble and little green shrubs. There are ruins of a large defensive tower in the northwest corner. It was originally built by the Thracians in the 5C BC, and was used in all historical periods up to the beginning of this century. There is a **secret tunnel** linking it with the river bank.

The Roman Theatre

Return by the same route and follow the hill to the south, past other outstanding houses, to the Roman theatre. This is slightly unhappily situated above an underpass tunnel, and road noise can be a problem with performances. It is heavily, although technically correctly restored, but remains a dramatic and impressive example of the later Roman style. It is all that remains of the buildings of the original Roman acropolis, the rest of which was destroyed by the Goths in 251.

The theatre is the largest building of its type designed for public performances so far discovered in the Balkans. The *cavea* which encircles the semi-circular orchestra is 28m in diameter, and is divided into two levels, with 14 rows of seats at the lower level, and six at the higher. The south side is occupied by the *scenium*, in front of which the actors performed. The original stage building was probably about 10m high. In these general features and design, it is an outstanding example of the Hellenistic style of theatre construction in the Balkans.

You can descend from here back into the town shopping streets. There are some of the best antique shops in Bulgaria dotted about the Old Town, some in historic houses repossessed by the pre-communist owners, so a visit to a shop can also be a visit to a fine interior.

7km south of Plovdiv at **Komatevo** the foundations of a very large Christian basilica have been found, in what was originally a Thracian settlement.

North and west of Plovdiv

Take the main road north out of Plovdiv past the airport towards Karlovo, turn left after about 23km towards Kalojanovo (3km). Bear right where the road divides 1km out of the village, and the road, which is mediocre, climbs towards the mountains.

Hisarya

Hisarya, 42km north of Plovdiv in the Sredna Gora mountains, is a very interesting **historic thermal bath resort**, where the hot springs have been in use since remote antiquity. Apart from the baths, it is well worth visiting to see the wonderful early Byzantine walls and Christian basilicas, and for the interesting location, in a prehistoric lake bed. The walls are the best preserved in Bulgaria, and date from the time when Hisarya, ancient *Augusta*, was a flourishing health resort for the rich inhabitants of Plovdiv in the late Roman and early Byzantine era. Due to its remote situation, in the hills and off the main through routes used by the barbarian invaders, the ancient town was not destroyed when the Empire fell, and the fortifications are much better preserved than in lowland towns.

■ **Hotels**. There are a number of hotels in the town connected to its development as a thermal resort in the communist period, when the four local villages of Miromir, Momija Banja, Verigivo and Hisarya were amalgamated to make the modern town. Some of the hotels seem to be permanently closed, presumably owing to property restitution disputes, and some are not exactly palaces, but it is usually possible to find a bed somewhere. **NB**. If visiting in the winter, full thermal equipment and a sleeping bag are recommended.

History of Hisarya

The lake basin has been inhabited since neolithic times, with Bronze Age tombs having been found nearby. It was inhabited by the *Bessi* Thracian tribe, who were part of the kingdom of the *Odrysae*. An important Thracian royal necropolis was found at *Duvsanli* nearby, with outstanding gold artefacts. In the Macedonian invasion of Thrace this kingdom was incorporated in the Macedonian state in about 340 BC. After the Roman invasion the first prosperity of the area was founded, with mineral baths being developed at what was called *Havuz*, a settlement dating from the 4C BC. In the early Roman period, the town was called *Augusta*.

In the later Roman period, a quite substantial little town grew up around the baths, and the area was peaceful until the advent of the Gothic invasions after AD 270, when the massive fortifications were constructed, enclosing a quadrilinear area covering 30 hectares. By this time the town was known as *Diocletianopolis*. The walls were badly damaged by the Visigoths in the third quarter of the

The Camel Arch

4C. A number of cemeteries lie outside the town walls, mostly alongside the road to Plovdiv.

Christianity established itself early in the town and it became the seat of a bishopric. A Slav settlement grew on the site, now called *Toplica*, named after the hot springs. In 1206 the town was laid waste by the First Crusade armies, with a later chronicler describing 'a fair town, with mineral baths which were the finest in the world'.

In 1364, the fortress was captured by the Turks, and called *Kjazil Kale*, meaning 'the red fortress', and by the end of the 17C a sizeable spa town had grown up. It declined in the later Ottoman period, and there was little activity on the site until 1925, when the modern spa town began to develop.

The town is quite small, and on a day with good weather it is easy to make a circuit of the **ancient walls**, which are still as high as 6m in places, and up to 3m thick. There is a very well-preserved and dramatically impressive **Camel Arch**. About 100m away are the remains of two Christian **basilicas**, which show the large size and population of the early Byzantine town. The **baths** need modernisation and renovation, but a dip in the warm springs is very pleasant. (Recommended.)

Return to Plovdiv by the same route. Pazardzhik is 36km west, on the main road.

Pazardzhik

Pazardzhik is a medium-sized town on the Maritsa river which makes a convenient stop on the way to Plovdiv, although it does not have much to delay the visitor now. One of a series of minor administrative centres that grew as the market town of an agricultural area under the hundreds of years of Ottoman occupation, it lost most of its interesting Ottoman buildings in the 20C. It is said that it was originally a settlement of Crimean Tartars who were planted there in the time of Sultan Bajezid II. There is a reasonably preserved but very depleted **Ottoman Quarter** with a 17C mosque. In 1876 More noted 'its wretched ill paved straggling lanes'.

26km west of Pazardzhik is **Goljamo Belovo**, on a high mountain terrace above the Thracian Plain. Remains of a very large early Byzantine **brick church** were found here in the 1920s, probably built in the early 6C. The settlement was part of a prosperous region then, which controlled early Byzantine trade routes linking the Plain of Thrace with the Mesta and Struma valleys. Similar churches and fortresses have been found near Velingrad at Barta, Rangela and Beglichka.

Velingrad and the Batak region

For Velingrad and Batak (44km), take the main road west and turn south at Zvanicevo (8km), and follow a signed second-class road to the southwest, along the attractive Cepinska river valley.

40km southwest of Pazardlik is **Velingrad**. This is the centre of a wild and very underpopulated region of the western Rhodope mountains, and an interesting minor spa town. As a result it has quite a variety of modest hotels, and it is a good place to stay to explore an interesting and neglected region of the country. The Western Rhodope is, above all, the region of the Pomaks (see box), the 300,000 strong minority of Slav-speaking Muslims who have often played an important, if controversial, part in Bulgarian history.

■ **Transport**. **Roads** and **transport arrangements** in this part of the country are often poor—do not expect to be able to hire a car locally—and garages are few and far between. The roads in the hills are often excruciatingly bad; a four-wheel-drive vehicle is needed in most places. Unaccompanied travel is not recommended. Carry all food, drink and cigarette requirements.

The Pomaks

The origin of the Pomaks is disputed by scholars, although it is clear that they were ethnic Bulgarians who converted to Islam in the 15C, after Ottoman rule became established over the territories of modern Bulgaria. In addition, large numbers of Muslim settlers were brought to Bulgaria at various stages of the Ottoman period, such as the Tartars along the Black Sea coast, the Circassians of the Danube valley, and the Yoruk people of eastern Anatolia who were settled around Haskovo. Although many of the descendants of these people are classified as 'Turks' in the minds of most Bulgarians, while 'Pomaks' are a separate minority, in practice quite a degree of racial intermingling seems likely. The official Bulgarian 'line' on Pomaks for many years was that they were forcibly converted to Islam, whereas some independent historians have claimed that they converted voluntarily in order to obtain economic privileges under the Empire, hence the etymology of the word Pomak, from *pomagach*, meaning 'helpers'. Irrespective of these disputes, it is a fact that some of the Pomaks played a role in the Bulgarian National movement in the 19C similar to the Ulster Protestants in Ireland at the same time, where religious affiliation meant they played a useful role on the side of the Imperial rulers. Pomaks provided gangs of Muslim thugs to attack Bulgarian nationalist activists.

In the 20C the Pomak identity has been maintained and in the Rhodope communities, at least, intermarriage with outsiders is discouraged. The Pomak culture is conservative, and visitors to this area will notice that women generally cover their arms in public, wear high-collared long dresses, and rarely go out on their own. The Pomak communities were less disturbed by the 'Bulgarianisation' campaigns of the 1980s than ethnic Turks living in the southeast.

About 25km east of Velingrad is the small town of **Batak**, nestling under the Bataska mountains. It is nowadays a small, nondescript place, but is worth visiting as a Pomak centre, and as the site of the famous **19C massacres** of Bulgarians which became an international scandal and led to renewed pressure on the Turks to relinquish control of Bulgaria.

Batak can be reached from Velingrad, via Rakitovo (13km), or by the direct road south from Pazardzhik, via Pestera (33km).

History of Batak

In ancient times Batak was a tiny settlement on a minor road linking central Thrace with northern Greece. Legend relates that Alexander the Great passed through here on campaign, and in Roman times a small fort was built to guard the road south through the mountains.

The modern town was a Turkish creation, in the 16C. It remained a totally insignificant place until April 1876, when a general insurrection was in progress throughout Bulgaria against the Turks. Batak took a full part, but as a predominantly Bulgarian town surrounded by Pomak and Turkish villages, was vulnerable to attack. Mobs of heavily armed Muslims descended upon Batak. According to witnesses, about 3500 Bulgarians were massacred, but the Pomak atrocities were witnessed by the correspondent of the *London Daily News*, J.A. MacGahan, and his reports had a profound effect on European public opinion. In communist times a hydroelectric scheme nearby provided some employment.

J.A. MacGahan

J.A. MacGahan was an Irish-American who was an experienced foreign correspondent in 1876, having written accounts of the Russian–Turkish war in Turkestan, and a book about the North West Passage. He scooped *The Times* at Batak, who refused to print what it believed to be inflammatory reports by its own correspondent. His reports, particularly of butchered children, 'babes that had died wondering at the bright gleam of sabres', embarrassed the Foreign Office in London and caused world-wide indignation against the Turks. The reports were a major factor in the Russian decision to declare war against Turkey in April 1877. MacGahan died of typhus in Constantinople two years later.

Batak still has many Pomak inhabitants, and is not overwhelmingly welcoming to visitors with an interest in the past. A visit to the **church** is worthwhile, with what is claimed to be the blood of the massacred Christians still visible on the wall. There is very good hunting in the local forests, and hill walking on **Mount Batia** nearby.

Return to Velingrad by the same route.

Panagyurishte

4km north of Pazardzhik in the attractive Luda Jana valley is the town of Panagyurishte. For most of its history it was a backwoods place known only for hunting in the local forests and thermal baths. In 1876 More noted it was 'a wild and unsettled district seldom visited by Europeans'. In 1949 the **Panagyurishte Treasure** was found here, one of the greatest hordes of Hellenistic metalwork ever discovered. It probably belonged to a local Thracian chieftain who hid it prior to, or during, the Celtic invasion of 279 BC. The horde is now in the National Museum of History in Sofia (see p 95).

It is a pleasant place to visit, rather similar to the small towns of the Stara Zagora region, with some nice old houses and good local rugs and carpets.

Koprivshtica

■ **Rail**. From Sofia, about 2 hours.

Koprivshtica is in the Sredna Gora hills south of the main road between Karlovo and Sofia, and can easily be reached from Plovdiv and Panagyurishte, if travelling in this region. It is about 35km north of Panagyurishte below Mount Bunaja (1572m) to the south. Koprivshtica is a small hill town built at an altitude of about 1000m with some very fine **National Revival houses**, and is of some historical importance as one of the centres of national movement for liberation from Turkish oppression in the 19C. In April 1876 the Rising began here

National Revival house

that led to the Liberation War of 1877–78. The Church of St Nicholas has some good frescoes.

Koprivshtica was founded by refugees after the fall of the Second Bulgarian Kingdom from Veliko Tarnovo, and became a centre of rugmaking after a series of disastrous fires at the end of the 18C and the beginning of the 19C. The town merchants became very prosperous in the mid 19C, and had close links with Constantinople.

A great **folk festival** is held in the town every five years, with as many as 4000 performers taking part. It will be held next in 2000. It was established in 1965.

47km to the northwest is the important copper mine a Pirdop, which has recently been sold to Belgian investors.

East and south of Plovdiv

Haskovo

Haskovo, on the plain of Thrace, 76km east of Plovdiv, is very much a tobacco town. It is reasonably prosperous, by the standards of the Turkish minority (a substantial number of whom live scattered around the vicinity), as valuable varieties of Oriental tobaccos are grown locally, which are sought after on the world market.

Haskovo is on the main road to Turkey. It has some moderately priced hotels, and it is practical to stay a night here. The **Hotel Aida** is clean and cheap. It is a good place to buy cheap good quality Turkish goods, such as pot ery and metalwork.

History of Haskovo
The history of Haskovo is mainly Turkish, in that it was founded by the Ottoman conquerors, and called *Haskoi*, but there was a Greek-speaking population in the town for a very long time as well: most were driven out after the 1906 pogroms. The general area on this side of the Maritsa valley was quite heavily populated in Roman and Byzantine times, but there has been little archaeological exploration here, and much remains to be discovered about its history. In 1936 excavation at the Mineralni Bani, to the west of the town on the banks of the little Banska river, revealed Roman remains which had been destroyed by invaders, including a nymphaeum, baths and a hilltop fortress. Behind the **Mineralni Bani** on a high hill is the Roman fortress of **Sveti Duh**, which was destroyed by the rampaging Goths in 270.

Haskovo is still very much a Turkish town, and received little real attention or investment in the communist period, apart from the obligatory city centre redevelopment to produce a large square where the people could demonstrate their 'loyalty and affection' for the government. This neglect did have the advantage of preserving many of the old **Ottoman streets**, and it is the sort of place to visit if you like that ambience, very similar to towns in Albania such as Berat or parts of Korca. The **Mosque of Eski Dzhumaya** is a fine building dating from 1395, constructed in the early stages of the conquest. Muslims here practice their religion seriously; be sure to observe the normal dress and behaviour conventions in Islamic surroundings. In Ramadan business is slow and difficult.

Dimitrovgrad

Dimitrovgrad, 15km north of Haskovo on the Stara Zagora road, is a grim, run-down industrial town with the remains of communist industrial monuments in the chemical, cement, agribusiness and power industries. Local pollution is serious. **Avoid**.

History of Dimitrovgrad

Dimitrovgrad was named after the famous Bulgarian communist leader (see p 98) and developed on the basis of the nearby Marbass coalfield, the largest in Bulgaria. At the end of the Second World War there was little more than a few small villages on the site, but by the early 1960s over 50,000 people lived in the new town.

8km to the west of Dimitrovgrad is the village of **Klokotnitsa**, scene of the important battle in 1230 between Theodore Comnenus, the Despot of Epirus (a territory straddling the modern Greek–Albanian border), and Tsar Ivan Assen II. His Bulgarian army won a major victory, based in part on the strong defensive position around the old fortress of Klokotnitsa, which used to be on a site about 3km south of the modern village. As a result, the Tsar was recognised as 'Tsar of the Bulgarians and Greeks', and married his daughter into the Imperial family in Nikea.

Kardzali

Kardzali is above all a tobacco town, and one of the main centres of the tobacco industry in Bulgaria. It is also a centre of ethnic Turkish minority settlement. The area around the town has very low rainfall indeed, and in the communist period a major dam building and associated irrigation scheme was constructed using the Arda river and its tributaries, as well as a large zinc smelter and asbestos production plant. These developments played havoc with the local ecology, and the economy has been seriously damaged in the post-communist period by the collapse of most of the Russian market for Bulgarian tobacco.

In the late Zhivkov period many ethnic Turks from this region went into exile in Turkey, but many have since returned with the advent of democracy and the end of the government-sponsored anti-Turkish campaigns after 1989 (see Hugh Poulton, p 71).

History of Kardzali

The town is almost entirely an Ottoman creation, being founded by a local *ghazi* called Kardzi Ali in the 17C. It grew somewhat in the late Ottoman period as a minor garrison town and regional market, but boomed in the late 19C for a short time as tobacco smoking became a worldwide habit. Kardzali was the subject of political controversy when under the Treaty of Berlin in 1878 it was assigned to the Turkish Principate of eastern Roumelia. In 1885 the town and surrounding region was claimed by Turkey and it did not actually become part of Bulgaria until after the Balkan wars in 1912–13. Given the devastation the wars had caused, it was then little more than a village.

Harmanli

Harmanli, 11km along the main road towards Svilengrad and Turkey from Haskovo, is the main centre of the **silkworm industry** in Bulgaria. It grew as a garrison and market town in the Turkish period, and as a post station on the Constantinople–Beograd road. Harman means 'threshing mill' in Turkish, from which Harmanli takes its name, as it was an important centre of corn growing to supply the Ottoman army.

From Harmanli to Svilengrad, 34km. This main road has recently been improved with European Union funding.

Svilengrad

Svilengrad is the border town for both Turkey and Greece, being just off the main motorway through to Istanbul. It is a dull and nondescript place, with a heavy—in all senses—presence of lowlife types and equally sinister-looking heavily armed police 'monitoring' their activities. Drug smuggling from Turkey is a particular concern. Avoid overnight, unless a stay is really essential.

The **Mustafa Pasha bridge**, designed by Sinan and built by command of Mustafa Pasha, Grand Vizier of Sultan Selim I in about 1540, is the only interesting antiquity in the town, about 1km to the south, beyond the railway station.

History of Svilengrad

Svilengrad was a small Thracian settlement which became a Roman strong-point guarding the road to Constantinople. The fort and garrison town were completely destroyed in the barbarian invasions. A town was re-established by the Ottomans in the 15C, when fishing and river trade was the main economic activity. In 1529 the Mustafa Pasha river bridge was built, 300m long, with 13 fine arches, and the town grew as a roadside centre on the road to Belgrade. It was known as Mustafa Pasha until the Liberation. A large part of the present ethnic Bulgarian population is descended from refugees from Greece resettled hereabouts after 1913 and the later exchange of populations.

Mezek

8km west of Svilengrad is the important archaeological site of Mezek. In antiquity it was linked with Thracian *Uskudama* and Graeco-Roman *Hadrianopolis*, both occupying the site of modern Edirne, 25km away in Turkey, over the border. Near the remains of a medieval fort the site of a large Iron Age settlement has been discovered, with an extensive necropolis. It is the main Celtic site so far excavated in Bulgaria. A very large and beautiful tholos tomb was found by peasants in 1933 containing a statue of a wild boar, grave furniture, jewellery and other artefacts. The Mezek collar and Mezek candelabrum, along with other objects, are thought to have come from a Greek colony on the Black Sea coast.

Asenovgrad

Asenovgrad is a not very interesting little town, 19km south of Plovdiv on the Pamporovo/Smolyan road, but is near the outstanding **Bachkovo Monastery**. Asenovgrad grows very good tobacco, and the Mavrud wine, a good deep, full flavoured red. Local fruit and vegetables were used for the local and Plovdiv canning factories but with land privatisation much of this trade seems to have ceased. There is an efficient little branch line train from Plovdiv to the town, which takes about 30 minutes.

Bachkovo Monastery

Bachkovo Monastery is one of the most remarkable buildings in Bulgaria—many people consider to be the finest of the Bulgarian Rhodope monasteries—and should be a priority for visitors to this region. It is of central importance in the history of Bulgarian monasticism as it represents the intermingling of the Old Georgian, Greek and Bulgarian traditions. It combines buildings of great antiquity, starting from the early days of the 900-year span of monastic life, such as the ossuary, with more modern buildings in a harmonious and inspiring whole.

History of the monastery

Bachkovo is one of the oldest continuously inhabited monasteries on the Balkan peninsula. It was founded in 1083 by Gregorios Bakouriani, the Grand Domesticos of the Western Army of the Byzantine Emperor Alexis I. It was initially developed as a centre of Georgian monasticism.

It remained essentially Georgian until the end of the 14C, and under the influence of the Georgian neo-Platonist philosopher Italos the Georgian (1050–1130). From the 13C onwards, the monastery was on the boundaries of the Byzantine and Bulgarian Empires. In 1344 the region was ceded to the Bulgarians by the Byzantine Empress Anne of Savoy. It was conquered in 1364 by the Ottomans, after which it seems to have become largely Bulgarian, although some Greek influences must have remained in practice given the ethnic Greek population movement out of Plovdiv to mountain towns in the 17th and 18C.

Bachkovo Monastery

A large building programme started in this period, including the principal church. In 1745 the monastery passed to the authority of the Patriarch in Constantinople, and many Greek-speaking monks moved into the monastery. In the 19C Bulgarian influences were renewed and after a period of political struggle over the future of the church, Bachkovo finally came under the authority of the Bulgarian Exarchate in 1894. Some Greek monks remained but finally left in 1906.

To reach the monastery from Plovdiv, the simplest route is by local train from Plovdiv to Asenovgrad, which takes half an hour, than take a taxi to Asenovgrad up the very attractive **Chepelarska river gorge**, to Bachkovo village (8km). The climate is very mild, and the valley is known for peach and apricot growing. The monastery is 2km beyond the village, on the left, nestling among trees at the foot of a steep hill. Walk 1km up a sloping Ottoman road, towards the imposing fortress-like front wall. Through a low arch there is the very fine inner courtyard, with the monastery buildings set in a large rectangle.

In the middle are one or two large trees, and the **Church of the Archangel**, a wonderful small 12C structure, and the **Church of the Holy Mother of God**, from the 17C. They are surrounded by a two-storey galleried set of monastic buildings, including guest rooms and a refectory. The Church of the Archangel contains a **miracle-working Georgian ikon**, the metal 'Holy Mother of God', which was made in 1311, a masterpeice of Old Georgian art. The atmosphere is gentle and pastoral, the buildings in perfect harmony with the wooded environment, with sheep grazing in the courtyard.

Over the road, 300m to the east of the monastery, is the **ossuary**, a venerable structure with some very fine frescoes that date from the time of the original foundation of the monastery in the 11C.

Return to main road by the same route and proceed south, passing through **Narechenski Bani** after 26km, a very attractive old village by the river with wooden houses and some new buildings connected with the thermal baths here, which have been used since Ottoman times, if not before.

Pamporovo

Pamporovo (64km south of Assenovgrad) is one of the best mountain resorts in Bulgaria. It is well known for skiing in winter, when most visitors come, but it is also a very pleasant place throughout the year, with much brighter and sunnier winter weather than some Bulgarian mountain resorts. It is promoted as being particularly suitable for novice skiers, but there are also more demanding runs and very good cross-country skiing nearby.

The resort is at a height of 1620m, and the highest ski point is 1937m. There are 25km of marked runs, and 38km of cross-country trails, three chair lifts and six drag lifts. The resort is scattered over the lower slopes of Mount Snezhanka (1928m), with most of the hotels and facilities in the lower resort of Svetitsa (1602m). The ski school and nursery slopes are mostly in the Malina district, originally a shepherds' summer encampment about 2km to the south. There is a triple chair lift from Malina to the top of Snezhanka mountain, which has spectacular views over the whole of the central Rhodope and the Plain of Thrace. One of the main assets of Pamporovo is that it is not simply a skiing resort: there is tobogganing above Malina, and the best hotel, the **Perelik**, has a good indoor pool and there are some conventional, though well-organised day trips, available, to traditional Rhodope homes, to Bansko (see p 216), and to Smolyan and Bachkovo Monastery. Nightlife is centred in Pamporovo itself, with an English pub, two discos and plenty of bars.

■ **Hotels**. The best hotel in Pamporovo is the three-star **Hotel Perelik**, with 234 rooms. It is built in traditional Alpine style, and has a swimming pool, bowling alley, shopping centre and several bars and restaurants. Other hotels include the **Orpheus**, the **Rozhen**, the **Mougarvets** and the **Markony**, all two or three star. There is not much difference in price; the more expensive hotels have better indoor facilities.

Continue on the road south towards Smolyan (12km). Weather conditions in the winter can be severe.

Smolyan

The road into the mountains south towards Greece ends at Smolyan (80km from Plovdiv). Villages up to 20km south are right on the border with Greece, and it is planned to open a border crossing here (see p 22). It is a very good scenic drive up into the mountains, with vast forests stretching towards the border with Greece. The town is not very exciting, with few historic buildings, but is a good place to buy traditional Rhodope craft goods. It was chosen for tourist development in the late communist period, but it is 1000m up, with quite a severe winter climate and it has never really taken off, and many inhabitants are poverty-stricken ex-mineworkers and family members try to get a job over the border in Greece in order to survive. As many are Pomaks, or Roma, this is often difficult. There are functioning mines and ore concentration plants nearby, some of which have caused serious environmental pollution, particularly the old heavy metal flotation plant at Rudozem. Avoid local tap water.

History of Smolyan

In medieval Bulgaria Smolyan was known as *Ezerovo*, the 'town of lakes', then *Pasmakli* after the Ottoman invasion. It was renamed after the *Smoliani*, a Slav tribe who used to occupy this area. Mining has taken place hereabouts since Roman times, if not earlier.

At Raykovo, on the edge of the town, is the **National Museum of the Rhodopes** (open 10.00–17.00, except Mon), a very good ethnographic and historical museum. The other main attraction around the town are the **Smolyan lakes**, which are peaceful and good for walks, on the edge of the remote and deep forest on the Momina Skala mountains. To the west of the town is an equally remote and virtually uninhabited area leading to the Greek border (no usable roads).

Return to Plovdiv by the same route.

From Plovdiv to Kardzali, 85km. Alternatively, there is an interesting but rather mediocre road direct to Kardzali across the hills from Smolyan via Bjal Izvor, and running near the big zinc- and lead-mining centre of **Madan**. **NB**. Four-wheel-drive vehicle required. The area is a stronghold of Islamic identity, most inhabitants are ethnic Turks and Roma who fled from the plains after the 1876 Revolution.

52km south of Haskovo is the town of Kardzali, across the hot dry southern edge of the Thracian plain.

Stara Zagora, Veliko Tarnovo and the Central Mountains

- **By car**. From Sofia, 224km, 89km from Plovdiv, 161km from Burgas.

- **By train**. There are regular trains from Plovdiv, and less good services north to Veliko Tarnovo.

- **Excursions coach**. Trips to Veliko Tarnovo by coach can be booked from Sofia hotels.

Stara Zagora is a modern commercial town dominating part of the Plain of Thrace, and on a route into the Central Mountains. But some of the seminal events in Bulgarian history have taken place in this region, from the great battle at the Shipka Pass during the War of Liberation against the Turks in the 19C, and reaching back into history to the great city of **Veliko Tarnovo**, the heart of medieval Bulgaria, and the centre of the Second Bulgarian Empire (1185–1393). Most other sites in the region can be seen in passing, or as part of a day excursion, but at least two days are needed to see the outstanding buildings and dramatic site of Veliko Tarnovo properly, with the nearby Roman site of **Nicopolis ad Istrum**. Weather conditions in the mountains can be difficult in winter, and some caution is needed if snow is expected.

A separate visit is needed for the capital of medieval Bulgaria, **Veliko Tarnovo**, the town that is perhaps closest to the spiritual heart of all Bulgarians. **Kazanlak**, in the **Valley of the Roses**, is another important historic centre with its great Hellenistic tomb, one of the outstanding ancient monuments in Bulgaria.

Stara Zagora

Stara Zagora (pop. 82,000), Ottoman *Eski Saghri*, is an important industrial centre on the Plain of Thrace, with a mild climate—in the summer it can become particularly hot—and good agriculture. It is essentially a 19C town, with the usual communist redevelopment, after it was totally destroyed by the Turks in 1877. It is a convenient base to expore the central mountain region, with historic towns such as Gabrovo.

History of Stara Zagora

In antiquity Stara Zagora was known as *Beroe*. In Roman times it was renamed *Trajana*, after the Emperor Trajan who improved it as part of his policy of building up the urban economy in the province of Thrace. It grew as a market town and military garrison town on the road crossing between the east–west road from Philippopolis to *Anchialos*, modern Pomorie, and the north–south route between *Nicopolis* and *Adrianopolis*, modern Edirne in Turkey. It was overrun by the Slavs, then retaken by the Byzantines and renamed *Irinopolis*, after Empress Irene. In the 9C it was captured by Khan Krum and became part of the First Bulgarian Kingdom under the name *Boruy*.

The town was captured by the Turks in 1370, but did not particularly prosper under Ottoman rule, and remained a minor garrison town, called *Eski Hisar*, then later, in the 17C, *Eski Saghri*, 'fertile land'.

Stara Zagora was an early centre of Bulgarian nationalism, with Vasil Levski founding a secret revolutionary committee in 1869, and the town welcomed the Russian army in 1877, leading to its total destruction by fire when the army of Suleiman Pasha entered the town.

It was a favoured centre under communism and received quite a substantial amount of investment, mostly linked to the agriculture of the region, with important meat and vegetable processing factories. Since 1989 it has become rather run-down.

It is worth going into the old quarter to see the **Mosque Eski**, one of the oldest mosques in Bulgaria, dating from 1409. It has a very large single dome, and is evocative of the early days of Ottoman rule in Bulgaria. It is in poorish structural condition and urgently requires renovation.

A **Roman theatre** from ancient *Beroe* has been discovered behind the town hall, but restoration works are currently at a standstill due to lack of funds. *Beroe* was an important Thracian town, with traces of previous occupation going back to the amalgamated Thracian tribal state of the *Odryssae*. Under Roman rule the potential of the site as the hub of the new Balkan road network was soon recognised and a large town, *Augusta Trajana*, was established, very near *Beroe*. This grew to be one of the largest Roman towns in the Balkans. A south gate, defensive towers, a forum, theatre and numerous ancient wall sections have been discovered, most of them in and around the site of the modern town. The town walls enclosed a site of about 48 hectares.

It is difficult to see much of the ancient city, as modern buildings constructed after the total destruction of the old town in the Liberation War of 1877–78 occupy the same site, but rescue archaeology has discovered some very large buildings underneath the modern town. *Augusta Trajana* was prosperous under Constantine, but severely damaged in the Visigothic and other barbarian raids. There are the remains of a Roman house in the Boulevard Ruski, and sections of walls and foundations of other buildings visible elsewhere.

Apart from one or two other churches and mosques of passing interest, the most significant site nearby is the **neolithic village**, near the hospital on the west side of the town. It dates from the sixth millennium BC and illustrates the way of life of some of the earliest efforts at urban civilisation in this part of Bulgaria. The two **small houses** enclosed under a shed offer a curiously modern and domestic view of Bronze Age life, with domestic objects such as cats depicted on ceramics, and children's jewellery that would fit the wrist of any modern child. It is thought to have been destroyed by fire, perhaps started by a hostile invading tribe, in about 5500 BC.

15km south of Stara Zagora are the **Baths of Stara Zagora**. Turn right off the main Plovdiv road, going south. The site has been in use since ancient times, with a natural hot spring issuing from the Sredna Gora foothills. There are picturesque ruins in the wooded countryside, with low walls of a Turkish *hammam* that was built using original Roman masonry in the 18C. The Roman complex was large, consisting of 12 rooms that covered more than 2500 square metres. It is thought to have been built in about 163, and remained in use for over 1000 years. Until recently, the water was believed to give miraculous cures.

At **Trite Mogili**, 4km north east of Stara Zagora, an important Thracian tomb complex containing **chariot burials** was found in 1960. At Chatalka, 18km southwest Stara Zagora, there are the remains of a **villa** of a wealthy Romanised Thracian, and a complex including baths and farm buildings. Low walls can be seen near the banks of the Chatalka stream. Some of the very fine jewellery and a **Thracian helmet mask** found here are in the Stara Zagora museum.

The road runs directly north into the mountains, via Kazanlak (33km), to Gabrovo (80km), and Veliko Tarnovo (126km). In winter there can be problems with snow and ice on the central section.

Kazanlak and the Valley of the Roses

Kazanlak is a minor regional centre, mainly significant for its agriculture. It was an important administrative centre in Ottoman times. It is the centre of the rose oil industry, something for which Bulgaria has always been justly famous.

The Valley of the Roses, Ottoman *Ghyulteknesy*, near the town, was a heavily promoted tourist attraction in the communist period, for reasons that escape the present writer, as the sight of millions of rose bushes growing is not, in itself, more exciting than millions of other plants or trees. Plums and nuts are other local products.

History of Kazanlak

Kazanlak was notable in the ancient world for being the site of the capital city of the Thracian kingdom of *Seuthopolis*. This was a short distance west of the present town, and is submerged under the lake and dam on the Tundza river which was built in the early 1950s. *Seuthopolis* was founded towards the end of the 4C BC by King Seuth III, and was a major centre, with a population of perhaps 50,000 people. It was totally destroyed by fire and Celtic invaders at the end of the 3C BC. The Thracian state had developed after the retreat of the Persian invaders from the area in the 5C BC.

The modern town seems to have developed from a nearby medieval fortress and settlement called *Kran*. It was an important town under the Turks, with a large Muslim population and 16 mosques, most of which have now disappeared, and most of the old Turkish quarter has been replaced by ugly modern buildings. A small part remains, near the station, with some nice old bars and coffee shops, and a mosque, in rather poor condition.

Kazanlak was the site, in 1944, of the discovery by workmen constructing an air raid shelter to the north of the town, of a remarkable **Thracian tomb**. It was excavated soon afterwards, when the mound of earth above it was removed. A protective structure was built over it in 1960. The earth mound is about 7.5m high and 36.5m across. The original tomb has been sealed, to protect the outstanding **paintings** from atmospheric deterioration, but a good replica has been built nearby, which is well worth visiting.

It shows Hellenistic wall painting of the highest quality, and is thought to be the grave of a tribal chieftain from the early 3C BC, with a low single entrance with a pointed arch beyond which was a low narrow passage leading to an inner chamber. The tomb was robbed, probably in early antiquity, and no significant artefacts were found. It is likely that as well as the tribal chieftain, a favourite wife and horse would have been slaughtered and buried with him.

Wall painting of Thracian chieftain's horses from the domed chamber

In general design the tomb belongs to the round domed genre that has been found widely in Thrace, Asia Minor, southern Russia and elsewhere. It resembles other domed tombs found at *Seuthopolis* when the ancient city was excavated in 1948, before the site was flooded.

The **paintings** even in replica reproduction are quite marvellous, with the depiction of the deceased and their favourite horses and servants equal to the quality of ancient paintings from Pompeii and ancient Egypt. The degree of **Hellenisation** of the political elite depicted is a highly politically controversial question. The authoritative work on the tomb in Bulgarian was written by the daughter of the party leader, Ludmila Zhivkov, and stressed strongly the 'Thracian' nature of the world depicted, whereas some Greek writers on the art have seen the paintings as exclusively 'Hellenistic', not merely in period, but also in content, style and execution. Whatever the exact degree of cultural influence, the paintings are among the masterpieces of ancient pictorial art, and a visit here is highly recommended.

Beyond the town, travelling north, the road soon runs into the Sipcenska mountains, and up to the **Shipka Pass**, site of the famous battle of 1877, when the 7000 Russian and Bulgarian troops successfully prevented the advance of 27,000 Turks who had been sent to lift the siege of Pleven in the August of that year. On the left, after 12km, you pass the Shipka **Church of St Nicholas**, with a very fine gold dome in the Russian style. It was built to the designs of Russian architects as a memorial to those who fell in the anti-Ottoman campaign, and the interior decorations are interesting, in the popular style of the time.

Beyond the church and village, the road rises very steeply with many hairpin bends to the top of Shipka Pass. This is well worth the journey for the **magnificent views**. On Mount Stoletov is the **Freedom Monument**, a tower with a huge bronze lion 8m long and 4m high, a grandiose but remarkable edifice built in 1920s, after the Liberation. It is possible to drive up to it. It is a lonely, dramatic spot, often in low cloud, somewhere to ponder on the elemental nature of the struggle against the Ottoman Turkish oppression.

Gabrovo

Gabrovo is, and has always been, the gateway to the Shipka Pass over the central mountains and an important strategic centre. It has some interesting old streets and Ottoman-period buldings, although there was considerable redevelopment as an industrial centre in the communist period, with all the usual problems of visual and ground pollution, and subsequent industrial decline.

History of Gabrovo

Gabrovo is named after the Bulgarian word for hornbeam, *gabar*, and was a very small Roman and Byzantine settlement. A town only developed in Turkish times, from the beginning of the 16C onwards. Gabrovo had a good power supply from water mills on the Yantra river, and in the 18C it grew as a centre of craft industry such as gun-making. In the 19C textile mills were built and a leather industry developed. Local folklore is famous in Bulgaria, particularly Gabrovo jokes.

The Shipka Freedom Monument

The centre of the town is dominated by the **clock tower**, a fine early 19C National Revival construction. Walk from the main square into what is euphemistically called locally the 'old quarter', but is actually the remains of the old town centre. There are two very fine bridges crossing the River Yantra, one known as the Baev Bridge, the other as the Igoto Bridge, and some picturesque little streets with good cafés, and National Revival houses in varying styles and states of preservation. There is also a nice statue to **Racho the Farrier**, a local folk hero who is supposed to have been the first citizen of the town, and to have set up his blacksmith's forge under a hornbeam tree. In the centre of the old town is the **Aprilov School**, named after one of the pioneers of education in the Bulgarian language. Vasil Aprilov was an early 19C Slavophile who rejected the Greek tradition in education that had hitherto prevailed in Bulgaria and based his educational theory and practice on what he had found in the Ukraine and Russia. As such he was a fêted hero under the communist regime and the extent of his actual achievements may well have been exaggerated. His body is buried in the school courtyard. Nearby there is an attractive **Turkish fountain** dating from the 18C.

Gabrovo is only an hour's drive from Veliko Tarnovo, and can easily be visited on a day trip if you are staying in Tarnovo. The road passes through **Dryanovo**, a small old town that used to be important for silkworm production before the industrial revolution, but declined after it. As a result it has some attractive 18C and 19C streets and atmospheric old churches. It is worth a brief stop.

4km outside the town in the gorge of the Dryanovo river is the **Dryanovo Monastery**, a rather isolated and fortress-like small foundation. It was a refuge for Bulgarian rebel leaders against the Turks and several leaders of the 1876 Rising are buried here. 8km south is the **Etar** outdoor folk museum.

Follow the main road northwest to Veliko Tarnovo (46km).

Veliko Tarnovo

Veliko Tarnovo (pop. 37,550) is a very well-preserved **medieval and Renaissance town and citadel** that has survived the passage of time much better than many comparable places. It was the centre of medieval Bulgarian power and a visit helps in the understanding of the history of that period more than anywhere else in the country. It is built in a very beautiful and dramatic setting above the Yantra river, which flows through a steep gorge below the town, and is generally regarded to be the most picturesque town in the country. The **old town** is centred on a narrow rocky hill, surrounded on three sides by the river gorge, and a natural defensive stronghold. It is by far the most arresting medieval town in Bulgaria, magnificently situated with many architectural gems. A visit should be on every holiday itinerary.

Tarnovo has always played a central role in the national identity and consciousness of Bulgarians, as it was the seat of the capital of the Second Kingdom, and of the Patriarchate, and it remained a functioning town and centre of religion, literacy and the language throughout the Turkish period. Most of the 20 or so monasteries in the vicinity founded by the early Bulgarian rulers have survived in one form or another.

Many central events in relatively recent Bulgarian political history have also taken place here. That said, some Western visitors have problems in assimilating Tarnovo, especially those with little prior knowledge of Bulgarian history. The town has suffered in its atmosphere from the attentions of narrow-minded nationalists and from a strange kind of religiosity that seemed to affect politicians and architects of the late-communist period in their building restoration works in the town. It is perhaps best for the visitor who is not unduly absorbed in the world of Bulgarian history to take the town in moderate quantities. Guide books to the town need to be read critically, particularly on matters connected with Greek settlement in the town, the Church, and relations with Byzantium (see below). In the post-communist period, some parts of the old town have suffered from privatisation of property and have been damaged by insensitive commercial development.

■ **By rail**. There is a good rail service from Sofia to the town if you take the express train to Varna and alight at Gorna Orjahovica. A bus or taxi to Veliko Tarnovo takes about ten minutes or so from there. There is a closer station, for Tarnovo itself, on the Ruse–Stara Zagora line but trains are said to be slow and irregular and, if approaching from this direction, a coach is likely to be a better bet.

■ **Hotels**. The hotel situation in the town is fairly chaotic, with the marked reduction in numbers of foreign visitors causing the closure of at least one large hotel from the communist period, others continuing to lead a shadowy life as *Mafiya* clubs, and some nice new little private places springing up, and so on. The **Hotel Etar** is the centre of town in Opelchenska Street is recommended for clean, standard accommodation (about $US30 a night) ☎ 062 20236, fax 062 21807. For wealthier visitors, stay at the **Arbenassi Palace** (see p 204). **Recommended**.

■ **Restaurants**. All sorts of new restaurants and cafés are springing up with privatisation. Tarnovo used to be a good place to hear live Bulgarian music but unfortunately many of the new cafés have replaced it with the worst sort of disco muzak in an effort to 'Europeanise'.

History of Veliko Tarnovo

The Veliko (meaning 'old') Tarnovo region has been inhabited since very early times, as its mountainous situation above the centre of the country has always provided safe refuge against enemies and invaders. Stone Age implements have been found near Dryanovo, and material from later prehistory is widely dispersed in the locality. It was a minor Thracian settlement, but prospered under the Romans who built a fortress above the town which guarded the road running from *Nicopolis ad Istrum*.

The hill was refortifed in Byzantine times and remained in Byzantine hands until the period of the First Bulgarian Kingdom. It then reverted to Byzantine rule. In 1185 the Byzantines were overthrown and Tsar Petar was proclaimed king of the Second Bulgarian Kingdom, and Tarnovo became its capital. For 200 years the town became the centre of Bulgarian life, reaching its height between about 1250 and 1390. After the death of Tsar Ivan II in 1393 the feudal lords overthrew the centralised monarchy, in a peasant revolution, put the pigkeeper Ivaylo on the royal seat. The town was unable to resist Tartar invasions, and much weakened, the Second Kingdom fell to the Turks in 1393.

Tarnovo remained a centre of clerical and monastic life under the occupation, and was an early centre of commitment to an independent church using the Bulgarian language in the 19C. In 1877 the Russian army entered Tarnovo and the first Bulgarian Constitution was adopted in the town in 1879. Ever since the town has been a shrine of Bulgarian national feeling, and was favoured with various industrial investment projects under communism.

The Tsaravets Citadel and Old Tarnovo

The citadel is one of the finest medieval castles in the Balkans and although the fortification walls and some parts of the interior have been heavily restored, it should be a priority for visitors to Bulgaria. **Open** 09.00–sunset.

If arriving by car, drive up through the **Old Town**, along many charming streets of mostly National Revival period houses, then find the car park below the citadel entrance. You see before you a magnificent edifice with long high walls loping around the natural contour of the wooded hill that has been a natural military strongpoint throughout the centuries. Evoking the great power and prestige of the Second Bulgarian Kingdom it stands above the winding gorge carved out of limestone by the river.

Walk up to the entrance arch and then along a long Ottoman period paved causeway, then enter the citadel proper. It is then possible to turn left, and walk along behind the fortifications, for about half a mile, with **magnificent views** of the other hills of Tarnovo, particularly the bare wooded little hill of **Trapezitsa** (from the Greek 'the little table'), so named after its flat top. The rows of medieval and Ottoman houses clinging precariously to the sides of the hills have been understandably praised by many famous architects, such as Le Corbusier. In some places the walls have heavily restored—some would say over-

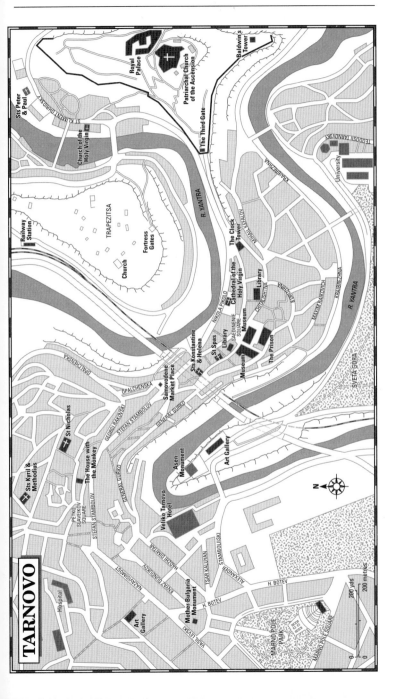

TARNOVO

Royal Palace

Patriarchial Church of the Ascension

Baldwin's Tower

Sts Peter & Paul

Church of the Holy Virgin

ST KLIMENT OHRIDSKY

The Third Gate

TEODOSII TARNOVSKI

University

R. YANTRA

KRAIBREZHNA

TRAPEZITSA

Railway Station

Church

Fortress Gates

The Clock Tower

MIHAIL LEFALOV

Cathedral of the Holy Virgin

Library

CHITALISHTA

NIKOLA PIKOLO

SAEDINENIE SQUARE

Museum

R. YANTRA

MAXIM RAIKOVITCH

KRAIBREZHNA

OPALCHENSKA

Sts Konstantine & Helena

St Spas

Library

Museum

The Prison

SVETA GORA

OPALCHENSKA

Samovodene Market Place

GEORGI RAKOVSKI

STEFAN STAMBOLOV

GENERAL GURKO

St Nicholas

The House with the Monkey

GENERAL GURKO

Asen Monument

Art Gallery

N

Sts Kyrii & Methodius

PETKO SLAVEIKOV SQUARE

STEFAN STAMBOLOV

Veliko Tarnovo Hotel

HADZHI DIMITAR

STAMBOLIISKI

ALEXANDER

H. BOTEV

Hospital

NEZAVISIMOST

KNYAZ DONDUKOV

Mother-Bulgaria Monument

H. BOTEV

ISAR KALUYAN

TSAR KALUYAN

Art Gallery

VASIL LEVSKI

MARNO POLE PARK

MARNO POLE SQUARE

0   200 yds

0   200 metres

restored—and this also applies when you begin to climb to the top of the citadel where you pass the early medieval fortress known as **Hugel's Tower**, which is currently covered in scaffolding but appears to have been almost entirely rebuilt in the last ten years. At the top of the hill is the **Patriarchal Church of the Ascension**, a fairy-tale fantasy building on the very centre of a small rocky outcrop. Nearby is a large rock on the edge of the precipice that was used as a place of execution in the Second Kingdom. The exterior of the church has a standard late 19C atmosphere, but the interior was redecorated in the late communist period with **dramatic Expressionist designs**, with a highly erotic Virgin and Child and portraits of masses of Christian toilers on the walls. Although the effect could be appalling, it somehow succeeds, rather in the manner of some French churches redecorated by disciples of the Christian worker-priests movement.

Take the steps below the church down the hill, past an impressive **carillion**, hung with four large bells. On the left, at the end of the fortifications, is a large defensive tower known as **Baldwin's Tower**, after a Crusader emperor allegedly imprisoned here.

In the **Old Town**, virtually all of the **museums** that existed five years ago are closed, either because of property restitution or the near-bankruptcy of the museum service here, and the lack of visitors. It is to be hoped that this situation will change in the near future. It is best to make enquiries at your hotel to see what may be open.

There is an impressive *son et lumiere* show at Tsaravets at about ten each night in the summer season, which can be watched from anywhere in town.

Environs of Veliko Tarnovo

Although there is pleasant hill walking country all around the town, the main interest is in the numerous **monasteries** in the vicinity (in Turkish times these numbered about over 30, nowadays about 20 have survived), the Ottoman village of **Arbanassi**, and the ancient site of **Nicopolis ad Istrum**, 17km north of the town, up the main road to Ruse. British archaeologists from Nottingham University have been working there recently.

Arbanassi

Arbanassi is an old Ottoman village about 4km north east of Veliko Tarnovo. It has some very fine **Ottoman domestic houses**, and one of the holiday homes of the communist leader Todor Zhivkov, now the Arbanassi Palace Hotel. Take the small road north east out of Veliko Tarnovo, across the river bridge by the Church of the 40 Martyrs. Turn right by the sign off the main road, then drive 1km to the village.

■ **Hotel**. The **Arbanassi Palace** (☎ 62280/6230176, fax 62 23717, telex 66739) is a 5-star hotel, developed from the Todor Zhivkov residence. It is at the top of the village with a wonderful view over Veliko Tarnovo. It is not cheap, about $US110 for a single room, but it is worth considering for the ambience, of late-Stalinist chic. It is part of the Interhotel group.

History of Arbanassi

The name of the village is of Albanian origin, and it was probably founded by Orthodox Albanian followers of Skanderbeg in the late 16C. The houses follow the classic Berat style of construction, with thick stone walls, a strong defensive orientation and wooden upper storeys. In 1582 the village became the property of the Grand Vizir Rustem Pasha.

In the 17C and 18C it became an important trading centre, linked to the Phanariot Greek traders of Romania, and was known for metalworking and silkworm cultivation. Trade links with the Habsberg lands were important. By the end of the 17C there were seven churches in the town.

In 1779 the first Greek language school in modern Bulgaria was opened at Arbanassi. In 1798 the village was ransacked by Turkish irregulars, and never recovered its former importance. The rich merchants' quarter was almost totally destroyed.

Apart from the pleasures of walking the village streets and seeing the fine Ottoman houses, there are three very beautiful churches. The earliest is the **Church of the Nativity**, which was consecrated in 1597. It has very beautiful 17C frescoes and a superb carved ikonostasis. A little way to the south are the **Church of the Archangel Michael** and **St Atanassius's Church**. Both were built in the 17C, and were decorated by artists from Mount Athos. On the outskirts of the village is the **Nunnery of St Nicholas**, a 19C rebuilding after the original church was ransacked by Turks in 1798. In the village the **House of the Konstantsalieva Family** has been made into a museum, and is open to the public (10.00–16.30, except Mon). It has a nice coffee shop.

Nicopolis ad Istrum

To reach the site, drive north out of Tarnovo towards Ruse, or take a bus, and stop about 3km before the village of Nikup, which is about 2km west of the main road in open farmland. Look for a small lake, about 200m from the road. The site entrance gate (no vehicles allowed) is beyond the stream flowing from the lake.

History of Nicopolis ad Istrum

Nicopolis ad Istrum was an important Roman town in the province of Lower Moesia that was founded in AD 107 by the Emperor Trajan. It was built on the junction of several important roads, to celebrate the defeat of the Dacian revolt that had taken the preceding six years. Inscriptions show it was founded as a Hellenistic city, and Greek was the first language of law, commerce and government, although this became diluted with later immigration and economic growth. It was settled mainly by Roman army veterans from wars in Asia Minor, Syria and Egypt, as well as the Dacian campaigns. It reached a peak of prosperity between 220 and 249, when very large quantities of coins were minted.

The city was attacked by the Goths in 250, and became the seat of a bishop in 346. The centre of urban life moved south at this time and a new fortification was constructed, involving the construction of 20 defensive towers. The town was again assaulted by the Visigoths in 376–82 which seriously affected its economic life and culture.

It was partly destroyed by barbarian invaders in the late 5C when the remaining inhabitants are thought to have abandoned the exposed and largely indefensible site for Tarnovo and the mountains. Some contact with the Roman city must have remained as it was the seat of a bishop, and stone quarried in the town has been found in the construction of some Tarnovo buildings.

The site was discovered by archaeologists in the 19C but the discovery of important works of art such as the copy of Praxilites' *Eros* led to unsystematic treasure hunting, which even continues today.

The remains of the town show an extensive settlement that in its time must have been wealthy. A very large area of the city remains unexcavated but aerial and ultrasound surveys have shown a very large and well-planned central area, around an enormous forum with a well-paved main road running through it. There is an outer fortification wall, not very well restored in many places, and low walls and street outlines of domestic buildings.

Bulls' head decoration

Enter the site through the metal gate and there are low walls, ruins of a large gatehouse, note the **bulls' head decoration** on the stones indicating the importance of cattle rearing here in antiquity. There is a very fine paved **Roman road** running 800m straight into the site, with some funereal monuments, although one or two appear to have been looted recently.

After 400m, you enter the remains of the **forum**, with parts of a small **temple pediment** to the left, and site offices. There is a very attractive grassy area with foundations of numerous buildings, and some standing columns. The **wild flowers** in spring and summer are very beautiful, and the herds of animals nearby grazing peacefully are redolent of a pre-industrial world.

Return to Stara Zagora by the same route. If the weather is bad over the Shipka Pass it is possible to take the lower road through the Trevnenska mountains via Vonesta Voda, which is only 700m high.

Sliven

Sliven, 55km north east of Stara Zagora, is quite an interesting historic town although it has more than its fair share of the usual communist redevelopment problems, common in places where a combination of wartime damage, anti-Ottoman prejudice and Stalinist bad taste and authoritarianism have given rise to some truly horrible post-war buildings. Apart from the town itself, the **Blue Rock** area in the forest park to the east of the town on the Burgas road, is very interesting (somewhat similar to the ambience of Belogradchik), where a great natural rock formation was used by both the Romans and Ottomans to build secure fortifications. **Kotel**, to the north, is a very pretty old carpet-making town with some well-preserved National Revival houses. In the 19C the Sliven area was famous for banditry. Sliven is a centre in Bulgaria for **Sarakatsan** settlement, semi-nomadic herdsmen who travel long annual migrations with their flocks of sheep and goats. The town can be very subject to a violent wind, the *bora*, at certain times of year.

History of Sliven

Thracian and Roman remains have been found near Sliven but there does not seem to have been much of a settlement here until medieval times when a small town grew up. This was largely destroyed during the Ottoman invasions and, under the early Empire the town, now renamed *Enidze Kariesi*, the 'new town', was little more than a small garrison centre. This changed in the agricultural boom in this region in the 18C when silkworm rearing was developed, along other agricultural exports. In the 19C tobacco growing also helped boost economic growth, and the beginnings of the important 20C textile industry. The resistance movement in Sliven in the Second World War was strong, and there were a number of important battles with the German occupiers.

Melnik and the southwest

The southwest region of Bulgaria is one of the most accessible and interesting parts of the country, enjoying a much less severe winter climate than most of Bulgaria. The **Pirin Mountains** have some of the most dramatic and beautiful scenery to be found anywhere in Bulgaria, with the famed **Pirin National Park**, a UNESCO World Heritage protected area. On the border with Greece, the **Rhodope mountains** run across the border for hundreds of kilometres, and include some interesting resorts and outstanding scenery and wildlife.

The northern section of the region is dominated by the **Rila mountains**, with the fashionable skiing resort of **Borovets**, some outstanding hiking country, and **Rila Monastery**, perhaps the most important national monument for the Bulgarian people.

The regional climate is dominated by the Struma river valley, which allows warmer air from the Mediterranean region to penetrate northwards into Bulgaria and it is a good region to explore in autumn or winter. It is easily reached by public transport from Thessaloniki, as well as from Sofia, and can be combined with a visit to northern Greece.

The southwest forms part of the geographical region of **Macedonia**, and has played an important part in modern Bulgarian history, and Balkan conflicts, and remains a centre of support for the **Internal Macedonian Revolutionary Organisation** (IMRO) today. The IMRO revolutionary hero Yane Sandanski is buried at Rozhen monastery near historic **Melnik**.

The economy is dominated by agriculture and tourism, with the favourable climate enabling crops such as peaches to be grown, as well as most of the Bulgarian production of early spring vegetables. Tourism centres on historic towns such as Melnik, with one of the best-preserved groups of Ottoman, Greek and Bulgarian National Revival buildings in the country. **Bansko** is a historic town of great interest and a winter resort, with good skiing and a centre for hill walking.

- **By car**. If driving from Sofia, allow about two and a half hours to reach Melnik, depending on traffic conditions on the main road south to Greece via Pernik (see p 221) and Blagoevgrad. If travelling north from Thessaloniki, it normally takes about two hours, depending largely on how busy the border is at Kulata. Follow signs south from Blagoevgrad towards Sandanski (76km); take left turn signed from main road to Melnik.

Melnik

Melnik is a charming, evocative little town that has outstanding domestic buildings and important historical associations. It is now only a fraction of its former size, with only a few hundred permanent inhabitants; in the 18C and early 19C, it was an urban centre of more than 10,000 people, with a substantial ethnic Greek merchant community, and dominated the trade route up the Struma valley between Ottoman *Roumelia* and Greece. Much of the early prosperity of Melnik was based on the wine trade, and the region still produces what many people consider to be one of the best red wines in Bulgaria.

Melnik is romantically situated in a narrow valley dominated by fascinating sandstone rock formations which have been eroded into unusual patterns, and with many deep clefts and caves. It is a landscape embodying the essential mystery, intrigue and conflict of much of the recent history of the region. Melnik is the best place to stay for a visit to Rozhen Monastery and the Grave of Yane Sandanski nearby. Rozhen is a wonderful building that embodies

Countryside near Melnik

the unity of spiritual and political struggle in this part of Bulgaria. The town of Sandanski has interesting Roman remains and was the birthplace of Spartacus, the famous Roman slave leader who was a Thracian.

The southwest of Bulgaria has very rich **mythological and astrological traditions**: Nostradamus's work is widely studied by the people. The region was the home of **Granny Vanga** (1913–96), the most famous soothsayer in modern Bulgaria whom even the communist leaders used to visit. She is thought to be the model for the 'Witch of Melnik' in Robert Liddell's novel *The October Circle*. The very rich popular mythology among the Greek peasants around Melnik and Pernik before the First Balkan War in 1912 was recorded by G.F. Abbott in his classic volume *Macedonian Folklore*.

Melnik has always been a centre of vampire and werewolf legends, and Bulgarian- and Greek-language stories from the Melnik region were studied by the British authority Montague Summers in his seminal volumes *The Werewolf* and *The Vampire*.

- ■ **Hotels**. The soulless state-owned **Hotel Melnik** (☎ 99727) often seems to be closed. In any case, it is much cheaper and more interesting to stay in one of the private rooms to let in their residents' houses. Many houses have Rooms to Rent signs in the windows, or ask at a bar or shop. Prices are about $US15 a night.

- ■ **Restaurants**. There are several good old-fashioned tavernas along the main street, although wine quality is sometimes not everything that it should be, surprisingly.

- ■ **Shopping**. Local souvenir shops are good for craft products, especially wood carvings. Melnik wine is available everywhere.

- ■ **Hiking**. Melnik is a good place for the serious hiker to begin exploration of the Pirin. There is a Hikers' Hut about 5 hours' walk from Melnik.

History of Melnik

This part of Bulgaria has always been subject to Greek influences, in antiquity, Byzantine and modern times. In Classical antiquity Greeks were involved in trade here, and very early ceramics and coins have been found. Melnik was then overshadowed by nearby *Petra*, modern Petrich. The village on the modern site was fortified by Tsar Samuel in the early medieval period. By the 13C it was a small Greek town, inhabited by people who had originally moved from the Greek community in Plovdiv. These people and their descendants built up the trade of the region, and some Turks moved into the place in later Ottoman times, when Melnik traders dominated the whole Struma valley.

At the time of the Liberation in 1878, the population was probably about 15,000 people, but the town went into sharp decline in the late 19C and early 20C, and was decimated by the political conflicts between Greek and Bulgarian nationalists during and after the Balkan Wars, in 1912–13.

In the Second Balkan War the area was occupied by the Greek army. The local Greek inhabitants, who had suffered badly from the Internal Macedonian Revolutionary Organisation, followed the Greek army back over the border and established a new settlement at *Nea Melnikon*, near Serres, in northern Greece. After the failure of the 1923 Rising, and the growth of violent internicine conflict within IMRO, a near-civil war raged between nationalists and many people left the region and moved to Sofia to escape it.

Melnik village is notable for the very large and impressive **merchants' houses**, and other buildings from its distinguished past. They straggle along the main street by the river bed, or are found strung along the hillsides above. Nearly all were originally Greek, and the most impressive is the fortress-like **Kordopulov House**, a Bulgarianisation of the House of the Kordopoulos family. It dates from 1754 and shows the great wealth of the Hellenic merchant class of old Melnik. The lower part of the house is a very large wine cellar while up above are beautifully furnished and decorated rooms in the Ottoman style, with separate men's and women's quarters, and very fine carved wooden ceilings. It is open as a museum on weekdays and sells wine and honey.

The Church of Sveta Barbara nearby is a sad roofless building that was destroyed in the Second Balkan War.

Another interesting building is the **hammam**, a very pretty little Turkish bath in the 18C style in the middle of the village. It is ridiculously described as a 'national revival' building on a sign nearby. It is in a poor state, overgrown by vegetation and the fine marble interior is heavily vandalised. It requires urgent restoration.

Rozhen Monastery

Rozhen Monastery is a great historic monument that should be visited by all travellers in this part of Bulgaria. It is not only a wonderful Christian edifice, beautifully situated at the foot of the Pirin range, but also a sacred shrine to the aspirations of IMRO and the Bulgarian struggle in this part of Macedonia.

The complex and bloody history of the Macedonian Question (see p 74) is often difficult to follow, even for those with some knowledge of the convoluted domestic and international politics of the region, with its often lethal mix of ethnicity, religion and nationalism, but a visit to Rozhen can assist the understanding of many of the old controversies that have revived since 1990, apart from being a visit to a beautiful and picturesque place.

The monastery is about 5km or so to the east of Melnik. By far the best way to reach it, if the weather is at all reasonable, is to walk up to it along the largely dried-up river bed of the Melnitsa river. This is a sublimely **romantic walk**, like entering a Garden of Eden, and even if you are unfit it gives the opportunity of seeing the unique sandstone rock formations easily, with their weird, eroded shapes and unusual patterns of vegetation.

Rozhen Monastery

To reach the monastery from Melnik, follow the path east through the village to the top, past the last houses, and enter the river bed. Unless there has been a recent storm, or very wet weather, it is a pretty dry affair, and the path winds up it through luxuriant vegetation. There is a very rich birdlife, with nightingales, woodpeckers and cuckoos common. Semi-wild goats live in caves in the rocks. The path narrows and there is often something of a scramble up the slopes to the top of the hill, which takes about two hours. At the top, there is a wonderful sense of a lonely Macedonian landscape—the only visible activity the occasional distant flocks of sheep feeding among the scrub and rough grass. The eroded sandstone produces remarkable visual effects. There is a narrow path, at the top, then a wonderful view of the monastery and church nestling in a lonely valley. Descend across open fields towards the antiquity.

History of the monastery

The exact date of the foundation of the monastery is unknown. It certainly existed by the beginning of the 13C, when the whole region of Melnik was ruled by Prince Alexis Slav, a nephew of Tsar Kaloyan (1197–1207). It retained a close connection with Mount Athos and was, in essence, Greek and was governed by the Patriarch in Constantinople. The original buildings were largely destroyed in the 16C, and rebuilt in the 17C, being completed by 1732.

The monastery is a fortress-like building, of a roughly triangular shape, with high stone walls, and very few windows, the latter only on the top storey indicating that it has had to be efficient from a military point of view to survive in many earlier epochs. There is a very beautiful inner courtyard with many wooden balconies lining the monks' accommodation.

In the centre is the **Church of the Holy Virgin**, with very good 16C frescoes, particularly in the narthex, and unique **stained glass windows**. The many paintings with fishermen, and fish, show the links this region had with the Aegean in the medieval and Ottoman periods. The northwest chapel of the church is dedicated to Agioi Anargyroi (the Holy Healers), Cosmas and Damian, whose cult in the area had continued since Classical antiquity, presumably linked to the healing springs nearby at modern Sandanski. The 18C **iconostasis** has very fine wood carvings.

In the courtyard buildings and residential complexes for the monks, the **refec-

tory is outstanding, with fragments of the original medieval wall decorations, and a gallery, redolent of a Jacobean hall in England, and the **ossuary**, built in 1597. Most of the rest of the external buildings date from the 19C reconstruction of the monastery.

About 400m from the monastery is the **Church of SS Kyril and Methodius**. This is a pleasant if architecturally undistinguished building, with an open, airy interior and attractive bell tower, but it is of considerable historic importance. It was built between 1912 and 1914, and contains an important and much venerated **ikon of St Nicholas**.

About 30m from the west door is the **grave of Yane Sandanski**, a simple dark grey granite slab. It is evocative and dignified, and usually covered with wild flowers left by Internal Macedonian Revolutionary Organisation supporters.

Yane Sandanski
Yane Sandanski (1872–1915) was, with Todor Alexandrov and Gotse Delchev, a central figure in the history of the anti-Ottoman and pro-IMRO revolutionary movements in this part of Bulgaria. He was primarily an IMRO guerrilla leader, a charismatic 'Robin Hood' figure, a brave hero to his Balkan friends, a dangerous hoodlum to his Turkish enemies.

Round trip to Gotse Delchev

An interesting round trip can be made into the Rhodopes from near the Greek border across to Gotse Delchev, then northeast to the Pomak areas around Batak (see p 188). It is an arduous mountain drive and although the road is generally fairly good, plenty of time should be allowed, and full supplies carried. After Gotse Delchev there are very few petrol stations.

First return to the main road and drive towards the Greek border, turning left at Marikostenovo (15km), then climbing towards Katunci (27km), across open rolling countryside. Walnuts are an important local crop. The road follows the Bistrica river valley and climbs towards the **Livardi Pass**. **NB**. Note the sign giving snow conditions in the winter months.

The road approaches **Pirin** village (40km), with magnificent views of the Pirin mountains and national park, then climbs with many hairpin bends through pine and birch forests. Wolves, brown bear and lynx live in this region. You reach the top of the Livardi Pass (1120m) at **Popovo Livadi**, the 'Glades of the Priests', with vast uninhabited forests stretching towards the border with Greece. **NB**. Beware landslides on this section of the road.

Descend towards **Dobrotino** (54km). There are soon very dramatic views down into the **Mesta** river valley, and the town of **Gotse Delchev** (63km). Today it is a modest regional centre on the banks of the Mesta river, the ancient Greek *Nestus*. It is a dull, very provincial town, although valuable Oriental varieties of tobacco are grown in the vicinity, and there is a solid local timber industry whose fortunes have improved since the end of communism with rising exports to Greece. It can be used as a base for exploring the eastern Pirin but it is not much of a place to stay.

It is a poor area, horse and cart transport is common.

History of Gotse Delchev

Gotse Delchev was founded as a significant urban centre by the Romans, who built *Nicopolis ad Nestrum* nearby, the modern city in Emperor Trajan's time. This was a military post that was meant to control the pass nearby on the road linking Constantinople with the north. A little town grew up nearby. There are remains near a local quarry at the village of Zagrade, nearby, although there is little to see, as virtually no excavation has taken place, and it is not worth visiting. Chance finds indicate it was a Greek-speaking town, with only one Latin inscription having been found to date.

Gotse Delchev

Gotse Delchev (1872–1903) was, with Todor Alexandrov and Yane Sandanski, one of the three leaders of the Macedonian revolution whose names have most resonance in modern Bulgaria. He was a schoolteacher by profession and, unlike the charismatic guerilla leader Sandanski, was primarily an ideologist and organiser. As such he appealed to the Bulgarian communists more than many other IMRO leaders.

He helped found the Macedonian–Adrianople Revolutionary Organisation (IMARO) in Thessaloniki (*Solun*) in 1893, and committed his whole life to setting up underground revolutionary committees. He was killed early in 1903, shortly before the start of the St Elijah's day uprising, later known to historians as the Ilinden Rising. About 240 pitched battles were fought in the region, as Delchev's life's work came to fruition, with 26,000 armed insurgents fighting a 290,000 strong Turkish army. About 70,000 people were made homeless by the Rising, many of which fled from what is now modern FYROM to make their homes in Bulgaria. He is buried in Skopje (see p 228).

Either return to the main road by the same route, or travel north to Bansko and Razlog, picturesque Pirin towns, through deep wooded valleys in the mountains.

Sandanski

Sandanski, 12km northwest of Melnik, is a mostly modern town on the main road to the Greek border post at Kulata. It is named after the IMRO revolutionary hero and has some important Roman mosaics. It was the birthplace of the famous Roman slave revolt leader **Spartacus** who was a Thracian. There is a mineral spa in the town.

History of Sandanski

The town of modern Sandanski was originaly settled by the Thracian *Medi* tribe, and was known as *Medius*. During the Roman invasion a large battle was fought nearby, and Medi tribesmen were taken prisoner and taken to southern Italy where they worked as slaves. Among them was **Spartacus**, who led their revolt against the Roman army under the command of Crassus. Spartacus died in battle in AD 71 in Lucania, in Italy.

The Romans renamed the place *Desudava*, and built a temple dedicated to Asclepius at the thermal springs. It was known for centuries for its healing properties and was called *Sveti Vrac*, the 'blessed doctor', in Slav. This town was abandoned in the Middle Ages as settlement began to be concentrated in nearby Melnik. The Turks rebuilt the town, and it became a local administrative centre. In the early 20C it suffered severe depopulation for the same reasons as Melnik, although there were never as many Greeks living here.

In 1949 the communists renamed the town *Sandanski*. The history of the Internal Macedonian Revolutionary Organisation always caused the Bulgarian communist authorities problems, with, for instance, the IMRO guerilla leader Yane Sandanski receiving the odd appellation of an 'agricultural innovator' in the 1960s' official guide to Bulgaria.

As you enter the town from the main road going south to Kulata, there is a colossal **bronze statue** of the slave leader **Spartacus** on the left, on top of a small mound. It is a good example of the socialist realist style, for once with an entirely suitable subject. The plinth has been vandalised and requires restoration. 400m on is the centre of the little town, with the spa baths on the left. On the right of the central square is a hotel. An ancient Christian basilica with some good mosaics was discovered here in the pre-war period. The **Hotel Spartacus** is open but is a bit dismal and is only recommended for short stays: it is useful en route to Greece. It has a large **casino** used by many lowlife-looking types. The blackjack tables are suspect. **Avoid**.

The border post at **Kulata** is 17km south of the town, follow the main road south. If it is difficult to get a bus to the Greek border from Sofia, or if you miss the through bus to Thessaloniki, it is possible to go by coach to Sandanski and then take a taxi to the border for a few dollars and walk across the border. The **border post** is open 24 hours, and is usually quite efficient and not congested. Under a European Union scheme, it is currently being extended and the road widened. There are good duty free shops, with exceptional value cigarettes, craft products and wine. On the Greek side there is little or no public transport. You often have to pay for a taxi to Serres, currently about £15, although you can be asked to pay much more, and then take a bus from Serres to Athens or Thessaloniki.

The nearest town to the border west of the main road is Petrich (10km). Take a turn off the main road after 3km, then a side road to the town.

Petrich

Petrich is a pleasant little town that is nowadays rather depressed economically, after the collapse of the extensive state farms devoted to peach and apricot growing nearby. The mountains to the south are very beautiful, and form the border with Greece. It is a good place to stay to explore the locality, with the important historic monument of **Tsar Samuel's Castle** nearby, and the border crossing point with FYROM at Zlatarevo (20km). There are very good walks in the Ograzden hills, with interesting landscapes derived from the activity of extinct volcanos. Petrich is a centre of support for the mainstream Internal Macedonian Revolutionary Organisation (IMRO), and the banned IMRO-Ilinden.

History of Petrich

A Thracian settlement of the *Medi* tribe existed near the modern town, called by the Hellenised name of *Petra*, meaning 'rock'. It was known as a town as early as 131 BC when it was inhabited by Peonians who were vassals of Alexander the Great and his successors. The Romans built a fort at Petrich after their conquest. In very early medieval times Tsar Samuel's Castle was built nearby, and the town was very prosperous until the Bulgarian Empire here was destroyed.

In the medieval period Petrich and this region was an important centre of Bulgarian power in the struggle against the Byzantines. After a long period of contested power, in September 1014 a great battle was fought between the Byzantine Emperor Basil II (Basil the Bulgar slayer) and Tsar Samuel's forces in a mountain pass near the town. The Byzantine attack from the rear resulted in the massacre of the Bulgarians, and 15,000 prisoners were blinded with hot pokers and force marched back to Tsar Samuel in his stronghold at Prilep (in modern FYROM). He dropped dead from a heart attack at the sight of the remains of his army.

Petrich was taken by the Turks in 1386. Under the Ottomans, the fertile land in the region was farmed by *beys*, while most of the population was Greek. It was an important place on the caravan routes across western Macedonia on the road to Constantinople, with a large trade in horses. In the 1840s bands of Albanians attacked the town. Bulgarianisation started in the 19C and was greatly accelerated by the Balkan Wars in 1912–13 when many of the Turks were murdered, and the Greeks were driven back to Greece. The town was on the Macedonian frontline during the First World War, and saw bitter fighting, described by the British war correspondent G. Ward Price in *With the Salonika Army*.

In the 1920s Petrich was bitterly divided by the conflicts within IMRO, and was notorious as a dangerous and anarchic neighbourhood, with assassinations and bombings of prominent individuals in public life. Most of the modern inhabitants are descended from refugees from Greece after the exchange of populations under the Treaty of Neuilly.

Petrich was an important military camp for Democratic Army activities in the Greek Civil War between 1947 and 1949, along with Berkovitsa and Smolyan. Population levels have never recovered from the disasters affecting the area between 1911 and 1918, and much of the land is hardly cultivated and is reverting to woodland. In the period of United Nations sanctions against Serbia, it was often used as a through route for large-scale petrol smuggling from Bulgaria to Serbia via FYROM, with as many as 20 tankers travelling in convoys in an atmosphere redolent of the Wild West.

The main excursion nearby is to **Tsar Samuel's Castle**, which is in open country near the river Strumesnica, about 10km west of the town. It is a beautiful spot in a landscape which has a remote pastoral quality, as if the god Pan might be found following the shepherds and their sheep across the low hills. Large earthworks show the scale of the medieval fort. A monument in a small wood commemorates the 14,000 Bulgarians blinded here by the Byzantines in 1014.

The road continues to the border crossing with FYROM after another 6km, at

Zlatarevo. To the south there is the very beautiful Belasica mountain range, on the border with Greece.

To reach Bansko, return to the main road and travel north towards Sofia for 44km, then turn right near Krupnik to Razlog (37km, along minor road) and Bansko (44km).

Bansko and the Pirin National Park

Bankso is a very picturesque, interesting historic town of 12,000 people which is well worth visiting to see the **domestic houses** and to use as a centre for the beautiful **Pirin National Park**, which offers excellent walking and mountain climbing. It is also a leading ski resort (see box). It is a tight-knit community with strong IMRO traditions, and in all periods of history has been at the forefront of the struggle for the Bulgarian cause in Macedonia.

The Shiligarnika ski region

The ski area is up the mountain from Bansko and is served by a free bus in the winter sports season: it is a 12km trip through pine forest. Most skiing activities are based here, including chairlifts to the slopes.

It is a quieter and cheaper resort than Borovets (see p 219), with a much higher proportion of Bulgarians. The main plus is the town of Bansko itself for après-ski, which offers a very pleasant and welcoming unpretentious environment, while the main minus is the relatively modest amount of piste runs. There is a ski school but no ski kindergarten. It is also worth bearing in mind that the resort is much lower than Borovets or Pamporovo, at 937m, and although the highest ski point is as high as 2501m, lack of good snow can sometimes be a problem. It is certainly not a good idea to book for Bansko much before Christmas. The recently renovated Pirin Hotel is recommended, also very nice rooms are available in local historic houses.

Blagoevgrad

Blagoevgrad is 61km north up the main road to Sofia from Sandanski. It is a regional administrative centre, a strong IMRO town with a definite 'Macedonian' consciousness, and has some worthwhile industries, but the town centre is dull and there is little reason to go there. It is the location of the new American University in Bulgaria.

There is a useful border crossing point with FYROM at **Delcevski**, 25km directly east of Blagoevgrad, although it is basically a minor road and is not very suitable for heavy vehicles. It can also be difficult in winter weather. On the FYROM side a minor road goes to Kocani, 58km, across largely deserted country. A poor road south goes to Strumica, in FYROM, 97km (not recommended except in summer). A four-wheel-drive vehicle is desirable although not essential.

History of Blagoevgrad

Although there were small Thracian and Roman settlements on and near the site, the town was really founded by the Turks in 1502, when it was called *Gorna Dzumaja*, meaning 'mountain marketplace'. Throughout the

Ottoman period it was a majority Turkish and Muslim town, although few traces remain today. The town was liberated by the Russian army in 1877, but was returned to the Ottoman Empire under the Treaty of Berlin.

An important rising was started here in 1902 by the Supreme Macedonian Revolutionary Committee (SMAC), which was intended to provoke the intervention of the Great Powers in the Macedonian Question. The region joined Bulgaria after 1912. Under communism it grew as a tobacco town.

The Rila Mountains

Rila Monastery

Rila Monastery is a national shrine for all Bulgarians, and a wonderfully situated monument of the highest architectural and historic interest. If the visitor is Sofia based, there are various tourist companies offering one-day bus trips, which are usually good value.

From Sofia, take the main road south to Kulata, and turn left after about 60km. The road goes across open farmland, then enters the valley of a small river, with the Rila range which rises to 2729m, with a severe winter climate. The road winds up towards the mountains through an increasingly narrow gorge, with houses clinging to the wooded hillsides and numerous peasant plots on the valley floor. There used to be a narrow gauge railway along here, which was specially built for royal use at the time Rila was the main residence of King Ferdinand.

Rila Monastery

History of the monastery

Rila Monastery was founded in the 10C by the ascetic anchorite John of Rila and soon became one of the centres of medieval monasticism in Bulgaria. It is situated in the western part of the Rila mountains at a height of 1147m, in a dramatic mountain setting. It expanded in the 14C, and prospered, but was attacked and partly burnt down during the Ottoman conquest. Redevelopment began during the 15C and 16C, in association with the Russian Orthodox monastery of St Panteleimon on Mount Athos. In 1469 the relics of John of Rila the founding saint were returned to the monastery from Veliko Tarnovo. It was subject to a major programme of reconstruction that lasted throughout the 19C, starting in 1818. It was a favoured residence of the Bulgarian monarchs after the Liberation, particularly King Ferdinand.

Entering the **courtyard** of the monastery through the fierce-looking outer walls, and the central entrance arch, there is an immediate sense of entering a great national shrine, as there are nearly always large numbers of Bulgarians here, paying homage to one of the seminal buildings in the history of the nation.

In the centre of the great courtyard is the **church**, next to which is the central **Hrelyo's tower**, a brutal-looking construction with deeply indented walls that is the only surviving part of the monastery dating back to the restorations of the 14C.

The outer ring of buildings consist of very large four-storey galleried wooden and stone monastic quarters, with white arches standing out against the darker background of the woodwork. There is a poetry of shape and colour, a harmony of design that is more fully developed than in any other comparable 19C monastery.

There are many remarkable works of art of all kinds to be seen. Perhaps the finest is the **external fresco paintings** on the monastery church, a wonderful symphony of Biblical scenes showing the descent of sinners to Hell, with graphic depictions of the Seven Deadly Sins.

The grave of James Bourchier

Across the monastery car park, and up a small path, about 150m, is the grave of James Bourchier, the famous 19C Balkan correspondent of *The Times*. He was a close friend of King Ferdinand and chose to be buried at Rila. The grave is a simple granite slab lying in an open wooded glade. A ceremony to commemorate the 75th anniversary of the death of Bourchier was held in January 1996, with the grave restoration financed by *The Times* and the Reuters Foundation.

Grave of James Bourchier of The Times *in Rila forest*

James Bourchier

James Bourchier (1850–1921) was a prominent British 19C journalist who was a strong supporter of the Bulgarian cause. He was born to an Anglo-Irish family in County Cork, and was an outstanding classicist, becoming a teacher at Eton College. Tiring of teaching, he began to travel in the Balkans and file stories for *The Times*. He soon became the most outstanding Balkan correspondent of his time, a confidant of monarchs and ambassadors. He represented *The Times* in the region for 33 years. He was a close friend of King Ferdinand and often stayed at Rila Monastery, a place he loved, and he gave instructions in his will that he wished to be buried at Rila.

Borovets

Borovets, taking its name from the Bulgarian word for pine, *bor*, is the oldest ski resort in Bulgaria, a product of the enthusiasm of the late 19C Bulgarian monarchs for winter sports. Founded in 1897, it started to become well known in the early 1930s. It is, in a general sense, the most prestigious resort in the country, with a proportionately large number of foreigners among visitors, and with most Western diplomatic missions having a ski chalet in the resort. It is 10km from the historic town of Samokov, and 72km from Sofia.

There are eight ski lifts, and a total of 40km of marked piste, with 18km cross-country skiing. The two ski schools have a minimum age of seven, but there is also a ski kindergarten. In theory the season runs from the end of November until the end of May although in these days of the greenhouse effect and reduced snowfall, it often does not do so. There are three hotels with more than 300 beds in the resort.

The resort nestles at the bottom of **Mount Musala** (2925m), one of the highest of the Rila mountains range. Skiing takes place in three subregions: **Yastrebets**, with difficult runs, **Sityakovo**, with predominantly difficult and slalom runs, and **Markudjika**, at the top of the mountain, where runs are used for giant slalom competitions.

■ **Hotels**. There are several large hotels in the resort. The best hotel is the four-star **Hotel Samokov**, an imposing concrete block with 614 beds that was designed for the upper end of the package holiday trade. Other hotels, such as the **Rila** and **Mura** are three star, and there are also two-star hotels and a variety of chalets and more informal accommodation. As elsewhere in Bulgaria, the main differences in classification are related to the indoor facilities, so that the Hotel Samokov is the only hotel in the resort with an indoor swimming pool.

It is much cheaper to book a SkiPack of locally hired equipment in the UK before leaving than doing so later in Bulgaria.

Samokov

Samokov makes a pleasant drive from Sofia, especially if you take the minor road off the Sofia ringway, via Zelenicia, about 46km in all. The road (badly potholed in places) is based on an old minor Roman road. It runs through pleasant woods and rolling farming country.

Samokov was an important centre of the national movement and for the early industrialisation in Bulgaria. In medieval and Turkish times it had a Jewish community. It was a favoured town under communism. Now it is rather run down, but it is worth a short visit to see the **Bairakli Mosque**, built in 1840, a quiet poetic building with very fine interior paintings. The twisted minaret is very engaging. There is an attractive **Ottoman pavillion** nearby.

Borovets is 10km to the north, along the main road.

Pernik, Kyustendil and the Western Borderlands

- **By car**. The road from Sofia to the border with FYROM is good asphalt, passing through Pernik (24km), Radomir (29km) and Kyustendil (75km) to the border with FYROM at Gjusevo (97km). The last section in the mountains is sometimes subject to very heavy snowfall in the winter. If crossing to FYROM, allow plenty of time for border formalities, as congestion is common.

- **By rail**. The Sofia–Gjusevo rail line offers a fair service, the journey taking about two hours.

- **By coach**. There is no through coach service to the border at the time of writing, take a taxi to Gjusevo from Kyustendil. The border duty free shops are outstanding value for spirits and tobacco products.

This district is dominated by the road to former Yugoslav Macedonia, following the Struma river valley, and passing through the important but declining industrial centres of **Pernik** and **Radomir**, one of the original heartlands of the Bulgarian trades union and socialist movements. Pernik has an impressive ruined castle, and a very interesting museum. The road then crosses the rolling uplands to the Bistrica river and the beautiful Konjavska mountains to Kyustendil.

Kyustendil, ancient *Pautalia*, was an important Roman and Turkish administrative town and under the Ottoman Empire was the centre of a very large and rich *vilayet*. It has some good Roman remains and Islamic buildings. The road climbs to the border in the Osogovska mountains.

From Kyustendil, it is only a short taxi ride to the border. The railway line was supposed to be built as far as Kumanovo, in FYROM, in the 1920s, but because of political difficulties between Yugoslavia and Bulgaria, it was never finished. Construction has recently resumed on the FYROM side of the border.

To the north, there are pleasant hill villages and thick woodland, which were the scene of important battles in the **Partisan war** against the German occupiers in Second World War. The Bulgarian resistance movement was very strong along the eastern border with Yugoslavia. The village of **Trun** was particularly important, and several of the leaders of the first Bulgarian communist government came from this area. Northwest of Mount Ruj is the Dragoman Pass, leading to the border with Serbia, and the interesting historic town of Berkovitsa (see p 126).

The main road leaves Sofia to the southwest, passing the attractive wooded suburb of **Boyana** on the left. This can be reached by a small detour, taking the turn up the hill by the 'Macedonia' restaurant. See p 113. Care is needed on this route throughout; although it is basically a good asphalt road, it is often heavily congested and is badly potholed in some places. On the outskirts of the city, you pass an ugly socialist realist monumental statue, and climb to the uplands and open grazing country towards Pernik and Radomir.

Pernik

Pernik (32km) is a grim industrial centre in deep decline, but it has a very interesting **museum** and a fine ruined **castle** which are worth a short detour.

■ The Pernik Folklore Festival is held at intervals on 14 January.

History of Pernik

The name of the town is thought to come from the Slav god Perun, and in the 9C it was known as *Peringrad*. The fortress was first built by the boyar Krakra to try to control the movements of the Byzantine armies, but was taken by the Emperor Basil II in 1002 and 1006. It was destroyed by the Serbs in 1189, assisted by the anarchy in the area caused by the appearance of Crusaders. A rebuilt fortress was taken by the Ottoman invaders and soon fell into decline. Pernik was taken by the Austrian general Schenkendorf in 1689, but remained an insignificant place until the 1890s, when exploitation of the coal measures underneath the town began. By 1925, Pernik was producing over 80 per cent of national output, and in the post-war period nine pits were in operation. A thermal power station was built, a steel works, and glass, metal and engineering factories.

Pernik at first sight is an ugly mess of engineering works and derelict industrial installations, but the old town to the west of the main road has some pleasant tree-lined streets, and a few good cafés and restaurants. The very interesting **museum**, near a small open square, is certainly worth visiting, with one of the best collections of the smaller Bulgarian museums. It is often not open but the staff are very helpful and, if it appears to be closed, it is worth ringing the bell and requesting a short tour of the exhibits (curator: Mr Kamen Borissov).

The collections are divided into two main halls, or pre-Ottoman and post-Ottoman periods. The **entrance hall gallery** has material from neolithic settlements, including bead jewellery, votive objects and a large ceramic vessel with inscribed circular decoration. A Bronze Age exhibition follows, showing the development of a Thracian hilltop settlement, with fine Thracian sculpture along with imported pottery and other objects showing strong trade links with Greece. The central gallery shows the Roman settlement, with a water system for the castle, ivory carvings and domestic items.

In the next room, there is an outstanding suit of Byzantine armour, from the 11C, examples of Byzantine ceramics, imported Venetian glass and Slavonic pottery. The **Ethnographic section** is remarkable, with the wonderful and dramatic original costumes for the Pernik Folklore Festival. There are also reconstructed interiors of a typical Pernik region peasant's house from the 19C, and objects such as beehives, looms and agricultural implements.

Souruakars from the Bela Voda quarter, Pernik

The **Fortress of Krakra** is best reached by taxi from the station, where there is a track leading to the foot of a wooded hill. At the top is a very extensive hilltop fortress, originally constructed in the 10C, although evidence of human habitation has been found on the site from neolithic times. The earthworks, over 20m high in places, took advantage of the site contours for defensive purposes. The external fortifications were of a massive scale, with exposed foundations over 2m thick. In the southeast corner, there is the foundation of a large defensive tower. The fort is about 800m x 400m, with remains from different periods, mostly earthworks and foundations of buildings with large stone block walls exposed above grassland. In the centre of the fort, there are the foundations of various domestic buildings from the Ottoman period. There are fine **views** in all directions, especially down the Struma valley towards Radomir.

There is a small Roman **temple foundation** to be seen between the lanes of the dual carriageway to Radomir on the town outskirts. A Roman **villa** was found southeast of the town, at **Kralev Dol**, dating from the end of the 2C AD, and another at **Meshtitsa**, to the north.

From Pernik, a small road runs northwest towards **Trun** (44km) via **Breznik** (21km). Both towns have traditionally been known for their stone masons and building workers. Trun was very important in World War II Partisan warfare. This is an interesting detour, into fine mountain country, although the trip can be hazardous in mid-winter as Trun has a severe climate. The little town lies on the **Erma**, a small Serbian river that flows for about 30km through Bulgaria.

Radomir

After km, you pass through Radomir. This is now a run-down, depressing industrial centre but it played an important part in Bulgarian history when in September 1918 it was the headquarters of the short-lived '**Radomir Republic**'. This early attempt to form a Soviet government in Bulgaria was initiated by revolutionary soldiers from the defeated royal army retreating towards Sofia in the aftermath of the debacle in Macedonia in the First World War. The area generally had been at the heart of the early trades union and socialist movement in Bulgaria. Many inhabitants live in considerable poverty and unemployment is very high.

History of Radomir

Radomir was originally a very small Roman settlement linked to nearby Pernik, then an Ottoman town, the seat of a *cadi*. An important Bible manuscript, the *Gospel of Radomir*, was written here in 1565. It was visited by the Turkish traveller, Hadji Kalfa, who found little of interest here.

On 26 September 1918 about 3000 mutinous soldiers from three army divisions seized Radomir and proclaimed a 'revolutionary Republic', with the initial aim of overthrowing the monarchy, with the participation of the Agrarian leader Stamboliiski and the rebel leader Raiko Daskalov. They called for the execution of King Ferdinand and the overthrow of the corrupt political leaders who were responsible for the wartime catastrophe. The revolt was put down, with considerable bloodshed at the end of September by royalist forces based in Sofia, after pitched battles had been fought around Boyana and Kniajevo with the government troops and German mercenary reinforcements. On 2 October Radomir was retaken, and the 'Radomir Republic' crushed. In the 1930s it had 6500 inhabitants. Under communism the town was developed as a centre of heavy engineering.

9km from Radomir, in the Svetlja valley, is the village of **Kovacevci** where the Bulgarian communist leader Georgi Dimitrov was born. See p 98.

Monastery of Zemen

After Radomir, the road runs across open grazing country before the woodlands near **Izvor**. At the moment this part of the road is being reconstructed and there are detours. The road from Izvor to the village of **Lobos** (8km) is the best way to the outstanding Monastery of Zemen (19km), about 2km to the southwest of the village.

Zemen monastery was built in the 12C and is one of the best examples of that period of Bulgarian architecture, with a characteristic triform apse design in the monastery church. The interior **frescoes** are outstanding, and were painted in the time of Konstantine Deyan, around 1354, when he was the boyar lord of Kyustendil.

Return to the main road, either by the same route, or by the small road south to join the main road at Dragomirovo. Travel on southwest towards Kyustendil, climbing up through the beautiful deciduous woods of the Konjavska mountain range, then dropping to the rich and fertile **plain of Kyustendil**, with some of the best agricultural land in Bulgaria.

The plain of Kyustendil, at an altitude of about 500m and with a more temperate climate than that of Sofia has always been famous for fruit cultivation. The 16C Turkish traveller Celebi noted the size and variety of the crops, samples of which were offered annually to the Sultan as a mark of respect. In the 19C, after the Crimean War, trade expanded considerably and large quantities of plums were exported to Bosnia, and dried prunes to towns in the south of France such as Marseilles. Today apples and pears dominate the orchards.

Kyustendil

The road crosses the Bistrica river and open grazing land where large herds of goats are common. Kyustendil is seen in the distance, below **Mount Lissetz**, at the north end of the densely wooded Osogovska range of mountains that stretch north into Macedonia. You enter the town through modern outer suburbs, with small apartment blocks separated by dirt roads. It is a good base for regional excursions.

History of Kyustendil

The site of Kyustendil has been inhabited since early antiquity, initially by the Thracian tribe of the *Danteletes*. Later it was known as *Pautalia*. In pre-Classical times it was the tribal centre of the kingdom of the *Paeonians*, who spoke a unique language. Mines were an early source of wealth, the nearby hills yielding gold, silver and iron. The leading Paeonian tribe in the area was called the *Laeaei*, who ruled over a large realm stretching east to Stip, in modern FYROM.

In the time of Philip I of Macedon, *Pautalia* grew prosperous on the basis of its early expertise in coinage, which was forged from local silver and gold deposits. The Paeonians worshipped a god of healing called Darron, and heavy silver coins issued in his honour in the late 6C showed a distinctive winged horse. The natural hot spring was probably already being used by the cult priests for medicinal purposes. The upper Strymon valley at that time was known for cereal growing, wild oxen and an unusual type of beer. Tribal power in the region collapsed when the Persians under Darius overran *Pautania* and other undefended local towns in 511 BC.

In Hellenistic times, the town was established and became a minor regional centre. Under the Roman occupation of the Balkans it was refounded by Trajan and the walls were rebuilt by the Emperor Marcus Aurelius. It became an important junction on the roads linking Macedonia with *Serdica*, modern Sofia. It was the most Hellenistic in culture of towns in the locality, with Greek used as the legal and administrative language.

In the time of Diocletian it was a legionary fortress in the system based on *Naissus* (modern Nis, in Serbia). Under Theodoric the Goth, *Pautania* was his second city—after *Dyrrachium* (modern Durres in Albania)—in the southern Balkans. It was an early seat of a bishop, and was refortified by Justinian in the 6C. It was taken by the Slavs and renamed *Velbuzhd*, and by 1019 the local bishop came under the jurisdiction of the Archbishop of Ochrid.

In the Byzantine period the town stagnated, and took on the vulgar Latin name of *Patelense*. It was taken by the Serbs in the anarchy in the region caused by the Third Crusade. It alternated between Byzantine Greek and Serbian occupation until 1330 when the great Serbian Czar Stefan Dushan destroyed the Bulgarian army in battle and killed the King Michael Sisman. By the end of the 14C the baths had regained their importance and the town was renamed *Konstantinova Zemja*, Constantine's Land, by the peasants *Velbuzhdka Banya*, or simply *Banya*, then *Constantinobagno* by the Venetians.

It was named Kyustendil by the Ottomans and grew further in the 16C after the invasion to become the important administrative, military and economic centre of one of the largest and richest *sandjaks* in the Balkans. It included the towns of Melnik, Petric and Radomir, in modern Bulgaria, and Stip, Veles and Strumitsa, in FYROM. Numerous mosques, konaks and hammams were constructed, and a harem for the Sultan's use when he travelled between Constantinople and Nis. It never remained prosperous for long, though, and was severely damaged by earthquakes, then an outbreak of plague in 1655 led to parts of the town being burned down. It was rebuilt as a purely Turkish city.

The region played an important part in the Hapsburg–Ottoman wars between 1689 and 1737. The town was a centre for attacks by local insurgent bands on Ottoman property, from the bandit strongholds in the mountains south of Mount Lissetz. In the Russian–Turkish wars, it was occupied for a time by Russian troops, along with Kriva Palanka.

In the 20C is has reverted to being a middle-sized provincial town, with some continuing ethnic Turkish presence. There was some fashionable tourism from Sofia in the early years of the century, when use of the baths as a spa led to the purchase of holiday homes in the town by better off people from the capital.

■ **Trains and coaches**. The railway station is on the line from Sofia to Gjusevo that was opened in 1909. The train is rather slow, but is picturesque for the first half of the journey. There is a good **express coach service** to and from Sofia, which takes about two hours. Vehicles leave more or less hourly every morning from the coach stop in the square opposite the railway station in Sofia, less frequently in the afternoons.

■ **Taxis**. If arriving from FYROM at Gjusevo, there is a taxi telephone office for cars to Kyustendil. **NB**. Avoid other taxis at the border. The fare to the town is about $US10; negotiate beforehand, and expect to pay significantly more at night. Avoid night travel if possible. Taxis in the town can be found near the station and in ranks by the main square.

■ **Tourist office**. Balkantourist, 37D Kalyashki Street, ☎ 078 23035, 27206.

■ **Hotels**. As elsewhere in provincial Bulgaria, it is recommended that you stay in one of the main hotels, as they are very good value at current exchange rates and security is poor in some streets of the town at night: staying in private rooms nearly always involves late night walks back from restaurants and the possibility of getting lost. The three-star **Hotel Velbuzhd** near the station is a 12-storey concrete block that offers very clean rooms at about $US9 a night, and has good views from the upper floors and a decent restaurant on the 13th Panorama floor, ☎ 078 20242, telex 27428. (Recommended.) The **Hotel Pautalia** is more central, and more expensive, but the staff are deeply unfriendly and there seems little reason to pay more to stay here. The Pautalia has a good taverna, though, with fine folkdancing. (Recommended.)

The town can be seen in about half a day, although to enjoy the baths and to spend time seeing the outstanding monuments—plus there are some attractive Ottoman backstreets in some districts—it is better to allow two days. The town can also be used as a base for exploring a larger region, as places such as Rila Monastery are not too far away if you have some transport; the hotels organise day trips in the season.

It is difficult to obtain access to the interior of the mosques unless it is a Friday. If travelling by car, park near the **Mosque of Fatih**, whose minaret dominates the centre of the main street. This building is in a very poor state, and is closed to the public, although some urgent structural engineering work has been undertaken to prevent the collapse of the dome and an outer wall. This has involved placing steel girders under the dome, and a network of wooden scaffolding and support metalwork. The outstanding external feature of the mosque is the brickwork, with complex patterns involving the use of inset tiles. The minaret is very graceful, but the brickwork is in pitiful condition, with the loss of whole sections of brick facing at the top, and is in very urgent need of restoration.

About 200m to the west of this mosque is a very fine Ottoman **konak**, behind low walls with red tile roofs, but the building is currently closed to the public. It is possible, though, to get a good view of it through a hole in the wall on the south side, or by standing on a box and peering over the red tiled roof.

If you cross the road here, and walk about 300m up the side street heading south, there is the main town square, adjoining the **Church of Sveta Bogoroditsa**. This is the main Orthodox Church in the town, and a beautiful and evocative building with many unique features in its decoration. It stands in a large **garden** enclosed by railings, and with three very fine decorative **bell towers** above a long low sloping room. The church is sunk about 4.5m into the ground and is reached through a set of steps in the north wall. In the gallery to the left of these steps is a bust of King Ferdinand in a glass case. The aisle is a simple whitewashed, very light area, with a fine screen and wood panelling. In the garden is the original bell tower, a wooden structure about 9m high on a stone foundation.

To reach the **hammam complex**, follow the main street in the Sofia direction for about 500m, then turn left into a small open space with a public garden. Behind it is the 19C **public baths**, a low rectangular two-storey building painted ochre: entry is through the Askeplius Café, at the far left. The baths are fed by a hot mineral spring that always has an exact temperature of 74°. You find in the interior a communal bath along Russian lines, with numerous naked Bulgarians lost in a fog of steam and hot mist. Individual baths are also available. These baths are on the same site as the Roman Asklepion. Outside there is a wonderful slightly sulphurous smell from the steam

To the east of the hammam is the **Mosque of Ahmed Bey**, a very good 16C mosque that used to be the town museum. It has finely patterned brickwork and an imposing whitewashed portico with three small inner domes. The building has been returned to religious use, but is often closed except on Fridays.

Immediately adjoining the mosque to the south are exposed ruins of the Roman **hypocaust**, with large red brick tunnels and low walls, the size of which indicates the scale of the original Roman bath complex on the site. The exposed area is about 100m square, and in parts is covered with red brick paving. The Emperor Trajan was said to be cured of his skin disease here.

To visit the **castle** (the Hisarlik), there is a road up Hisarlik hill, on the southeast side of the town. The ancients built **small temples** by the side of the springs issuing from the hill, and **aqueducts** for the cold water supply to the town.

The top of the hill—a triangular shape about 250m long—is a magnificent natural fortress, that has probably been used as a place of refuge from the earliest times. The existing walls probably mainly date from Justinian's refortifications in the 6C, but the foundations date from earlier periods in the 4C when the basic structure was built, with four external round towers at the corners. They may have been built by the Emperor Julian as part of his defence programme for the province of Illyricum. The very steep slopes on the north, west and south were not fortified. On the west side are remains of Roman baths, to the south, on the dramatic site of a pagan temple, are the foundations of a basilica, with three naves and a single apse, that probably dates from the 5th or 6C. The site was excavated from 1906–12. Large coin hoards were found.

Environs of Kyustendil

The most important antiquity near Kyustendil is the **Kadin Most** (Kadin Bridge), on the outskirts of the village of **Nevestino** (13km). This is a very elegant Turkish structure in a good state of preservation. It has five arches, all perfectly proportioned, and is 100m long.

> In Ottoman times this road was an important thoroughfare for the caravans travelling between Sofia and Constantinople. The Byzantine bridge that crossed the Struma was demolished in 1465, and Kadin Most constructed afterwards. According to legend it was built at the request of a girl who was seperated by the Struma river from her bethrothed. The Sultan built her the bridge as a wedding present, hence its name Nevestin Most, the Bride's Bridge. In Turkish this was *Kadankjuprjusu*, which combined to give the name Kadin Most. It also has the common Balkan legend of immurement associated with it where the wife of one of the builders was killed and walled up in the bridge, to give the structure the power to overcome the force of the current.

A **Roman villa** was found near the bridge in the early years of this century, and a Thracian **necropolis**. Excavations at the latter have revealed the continuity of the Thracian horse warrior cult in this part of Bulgaria well into the 4C AD. Minor traces of rural cult centres are common in the Kyustendil district, where the worship of the horseman was linked with that of Zeus, Athena and other Greek gods.

Remains of large **temples** dedicated to Zeus and Hera were found about 8km from Kyustendil, near the modern village of **Kopilovitsi**. They appear to have been very thoroughly destroyed sometime in the 4C AD.

Excursions into the FYROM

It is easy for people with US or EU passports to cross the border here into FYROM, although there can be delays at busy times, and officials work at a truly Balkan pace. There is no visa requirement on the FYROM side. An irritating new minor tax on travellers was introduced in the summer of 1997 by the FYROM authorities, 30 FYROM denar per crossing.

It only takes about an hour or so to drive to **Skopje** via Kumanovo from the border at Gjusevo, via Kriva Palanka, along a wide, good quality asphalt road all the way, with some dual carriageway sections. It is a beautiful drive, for the first part, down the Slaviste mountains into the Vardar valley, following the Kriva river. The villages are very backward, and rural culture is highly traditional. Mount Ruen (2252m), south of the borderpost can be a magnificent sight with winter snow.

Kumanovo is an ancient town in origin, with large ethnic Serb and ethnic Albanian minorities present nowadays. There are historic mosques and an open air market. It is a base for UNPREDEP United Nations Preventative Peacekeeping Force; currently most of the troops are American. The hotel, the **Kristal**, is very bad, with insect and vermin infestation. Avoid.

Skopje, Ottoman *Uskub*, has some outstanding Ottoman monuments, the hammam and Old Quarter mosques in particular, and the ruins of Roman *Skupi* on the outskirts. Skopje has a very large Albanian community that is soon likely to be in the majority. Skopje is known in Albanian as **Skup**. Avoid the horrible Galactic-city-type modern city centre. Decent hotels for an overnight stop include the **Bristol** and the **Tourist**, both in Marshall Tito Street, both about $US60 for a single room.

There are important antiquities and historic towns in the FYROM. In Skopje itself, apart from the fine Ottoman buildings in the Old Town, the *Uskub* **citadel**, and the evocative **old bridge** over the Vardar river, the most important IMRO site is the **Grave of Gotse Delchev** (see p 213) in the cloisters of the Church of Sveti Spas near the citadel. It has become a place of pilgrimage for nationalists. The historical information given in FYROM official guides is often inaccurate, for example, the old bridge was built by a medieval Serbian tsar. The **Carsija**, the bazaar, below it is one of the largest in the southern Balkans, and is predominantly Albanian and Roma inhabited. There are several very fine mosques, and nearby is the **Kursumli Han**, a very well-preserved and authentic example of the Ottoman merchants' *caravanserais* that were at the heart of the economic system of the vast old theocratic empire.

Roman *Skupi* is the most interesting site near Skopje, a large, partly excavated, but currently overgrown site with some very fine **Hellenistic tombstones**. Modern Skopje is an unattractive town and a much more interesting base is **Tetovo**, 50 minutes by bus to the west of Skopje, where the hotels are clean and very cheap. Tetovo has the finest **Islamic monuments** in western Macedonia, and is a small skiing centre. It is a beautiful and atmospheric Muslim Albanian town nestling under the lee of the imposing Sar mountains, with very wild country north and west of the town towards the borders of Albania and Serbia. The most important building which should not be missed in Tetovo is the **Coloured Mosque**, *Sarena Dzamija*, which stands on a small flat patch of land by the river. It is an exquisitely proportioned 16C building with remarkable internal and external wall paintings, the former of Constantinople, in a poetic and romantic style. The **Tekija**, the Dervish monastery, which is the finest remaining *tekke* outside Turkey, is another marvellous building which you should try to see. The monastery is about 2km south of the town towards Gostivar. After a long struggle with the Skopje authorities, the *tekke* has been returned to religious use, and a *Baba* is in residence. You can stay in the part that is a hotel for about $US40. **Highly recommended**.

For the traveller with a little more time, **Ochrid** and **Struga** are both interesting towns with, in the case of Ochrid, very strong Bulgarian elements in their history. Lake Ochrid is one of the most beautiful lakes in the Balkans (see *Blue Guide Albania*, p 216). As a major town, Ochrid was a vital centre of the medieval Bulgarian empire, and has remarkable churches and domestic buildings. **Struga** is at the source of the Black Drin river as it leaves Lake Ochrid for its long journey through FYROM and Albania before it flows into the Adriatic near Shkoder. The lake here is particularly beautiful on cold winter days. The lakeside Drin Hotel in Struga is recommended. Private rooms are plentiful in Ochrid. Advance booking is unnecessary everywhere in FYROM. **Debar** and **Mavrovo** are interesting mountain centres.

The drive from Ochrid back to Bulgaria takes about 4 hours.

Index

A

Abritus 143
Agathopolis 178
Agathoupolis 177
Ahtopol 177-178
Aladzha Monastery 153
Aleko Hut 112
Alexander the Great 188
Alexis I 193
Amadeus of Savoy 161
Anastasius, Emp. 156
Anchialos 163
Apollonia 152, 163, 170
Apollonia in Pontika 174
Arbanassi 204
Archar 128
Aristaeum 158
Asenovgrad 192
Asenovo 135
Ataturk 100
Attila the Hun 86, 128, 146
Augusta 186
Augustus 146
Avars, The 128
Azelius Emilianus 101

B

Bachkovo Monastery 193
Balchik 151, 154
Balgarevo 156
Balkan Wars 215
Bankja 119
Bansko 208, 216
Basil II 221
Batak 187-188, 212
Batulija 120-122
Bazajet, Sultan 129
Belene Forced Labour Camp 134
Belene Island 134
Belogradchik 118, 127
Beograd 119
Berendi 120
Berkovitsa 125, 126, 220
Bisoni 155

Bjala 157-158
Blagoevgrad 216
Bononia 129
Boris I 166
Boris III 94, 117
Borovets 208, 219
Botev, Hristo 123
Botevgrad 113, 122
Boué, Ami 112
Bourchier, James 99, 218
Boyana 109, 111, 113, 114, 220
  223
Breznik 222
Bulgarian hiking movement 112
Burgas 169-170
Burgas lagoons 170, 173

C

Calafat 128
Canetti, Elias 138
Cape Emine 158-160
Celebi, Evlija 132
Central Danube valley 131
Cherepish Monastery 122
Chernomorets 173
Cherven 139, 143
Chiprovci 124
Circassians, The 188
Claudius, Emp. 161
Commodis, Emp. 101
Communist party 113
Constanta 157
Constantine the Great 120, 136
Crassus 128
Crusaders. The 86

D

Danielopoulos, Yiankos 177
Danube, The 128, 134, 139-140,
  166
Danube Bridge 141
Darius, King 160
Decius, Emp. 143
Delcevski 216

Delchev, Gotse 213
Democratic Army 109
Devnya 164
Dimitrov, Georgi 98, 113, 117
Dimitrovgrad 191
Dionysopolis 154
Djuni 176
Dobric 154
Dobrotino 212
Dobrudzha 146
Dobrudzha plain 142, 144
Dobrudzha region 11, 151
Domitian 181
Dracula, Count 148
Dragalevtsi 111, 115
Dragalevtsi Monastery 115
Dragoman Pass 118, 120, 220
Druzhba 152
Dryanovo 200
Dryanovo Monastery 200
Durankulak 157

E

Edirne 192
Elenite holiday village 159
Emona 158
Erakli 158
Ereta 157
Erma 222
Euxinovgrad Palace 152
Exarchate of Bulgaria 181
Ezerec 156

F

Ferdinand, King 217-218, 222
First Bulgarian Kingdom 127, 165-167, 181, 202
First Crusade 86
FYROM 227, 228

G

Gabrovo 200
Galata 157
Getae 174
Gigen 136
Golden Sands 153
Goljamo Belovo 187
Gorna Orjahovica 201
Goths, The 102, 181

Gramatikovo 178
Granny Vanga 209
Greater Bulgarian Union 166

H

Hadrian, Emp. 161
Hadrianopolis 192
Harmanli 192
Haskovo 190
Heliopolis 158
Hemus 157
Heraclitus I 135
Herodotus 123, 160
Hisarya 185
Homer 158
Huns, The 102, 132

I

Illyricum 226
Irecek, Constantin 114
Iskar Gorge 120-122
Ivan II 202
Izvor 223

J

John of Rila 217
John V Paleologus 161
Julian, Emp. 226
Justinian 86, 90, 102, 128, 132, 146, 181

K

Kadin Most 227
Kaliakra peninsula 155-156
Kalojanovo 185
Kalotina 120
Kaloyan, Tsar 211
Kamcija 157
Kamen Brjag 156
Kardzali 191
Karlovo 102, 185
Kavarna 155
Kazanlak 116, 196, 198
Kham Malamir 181
Khan Asparuh 161
Khan Krum 86, 161, 163, 170, 196
Khan Omurtag 167
Klokotnitsa 191
Kniajevo 223

Kolarovgrad 165
Konstantinov, Aleko 112
Kossuth, Lajos 165
Kotoljan, Sevastokrator 114
Kovacevci 223
Kozloduj 125
Krakra, Fortress of 222
Kralev Dol 222
Krapec 156
Kremikovci 130
Kriva Palanka 224
Kulata 213-214, 217
Kumanovo 227
Kyril 166
Kyustendil 220, 223
Kyustendil, plain of 223

L

Lala Salin, Pasha 181
Ledenika cave 123
Levski, Vasil 102, 133, 197
Livardi Pass 212
Lobos 223
Lom 118, 125
Lovec 132
Lower Moesia 161, 205
Lozenec 177

M

MacGahan, J.A. 189
Madan 195
Madara Horseman 144, 157, 164, 166
Madara river 167
Mafiya, The 83, 169
Magyars, The 86, 132
Mahmud II, Sultan 146
Malko Turnovo 178
Marcianopolis 164
Marcus Aurelius 181, 224
Maritsa river 182
Maritsa valley 190
Maxwell, Robert 113
Medni Hills 173
Melnik 208
Melnitsa river 211
Mesembria 152, 158, 160-161, 170
Methodius 166
Mezdra 122

Mezek 192
Millers Inn 116
Milosevic, Slobadan 120
Mithridates VI 174
Moesia 161
Monastery of St John of Rila 124
Montana 123
Morava Gorge 120
Morava valley 120
Mount Batia 189
Mount Kom 126
Mount Lissetz 223
Mount Snezhanka 194
Mount Vitosha 83, 85, 109, 108, 111-112, 114
Murad I, Sultan 146

N

Naissus 84, 120, 128, 224
Naroden National Park 176
National Film Studio 116
Naulochus 158
Neftochim 170-171, 173
Nesebur 152, 160, 170
Nevestino 227
Nicephorus, Emp. 166
Nicopolis 135
Nicopolis ad Istrum 132, 205
Nikopol 135
Nikup 205
1906 pogroms 70, 163
Nis 120, 128
Nos Sabla 156
Novae 134
Novi Iskar 121
Novo Panicarevo 178

O

Obrochishte 154
Obzor 158
Ochrid 228
Odessus 132, 144, 164
Oescus 136
Orient Express 84
Ottoman Empire 165
Ottoman Turks 175
Ovid 151-152, 163

P

Pamporovo 194
Panagyurishte 189
Pautalia 220, 223, 224
Pazardzhik 187
Pecheneg horde, The 86
Pernik 220-222
Petrich 214
Philip I of Macedon 224
Philip II of Macedon 85, 174
Philippopolis 179, 181, 196
Pirgos 169-170
Pirin 212
Pirin Mountains 208
Pirin National Park 208, 216
Pirot 120
Plavets 122
Pleven 131
Pliny 158
Pliska 144, 161, 164, 166
Plovdiv 109, 179
Pobiti Kamani 164
Pomak, The 188, 189, 212
Pomorie 160, 163
Pomorie saltpans 164
Popovo Livadi 212
Preslav 161, 164
Primorsko 177-178
Procopius 146

R

Radomir 98, 220, 222
Radomir Republic 222-223
Rakovski, Georgi Sava 106
Ratiaria 128, 129
Razgrad 143
Rhodope mountains 208
Rila Monastery 208, 217
Rila mountains 208
Romania 151, 157
Romans, The 165
Rozhen Monastery 209-210
Ruschuk 138
Ruse 138-139

S

Samokov 219
Sandanski 213
Sandanski, Yane 209, 212, 213,

214
Sarakatsan settlement 206
Scythians, The 160
Second Bulgarian Kingdom 181,
202
Selim I 192
Seraphim of Sofia, Abp 100
Serbia 120, 126
Serbs, The 86
Serdica 84-85, 97, 101-102, 224
Serres 214
Seuth III 160, 198
Seuthopolis 198
Sexaginta Prista 139
Shabla 156
Shiligarnika ski region 216
Shipka 199
Shipka Pass 140, 199
Shumen 164, 166
Shumen region 144
Silistra 142
Sinan 192
Sinemorec 178
Skopje 227, 228
Slavs, The 86, 132
Sliven 206
Slivnica 119
Smolyan 195
Smolyan lakes 195
Sofia 83, 86
Aeroflot Office 99
airport 84
Ambassador Hotel 110
Archaeological Musuem 96
Balkan Airways office 107
Bladzeki Theatre 108
Boyar houses 105
British Airways 87
British Council 105
British Embassy 105, 110
Bronze Statue of Alexander
Stamboliiski 108
Bulgarian Television 105
Cami Banya Bashi 91
car hire 84
Casino 87
Chapel of Sveta Petka Parskeva 94
Church of Sveta Nedelya 94
Church of Sveta Petka

Sofia, cont.

Samardzhiiska 91
Church of Sveti Sedmochislents
105
craft market 91
Danish Embassy 100
Deltcheff Bequest 104
Equestrian Statue of Tsar Alexander
II of Russia 108
Eternal Flame Monument 100
Ethnographic Museum 96
Flea Market 100, 108
Foreign Ministry 90
Georgi Dimitrov Mausoleum 97
God Loves Bulgaria 109
Grand Hotel 107
Grand Hotel Bulgaria 99
Greek Ambassador's Residence 105
Greek Embassy 105
Headquarters of the Internal
Macedonian Revolutionary
Organisation 92
Hotel Rodina 109
hotels 85
Ikon Museum 103
Institute of Balkan Studies 101
Intercontinental Hotel 109
Iranian Embassy 105
Ivan Vasov Museum 107
Kyril and Methodius Foundation
Gallery 104
Largo 87
Military Club 100-101
Military Museum 110
Ministry of Finance 107
Monument of Vasil Levski 103
Municipal Baths 92
National Bank 97
National Historical Museum 94
National Palace of Culture 110
Natural History Museum 96, 99
Novotel Sofia 109
Old Royal Palace 96
Opera House 108
Orlov Bridge 105
Party House 87
Patriarchal Cathedral of St
Alexander Nevski 103
Public Market 92

Sofia, cont.

Rakovski Street 100, 106
Residence of the Austrian
Ambassador 107
Residence of the British
Ambassador 106
Residence of the Orthodox Patriarch
of Bulgaria 103
Restaurant Budapest 107
Roman pavement 90
Rotunda of Sveti Georgi 90
Russian Army War Memorial 105
Russian Church of St Nicholas 99
Russian Cultural Centre 105
St Sophia Cathedral 101
Sheraton Business Centre 87
Sheraton Hotel 86, 94
Shipka Street 105
Slavyanska Besseda Hotel 107
Sobranje 103
Sofia Synagogue 93
taxis 85
trams and trolleybuses 85
TSUM 87
Turkish Embassy 105
University of St Clement of Ohrid
104
Zoo 111
Sopot 116
Sozopol 152, 163, 170, 173
Sozopolis 173
Spartacus 213
Sredna Gora mountains 185
Stamboliiski 222
Stara Planina 160
Stara Planina mountains 157
Stara Zagora 196
Stip 223
Stoker, Bram 148
Strabo 156
Strandjha mountains 177
Struga 228
Summers, Montague 209
Sunny Beach 159-160
Sveti Konstantin 145, 152
Sveti Nikolska Mountains 127
Svilengrad 192
Svishtov 131, 134, 135

T

Tartars, The 188
Tetovo 228
Theodore Comnenus 191
Theodoric the Goth 224
Theodosius the Great 102
Theodosius, Emp. 142
Thompson Railway Station 120
Thompson. Maj. Frank 121
Thrace 101, 161, 174
Thrace, plain of 187
Thracian tomb, Kazanlak 198
Thracian tombs of Vratsa 123
Thracians, The 165
Tomis 157
Trajan 85, 129, 205, 224
Treaty of Berlin 146, 181, 217
Treaty of Bucharest 120, 146
Treaty of Neuilly 215
Trimontium 181
Troyan 133
Troyan Pass 133
Trun 220, 222
Trunski, Slavcho 121
Tsar Samuel's Castle 214-215
Tsarevo 177
Turnu Magurele 135
Tuzlata 151, 155

V

Vaklino 157
Valens, Emp. 136
Valley of the Roses 196, 198
Varna 10, 132, 144, 146, 152, 164
  Aquarium 149
  Armenian Church of St Sarkis 149
  Bay 157

Varna cont.
  Cathedral of the Assumption 146
  Church of Sveti Bogoroditsa 149
  Clock Tower 148
  craft market 148
  Grand Hotel Varna 145
  Imperial Roman Baths 149
  Lagoon 145
  Museum of History and Art 147
  Opera House 148
  Port 148
  Roman Thermae 144, 150
  St Nicholas the Miracleworker 148
Vasiliko 177
Veleka river estuary 178
Veliki Preslav 167-168
Veliko Tarnovo 196, 200-201
Velingrad 187
Verkovic, Stefan 114
Vidin 118, 120, 124, 128
Vitalian 156
Vizica 178
Vostok Spaceship 105
Vrania 111, 116
Vratsa 121-122

Y

Yantra river 200
Yoruk people 188

Z

Zemen monastery 223
Zhivkov, Ludmilla 199
Zhivkov, Todor 113, 204
Zlatarevo 214, 216
Zograph, Zachary 133